W9-ABG-394

Language Diversity
and Education

Language Diversity
and Education

David Corson
*Ontario Institute for Studies in Education
of the University of Toronto*

LAWRENCE ERLBAUM ASSOCIATES, PUBLISHERS
2001   Mahwah, New Jersey   London

Lawrence Erlbaum Associates, Inc., Publishers
10 Industrial Avenue
Mahwah, NJ 07430

Cover design by Kathryn Houghtaling Lacey

Library of Congress Cataloging-in-Publication Data

Corson, David.
    Language diversity and education / David Corson.
       p. cm.
    Includes bibliographical references and index.
    ISBN 0-8058-3449-4 (pbk. : alk. paper)
    1. Language and languages—Variation. 2. Language
    and education. 3. Sociolinguistics. I. Title.
    P120.V37 C67 2000
    306.44—dc21   00-020306
                                            CIP

Printed in the United States of America
10 9 8 7 6 5 4 3 2 1

To the Staff of the Villa Serbelloni, Bellagio, Italy.

Contents

Preface   ix

1   Language in Social Life and Education   1

2   Language, Power, and Social Justice in Education   16

3   Different Cultural Discourse Norms   36

4   Non-Standard Varieties   66

5   Bilingual and English as a Second Language Education   99

6   Gender and Discourse Norms   152

7   Research Methods for Language Diversity and Education   188

References   223

Author Index   239

Subject Index   245

Preface

In writing this book, I had two audiences in mind:

- graduate students of applied linguistics, sociolinguistics, psycholinguistics, the social psychology of language, anthropological linguistics, and other related disciplines
- graduate students of education, including experienced teachers undergoing advanced courses of professional development

The book provides an introductory text for all the above areas. Its first, second, and last chapters give much of the background that beginning researchers need for studying language diversity and education. These chapters offer an update on the philosophy of social research. In doing so, they reveal how important language is for all the processes of learning that humans engage in, whether it is learning about the world through education, or learning about the nature of social life through research in the human sciences. The same chapters review the links between language, power, and social justice. And they look at dynamic changes occurring in 'language diversity and education' research.

The book's four central chapters attempt a comprehensive and state-of-the-art coverage of the chief areas of language diversity that affect the practice of education:

- standard and non-standard varieties
- different cultural discourse norms
- bilingual and English as a Second Language (ESL) education
- gendered discourse norms

SUMMARY

The early chapters also provide the necessary background for interpreting material in the four central chapters. The main themes of all the chapters are as follows:

Chapter 1 looks at language in social life, especially its central role in discovering and explaining a diverse social world. Leaving behind the positivist orthodoxy that dominated research in the twentieth century, the chapter follows the interpretative, discursive turn that now offers a way of understanding language diversity and education that is critically real yet thoroughly postmodern.

Chapter 2 reviews the links between discourse, power, and social justice. It looks at 'language and power' and at 'language and social justice'. Then it brings these two discussions together to suggest how the imbalances in power that language diversity creates, can be reduced in the interests of social justice.

Chapter 3 addresses the many students who bring different cultural discourse norms into schools. It discusses cultural identity; mismatches in discourse; different cultural values; the effects of dominant discourse norms; the power of classroom contexts and teacher practices; and ways of changing these contexts and practices.

Chapter 4 discusses the fair treatment of standard and non-standard varieties in education. Its topics include non-standard varieties and educational policy; recent research on non-standard varieties; and the practical issues of critical language awareness and critical literacy.

Chapter 5 reviews bilingual and ESL education. It deals with the advantages of bilingualism and of bilingual education itself; the education of immigrant children up to middle childhood; established linguistic minorities; the signing Deaf; the ESL education of older children; and valuing minority first languages in schools.

Chapter 6 looks at gendered discourse norms. Its topics include female discourse norms and male power; cooperative and competitive practices among adults and children; gendered norms reinforced by schools; influences beyond the school; the norms of immigrant girls; and reducing gendered school discourses.

Chapter 7 examines the changing role of the language disciplines in understanding the real world of human interaction. It points towards discourse studies that are broadly conceived, politically aware, and socially situated. Finally, it presents summaries of methods at work, each drawn from one of the four central chapters.

SPECIAL FEATURES

I have tried to create a clear, jargon-free writing style that invites careful reading. To help in this, I have asked a number of people to read parts of the manuscript and to comment on its accessibility for readers, including its argument and its presentation of evidence. While the ideas the book advances are far from easy, it is difficult to present them more accessibly than I have while still retaining their force and sense. All the ideas are well within the range of ideas that graduate students in the language disciplines or in education can assimilate and relate to their work. I have also kept theoretical ideas to a necessary minimum, and linked them with practical examples in every case. In addition, the book makes only minimal use of the controversial terms 'minority' or 'minorities' except in two types of context. First, when citing the ideas of other writers who used these words in their work, I follow their lead. Second, I follow the established practice of using 'language minorities' to refer to groups who use languages other than the majority one.

The book gives many examples and brief suggestions for policy and practice; but it does not begin to deal with the problems of implementing these ideas in specific contexts. Any suggestions, like the ones I offer, have to be interpreted against the backdrop of specific settings by people familiar with the flux and flow of real-world obstacles and pressures. Only then can ideas be made to work, usually by people quite removed from those who offered them. At the same time, it would be quite wrong to say that these ideas are limited in their relevance to the countries and contexts where they are already in use. This is because language diversity, everywhere in the English-speaking world, faces most of the same broad problems and many of the same structural constraints. Those actively reforming the new international world of language diversity and education know only too well that they have much to learn from the experience of other countries.

The reader will find extensive referencing to the book's up-to-date, international, and cross-cultural bibliography. The book has no footnotes, so the interested reader is urged to consult those references widely for elaboration. Finally, the 'discussion starter' questions at the end of each chapter will be useful for those who are reviewing their work after reading parts of the book. These questions will also be useful to graduate teachers using the book as a text. The questions highlight key points and try to stimulate informed, reflective discussion.

ACKNOWLEDGMENTS

In different ways, many people have contributed to the writing of this book. Some helped by collecting parts of the evidence that it uses: Michelle Goldberg, Sylvie Lemay, Kyoko Sato, and Hiroko Yokota. Some helped by commenting on single chapters, either in their draft form or in some earlier form: John Baugh, Judith Bernhard, Pat Corson, Martha Crago, Jim Cummins, Victoria DeFrancisco, George Dei, Penny Eckert, Mark Fettes, Rebecca Freeman, Tara Goldstein, Monica Heller, Hilary Janks, Claire Kramsch, Sally McConnell-Ginet, Brian Morgan, Sonia Nieto, Jim Ryan, Dave Smith. Others helped by supporting the project in essential ways: Tim Corson, Nancy Hornberger, Bonnie Norton, Naomi Silverman, and Leo van Lier. Finally, my thanks go to the Rockefeller Foundation, whose submission process for its Bellagio Fellowship prompted the idea for the book and whose Study Centre, on a lovely promontory in Lake Como, saw the project's completion.

—David Corson
Toronto

1

Language in Social Life
and Education

I think I have in fact been situated in most of the squares of the political checkerboard, one after another and sometimes simultaneously: as anarchist, leftist, ostentatious or disguised Marxist, nihilist, explicit or secret anti-Marxist, technocrat in the service of Gaullism, new liberal, etc. None of these descriptions is important by itself; taken together, on the other hand, they mean something. And I must admit that I rather like what they mean.

—Foucault (1984a, pp. 383–384)

Michel Foucault stands closer to the end of the story I tell in this chapter than he does to the beginning. Yet his description of himself here is very germane to my theme throughout. Foucault portrays himself as a person unwittingly identified with many competing orthodoxies at the same time, implying of course his preferred detachment from any single one. Similarly the role of language in social life is now more clearly seen as a series of witting and unwitting alliances that people form with the many diverse sets of discourses that they encounter. And each of these discourses is an orthodoxy that positions us, whether we resist its seductive pull or rush eagerly to embrace it.

This opening chapter suggests how important language is to the processes of learning that humans engage in, whether it is learning about the world through education, or learning about the nature of social life through research in the human sciences. As my opening paragraph hints, in recent decades the search for objectivity and for absolutes in understanding social life has gradually been replaced by a much more skeptical conception of discovery that is more in tune with the real social world. Accordingly, but gradually, human science disciplines are transforming themselves to take account of this diverging view. Furthermore, this quite different understanding of what people can really know about the human condition, is slowly filtering into school curricula, into the pedagogies that teachers

1

choose to use, and into the new modes of administration and evaluation that schools are introducing.

In this different social climate, which many call 'postmodernity', people are living increasingly in social spaces where orthodoxies of all kinds are losing their influence. While this development is worrying for some, it is welcomed by many others who see it as overdue recognition of the way the social world actually is. A spirit of tolerance about matters of diversity is becoming a necessary part of modern life: a recognition of diversity in world view and behaviour is gradually becoming more acceptable these days. And it is much more taken-for-granted as well. Alongside this development, we are seeing a rapid decline in the influence of positivism as a guiding ideology in social research. So to get at these changes, this chapter's first section traces that decline and outlines the new conceptions of discovery that have begun to replace or supplement the older positivist approaches. Later, I suggest how education is affected by these important changes that are now impacting on society and also on the work that teachers do.

DISCOVERING A DIVERSE SOCIAL WORLD

Positivism, Language, and Diversity

Not too long ago, it was still accurate to claim that positivism "is the philosophical epistemology which currently holds intellectual sway within the domain of social research" (Hughes, 1990, p. 16). In the context of that claim, an epistemology is a 'theory of knowledge' that describes what counts as knowledge and how people might go about acquiring that knowledge. Positivism dominated social research for most of the twentieth century, including most of the research done on language and education topics. And the variety of positivism practised in the social sciences was quite firm about its own epistemology. Beginning in Europe with Auguste Comte, positivism argued that society could be studied using ideas similar to those that the natural sciences used.

Key ideas here were that all natural (and social) phenomena can be fully described in terms of determinate laws governing the interaction of lower-order entities; and that such descriptions can be made independent of the observer. This positivist position was based on the firm belief that human action is not random. Rather, just like events in the physical world, human action was thought to conform to certain quite predictable and knowable patterns that can be re-applied to other human actions removed culturally and historically from the actions that informed the originally observed patterns.

At the turn of the twentieth century, Emile Durkheim's 'principle of correlation' set the scene for most social research that followed in that positivist tradition. This important principle still has wide application in research, as it does in many processes of disciplined thinking. Again, it assumes that human behaviour follows certain predictable patterns, even across societies and cultures. It also assumes that we can understand the social world by understanding the way those patterns vary one with another. For example, from the simple fact that murder rates in certain French cities covaried with one another in ways that remained fairly stable, even over long periods of time, Durkheim (1894/1966) was able to argue the validity of his principle of correlation. But, as I indicate below, this important principle can also mislead us, by making us overlook the real diversity hidden within these apparently predictable, social patterns.

Today, the role of meaning and interpretation, especially interpreting the meanings of natural language, has become central to most forms of social research. Yet it was the language of social research that obsessed the early positivists too, although only in a very narrow sense. What interested the positivists most was finding an objective 'observational language' that could be used to give agreed names to all the variables in their research theories. In practice, this meant that the words and expressions used descriptively in their ideas about the world had to be translatable into meaningful statements in this observational language. Indeed, almost all the debate that engaged the early positivist philosophers addressed this problem of reducing key terms or concepts into statements in a basic and objective observational language.

This concern with finding an objective language placed severe limitations on positivist social scientists and on their theorising. What were they to do about people's 'mental states', which cannot be described in anything like the neat and objective way they sought? Clearly, the workings of the human mind, and the unimaginable range of ways in which people's minds seem to work, are important factors for understanding the social world. Yet many positivists tried to dismiss their relevance, arguing that respectable social research needed to find ways around such slippery notions as these. Often their response was to ignore mental states altogether, by theorizing them out of existence, or more rarely by refusing to entertain the possibility of there being mental states.

For example, in psychology the science of behaviourism assumed that human beings and animals act as they do in response to a wide range of stimuli in their environments. The behaviourists set about discovering those stimuli and showing their effects. They did this by devising experiments that placed severe limits on the environmental conditions operating in the experimental settings created, thereby depriving their subjects of the need or the opportunity to exercise the range of choices and interpretations that would normally be available to them in a real social world. The stimuli and the subjects' reactions to them were the things of most concern to the behaviourists, and these things had to be observable in some way to really count. Accordingly, behaviourist research left little room for ideas like 'free will', 'moral values', or other abstract notions that grow from different people's mental states. Indeed, like others in the positivist tradition, the behaviourists seemed to think that everyone is basically the same as everyone else. This view contrasts sharply with more recent forms of social research which acknowledge that a key attribute of human beings is our capacity to reflect on what we have said or done, and to give an account of those unique reflections in language.

Language Games and Diversity: The Challenge to Positivism

Long before positivism was challenged in the social sciences, it was already becoming discredited in the physical sciences. Karl Popper's influence on the philosophy of science in the twentieth century was second to none; and there is no doubt that his work marks the historical and logical break between a positivist and a post-positivist view of the natural world, and eventually of the social world too. Nevertheless, Popper's is only the first word on the subject, not the last. Much progress has been made since the 1930s when his ideas began to circulate, and even since the 1960s, when he made a substantial updating of his early work (Popper, 1972).

Until quite recently, most social researchers applied the hypothetico-deductive model of scientific reasoning to their work. The theories they offered involved deducing a statement using premises based on empirical observations. Popper's point in opposition to that model was that this approach to the hypothetico-deductive process involves verifying what can never be known with certainty, because some counter instance might turn up in the future to show that any firm conclusion reached is wrong. This more skeptical account of knowledge was an attempt to throw off a belief in the strict regularity of the world, whose patterns one might infer inductively. Popper recognized the existence of unpredictable forms of diversity in the physical world: things that might overturn even the most strongly felt theory.

Accordingly, Popper's main innovation was to suggest that we do not verify our theories. Rather, we falsify them by finding counter-instances which we use to eliminate error from our conjectures. Indeed, this direct challenge to positivism set philosophy heading in quite new directions. At about the same time, another Austrian philosopher, Ludwig Wittgenstein, was discarding his own earlier positivist ideas which he had already set out in his famous *Tractatus*. He replaced them with a new set of ideas that was to underpin almost all modern approaches to interpretive research in the social sciences. By highlighting the role of natural language and other systems of signs in shaping the endless variety of world views that people develop, Wittgenstein threw open the door to an unlimited appreciation of human diversity. And this seems a key moment in intellectual history.

For Wittgenstein (1953; 1972), humans are participants in many different 'language games' that are all played within fairly closed linguistic circles. When we have knowledge or belief, we have it according to the linguistic rules that obtain in a given circle or game: in some discipline or theory, for instance, or in some other ideological framework, like a culture, a social group, a religious sect, and so forth. Although Wittgenstein's views were very different from Popper's, the sophisticated form of skepticism that both philosophers advanced offered a direct challenge to the naive certainties of positivism. Over several generations, this skepticism fostered the development of a more sociological view of knowledge.

An influential figure in the United States was Thomas Kuhn (1970). He argued that scientists tend to interpret knowledge from inside 'frameworks' or 'paradigms' of theory that tend to isolate scientists from the world they are interpreting. Indeed in practice these paradigms are quite like Wittgenstein's language games. Each one stands as its own cultural meaning system, and it allows those who view the world from within it to make sense of their own world by using the system's relevant 'rules' of use. In moving from paradigm to paradigm, the interpretative rules change somewhat, and often the facts drawn from the world take on a slightly different sense. The facts can be used to explain things in quite different ways, so that different theories develop from similar facts and, sometimes, these theories about the world are even contradictory or incompatible. This is because complex theories within paradigms always outrun the facts available to support them.

The expert thinking on this point is captured in W. V. O. Quine's conclusion (1953): Theories about complex things in the world are always underdetermined by facts. The facts we have about the external world are capable of supporting many different interpretations of it. In other words, our unique experiences of the world do not impose any single theory upon us. The different theories we develop and use depend on the particular language game or games we are operating within.

Meanings and Sign Systems: Interpreting the Social World

By the end of the twentieth century, an 'interpretative alternative' was beginning to replace positivism. Here, the very possibility of reaching theoretical neutrality in observations is discounted. Looking out from inside a language game, the knower is always a contributor to the construction of knowledge, and this colours any understanding of the social world that we have. It also places severe limits on research, as Max Weber (1969) observed. On the one hand, the complex nature of 'interpretative understanding' offers an opportunity to go into social and cultural questions much further than a natural scientist could possibly penetrate the inanimate world. But on the other hand, this deeper penetration comes at a price: it means a loss in objectivity, precision and conclusiveness. So when people accept the challenge of 'interpretation' as a better way of understanding the social world, they also accept its inevitable 'fallibility'. Like the verdict of a jury, our interpretations can always be overturned by new evidence. But even an overturned interpretation leaves us with only another interpretation of a text. As Charles Taylor (1979) puts it:

> We are trying to establish a reading for the whole text, and for this we appeal to readings of its partial expressions; and yet because we are dealing with meaning, with making sense, where expressions only make sense or not in relation to others, the readings of partial expressions depend on those of others, and ultimately of the whole. (p. 28)

Clearly, then, meaning is central to all this, although it is not just linguistic meaning that matters. Meaning is the basis of any sign or sign system. A 'sign' is not really a sign unless it has some meaning for someone. A burgeoning field of inquiry called 'semiotics' has sprung up just to study the theory of signs, including all the work signs do in their many manifestations. The occasional detective or spy novel helps introduce its readers to the theory of signs, which again has much to do with the diverse reasons and 'rules' that inform our interpretation of signs in the social world.

On the one hand, the reasons people give for their actions are always much more than just 'causes' or stimuli. It is not helpful to use a purely causal vocabulary when describing the social world, because this ignores things like values and cultural beliefs which always influence people's actions, and which are quite basic to living in the social world. The reasons people give for their actions are expressions of their values and beliefs, and these things cannot be understood without consulting the people themselves.

On the other hand, the 'rules' that affect people's social behaviour are rarely permanent ones. They are usually just social and cultural conventions that come and go in response to social conditions and historical circumstances. For example, sometimes people in a similar context are affected by different rules or conventions, so they behave quite differently from one another, for reasons of their own. To see the meaning behind their words or actions, then, means knowing more about the unique conventions or rules that influence them.

All this becomes clearer when we study another language to a reasonably high level of proficiency. In working with another language there is always what Quine called an 'indeterminacy of translation': Regardless of how happy we are with a translation, we never know if we have translated completely. And this is the salient issue at the heart of all research in the human sciences, yet many still operate as though it were not. When we look below the commonsense division between 'languages' like English, French or Spanish, and think instead of languages as diverse 'varieties' belonging to cross-sections of language communities of every kind, including the unique 'language varieties of individuals ' called idiolects, then the point becomes clearer. The 'indeterminacy of translation' operates between any two of these 'varieties' to a lesser or greater extent, just as it does when interpreting the texts of 'languages' in the more everyday sense. We never know if we are reading the signs correctly, and this can still be true even after we have consulted the reasons and the rules that lie behind people's words and actions.

But there are other complications as well. Even social realities themselves are constructed in and through meanings; they cannot be easily discussed except in the language in which they are embedded (Hughes, 1990). Yet language is not just the vehicle for reporting the world; it also performs actions in that world. So the structures that constrain social action, whether they be values or rules or behavioural norms, are created in and through discourses of various kinds. In their turn, these structures change discourse practices in a reciprocal way, so that what we say about the world changes that world, and the new structures that those changes bring about, go on to change what we say.

In this more contemporary understanding of the social world, two thinkers, Roy Bhaskar (1986) and Rom Harré, are quite influential. In the next chapter, I say more about Bhaskar and the external social world. And in the next section of this chapter, I say more about Harré and the more 'internal' social world. Both are key advocates for an understanding of this 'internal' world that respects the diverse world views that it contains. They argue that apparently incompatible explanations of the same world are usually answering quite different questions about it. At the same time, they believe that arguing the view that knowledge is socially constructed is not the same as arguing that knowledge is unconstrained by the world. Both thinkers are realists after all. Inevitably, knowledge reflects how things are in the real world, but it does so from different points of view. Our realist interpretations of the social world are only what is in people's 'minds' about the part of the world that is available to them through the discourses they have encountered. Each of those 'minds' is positioned in the interaction between a human organism and its environment, including its language environment.

If all this seems far removed from everyday reality, it does not take much to bring it back to the real world of children's lives in classrooms, schools, and communities: Every verbal or non-verbal exchange in schools assumes some background knowledge that is expressed in signs whose rules of use are only partially shared. The more that participants in discourse are unlike one another—in their culture, beliefs, age, language, experiences, and prior knowledge—the more likely it is that assumptions made about commonality of background will be mistaken, misleading, or prejudiced. So at the very least, this new understanding of the social world should make us more cautious about dealing with diversity. It is easy to see how the old positivist approaches to educational research, that focussed largely on simple learning and behavioural theories, on disciplinary subject matters, and on the marks and gradings that pupils achieve, risked getting matters dangerously wrong.

LANGUAGE IN SOCIAL LIFE

The Discursive Turn

In an important book, Rom Harré and Grant Gillett signal the appearance and the rapid rise of a genuinely new science called 'discursive psychology'. Their book tries to make the main tenets and the initial research efforts of discursive psychology available to interested non-expert readers. While their focus seems to be on psychology, this new field extends to all branches of the human sciences, involving anthropology, sociology and linguistics, in a synthesis of trends that are already appearing or established. "It is both remarkable and interesting that the old psychologies continue to exist alongside the new" say the authors, and they begin their description with a critical look at "the traditional experimentalist psychology that still exists, particularly in the United States" (1994, p. 2).

Discursive psychology's origin is in the well attested idea of the sociocultural world as a place that is constructed by discourse. As mentioned already, other current approaches to thinking about social research point in this direction too. Although this is an idea that has many sources in social psychology, it is Jerome Bruner (1973, 1990, 1996) in cognitive psychology who opened the way for thinking about human cognition in ways other than the experimentalist tradition. For him, it is culture that shapes mind, providing us with the toolkit we use to construct not only our worlds, but our very conceptions of our selves and our powers. Familiar conclusions from Bruner (1996), like the following, carry great weight for education:

> Culturalism takes as its first premise that education is not an island, but part of the continent of culture. It asks first what function "education" serves in the culture and what role it plays in the lives of those who operate within it. Its next question might be why education is situated in the culture as it is, and how this placement reflects the distribution of power, status, and other benefits. (p. 11)

In chapter 2, I return to these themes. Already, though, discursive psychology has gone beyond Bruner's path-breaking work by discarding the twin dogmas of cognitive science: that inner mental states and processes actually exist; and that they are much the same for all human beings. Recent studies in the physiological sciences have shown these dogmas to be little more than that. They have revealed the human brain as much more than a static and conservative organ. Rather, its neurobiological mechanisms alter as a result of different social environments and discursive practices, which means the uniquely personal events that begin at the moment of conception. It seems that the brain is physically shaped by the experiences its owner has, especially by the different narratives, sign systems, and other discursive events that people participate in.

Signs, Meaning Systems, and Following Rules of Use

Again, Wittgenstein's simple idea of following a rule is at the root of this discursive turn: Mental activity is not tied to some internal set of processes; it is a range of moves set against a background of human activity governed by informal conventions or rules, especially rules to do with the ways in which words and other signs are used within the structures of a language (Corson, 1995b). For Harré & Gillett, whatever existence the psychological world might have, it is not reducible or replaceable by explanations based on physiology, or any materialist discipline that does not get to grips with the structure of meanings in the lives of the cultural group to which a given person belongs. Getting inside those structures means getting inside the forms of life, norms, conventions, and rules; and seeing the relevant signs and meaning systems in the way that other person does.

Because the meaning of a sign is its 'use' in a language game, people have to adopt normative attitudes to their own responses when they use a sign to structure mental activity. In other words, they have to conform in some sufficient way to the sign's informal rules of use. Again, these norms or rules are set within some language game or other, where signs have their meanings and in which the range of moves and rule-following takes place. These language games embrace the different signs and sign systems that groups of people create to do complex things, and the relevant tools and actions that inform those discursive practices. Moreover, language games are often nested within each other. They also overlap in complex ways, depending on the diverse cultural, gendered, and class identities of the people participating. In keeping with Wittgenstein's more familiar usage, I am using the term 'language game' throughout this book, although a more complete label might be 'discourse game'; or even 'a Discourse' in James Gee's sense (1997).

By the end of the twentieth century, the subject matter of the human sciences had begun to change radically to include discourses, significations, subjectivities, and positionings, because this is where mental events are really located. For some time, discourse analysts, ethnographers, critical linguists, and sociologists of language have been setting this new course for the social sciences. But now, all these viewpoints are beginning to come together in a more coherent way. As Harré and Gillett (1994) conclude: "the study of the mind is a way of understanding the phenomena that arise when different sociocultural discourses are integrated within an identifiable human individual situated in relation to those discourses" (1994, p. 22).

In this new understanding of mental events, the mind of an individual is a nexus or meeting point of social relations, and of past and present discursive practices and subjectivities. So each human individual stands at a unique intersection of discourses and relationships: a 'position' embedded in historical, political, cultural, social and interpersonal contexts, that largely determines 'mind'. Yet even this dynamic concept of mind seems too static for some. In the allied perspective of 'ecological psychology' (Fettes, 2000), 'mind' is located in the active relationship of organism and environment. This yields a conception of the individual as an embodied being, constantly building on previous encounters with the world in a search for meaning and value carried out in an environment where social practices, including linguistic practices, play a very large role: one that is both constraining and enabling. Returning to language games, people who play in the same games, sharing the same discursive experiences as one another, are constantly being repositioned over time, but often in similar ways. So while diverse human groups develop everywhere, each group has members who tend to be rather alike in world view or in mind.

These language games might also be described as 'cultural meaning systems' because above all else they are cultural products. As Clifford Geertz (1973) observes, the cultural world consists of all the webs of significance humanity has spun for itself. And for Raymond Williams (1981), culture consists of sets of signifying systems through which a social order is communicated, reproduced, experienced, and explored. Incorporating natural language itself as they do, these meaning systems provide the best evidence of a culture's distinctness. As shared sets of symbols, meaning systems exist before each one of us comes into contact with them, and usually well before we even exist ourselves. Although they have bewildering surface differences and can change greatly over time, cultural meaning systems are shared, collective, and enduring (LeVine, 1984). This means they operate on a plane that is emergent from us, in the sense that they are independent of individual people. But we acquire our ability to use different meaning systems through the many discursive practices our unique life experiences give us. Again, of course, discursive practices are not limited to activities involving natural language.

Discursive practices extend to routine or special actions and customs that carry individual and sociocultural meanings. An act of violence committed against someone is no less a discursive act than thumbing your nose at them. So is washing a relative's feet in some cultures; or serving yourself last at mealtimes (Much, 1992). All these practices employ signs that are redolent with meaning and significance inside different cultural meaning systems. And even when signs like these are not accompanied by natural language, they still carry great weight. This latent power of non-verbal signs can be readily seen in the communication of toddlers at play with one another, as they use signs that reproduce gendered relationships learned from their significant others (see chapter 6). Again, the power of non-verbal signs can be seen in the new forms of domination and resistance that computer technology is producing, as it creates signs and symbols within language games that privilege some while silencing others (Herring, Johnson & DiBenedetto, 1995). Even more powerful are the multisemiotic, visual images of the media and of advertising that are an increasingly prominent feature of present-day discourses (van Leeuwen, 1997).

Clearly, then, our ability to use signs of all types lies at the heart of a discursive account of mind and the social world. These symbols provide all the important means for forming and refining thought, based on meanings that derive from their use in discourses. For Harré and Gillett (1994), the role of words in forming and refining thought is increasingly confirmed across a range of disciplines. Thinkers are competent managers of systems of signs, and our most efficient signs, in most contexts, are the words of a language: "To be able to think is to be a skilled user of these sign systems, that is, to be capable of managing them correctly" (p. 49). This is not to say that words and other signs actually structure cognition, only that discourse itself is the medium in which cognitive activity takes shape. Harré and Gillett (1994) sum it up this way:

> Thus the grasp [of the meaning of a sign] is an active discursive skill. It is selective in the face of a rich set of experiential possibilities. It is built on participation in discourse, and it is governed by rules or prescriptive norms that tell the thinker what counts as an item of this or that type (e.g. what counts as a DOG in the fireplace or in the kennel, a FROG in the pond or in the throat, or a HEAVY METAL BAND in the dance hall or around the ankle). Thinkers' awareness of these rules shows in their rec-

ognition that there is a right and a wrong way to capture in thought the object or property that is thought about. (p. 48)

So when we have knowledge, we have it according to linguistic rules that obtain in a given language game or meaning system. In order to play in the game to optimum levels of proficiency, we need to learn the full spectrum of special rules that attach to each of the signs at work in the system, so that we can use them in productive ways. Again, these 'rules' are no more than imperfect conventions. They are forms of order laid down at some time after the meaning system began to develop. As these rules slowly emerge from the ongoing co-ordination of individuals' awareness and actions, they tend to privilege some people and disadvantage others. Sometimes this happens deliberately, through the conscious imposition of rules of use that discriminate between people in some way. Much of the discussion, in the chapters that follow, relates to that point.

At the same time, these rules are not as abstract as they might seem. Everyday words have quite basic and commonly agreed rules for their use, based on the tacit assumption of all language users that there are right and wrong ways to use all signs within language games. Harré and Gillett give some examples, like the rules behind the use of words like *red* or *square* that prevent us from thinking readily of a red object as blue or a square object as round.

Similarly, the sentence "sheep are carnivorous" is not false, just senseless. This is because the rules governing the use of the sign *sheep* and the sign *carnivorous* are not compatible with placing the two words together in the sentence 'sheep are carnivorous'. The sentence is inexplicable because it is outside the language games and forms of life where people who follow these rules live their lives. Instead, the idea of 'carnivorous sheep' enters other realms where conventional rules of use are deliberately ignored, like science fiction, horror movies, or satire. In fact, the very thought of 'carnivorous sheep' could be very appropriate within the language game of a satirical show, like *Monty Python,* or in a child's cartoon, where the prevailing rule is that some of the rules that apply in other language games can be ignored. So these ideas about words and their rules of use are not abstractions. Rather they are tied closely to the real world of life forms, material practices, and human interaction. Use really defines meaning.

While 'meaning' and 'use' are not exact equivalents, a consideration of 'use' does open up possibilities that are overlooked if we concentrate simply on the 'meaning' of a sign:

> Questions of meaning do appear to be, invariably, questions of use, but the converse does not hold: the use of a word, but not its meaning, can be fashionable, ill-advised, or unjustified; it can be encouraged or prohibited, accompanied by gestures, occasion disputes, and reveal something about the speaker. Not so its meaning. (Rundle, 1990 p. 9)

In chapter 2, I consider some of these powerful uses that attach to signs, especially in settings like education where the evaluative use of signs and sign systems distinguishes different people in different ways. When we think about a sign's use, we do have to operate at the point where world and sign meet, so as to keep in touch with its meaning. This always returns our thinking about meaning to the real contexts of diversity where words and other signs are used.

Discourse, Social Life, and Personal Feelings

The influences that shape individual cognition are social and interpersonal, and it is the discourse of these interactions that shapes individual psychology. Harré and Gillett (1994) find this point highlighted in theoretical, clinical, and experimental work in cognitive psychology. In conclusion, they paraphrase the Russian psychologist, Alexandr Luria (1973): "Discourse and usage, particularly of the tools made available in natural language, penetrate deep into the organizational structure of the brain," so that "brain structure is transformed to provide the machinery that an active human agent puts to work in exercising those skills in a multiplicity of tasks of everyday life" (p. 86). In much the same way, our most personal feelings about the world are intricately bound up with the discursive structures in which we move and have moved (Harré, 1987).

After examining contemporary neuropsychological data, including findings on split-brain patients and connectionism, Harré and Gillett see language having a dual role in the discursive origins of 'the self'. As well as the medium, along with the body itself, in which most cognitive activities take place, it is also an analogue for episodes of non-linguistic actions that are really alternative systems of signs, such as prosody, gestures, or other meaningful sets of actions. So the development of self is 'a continuous production' structured by discursive events, rather than something that goes on exclusively inside a person.

In studying personality, for example, the task is to understand the individual's self-locations and the discursive contexts in which they are formed and expressed. There are clear links between emotion words and emotion acts. Indeed, most displays of emotions are recognizably discursive acts, based upon natural and inculcated patterns of bodily reaction, whose meanings are defined by their role in the discursive relations of a culture. Like perception and even consciousness itself, our emotions derive from discursive practices, although sometimes the world itself is our interlocutor, rather than other people. Often, our interactions with the world's potential to arouse grief, delight, horror, or amusement make us conceal or display our emotions in less voluntary ways.

Perception exists in techniques and forms of life that render us skillful in extracting information from the environment. And those skills are both enabling and constraining: Sometimes they open up options and become practical and universal ways of adapting to features of the world. For example, much of the basic content of elementary education—learning about the number system for instance— is placed on the curriculum for its practicality and universality in adapting to the world.

Sometimes too, the perceptual skills that we acquire draw features from the uniquely different settings in which each perceiver has been positioned. People from more local cultures, for example, are much more adept at perceiving salient features in that local environment than strangers to it.

And sometimes these perceptual skills can expose us to 'non-negotiable' features in the environment that reflect taken-for-granted components of the many discourses that we experience. This last category includes benign things, but also malignant things. For example, it covers many of the early, pre-literate perceptions of the world that little children acquire in order to give structure to their own culture and move around within it. But it also ranges over the more political perceptions of the world that individuals and groups formulate, including distortions that protect powerful sectional interests, such as the distortions of political ideologies, propaganda systems, stereotypes, religious and political indoctrination, and other forms of groupthink. To illustrate this last category, Harré and Gillett give the example of a person who holds a racial stereotype: That person's mind has been shaped by many different situations and discourses in which the stereotyped group, seen as individuals or collectively, was either directly experienced in a negative, stereotype-reinforcing light or portrayed in that way. The meanings or 'rules' of use derived from such experiences would now have come to dominate all real or imagined encounters that person has with members of the stereotyped race.

Finally, discourse has a role in expanding consciousness itself: As people extend their discursive skills, so they also expand their consciousness, which is the range of meaningful things of which they are aware. The wider the range of discourses and the associated skills, the more critical individuals can be, in principle, of disabling perceptions of their world. This is not to say, of course, that they will necessarily use that level of critical awareness for emancipatory ends, either for themselves or for others.

Moreover, self-consciousness is just as tied to discourse as is consciousness itself. For instance, even conventional mental states like 'apathy', 'complacency', and 'complicity' are structured for individuals through their participation in a moral reality that is lacking in discursive practices that would arouse greater levels of self-consciousness.

Clearly then, this dynamic and vital 'discursive turn' responds to the differences that linguists, sociologists, historians, and anthropologists have long discovered in the discursive practices and thought processes of culturally, socially, and historically remote peoples. By studying the discourses of people who are positioned differently by their sociocultural experiences, we can establish with a little more certainty the ways in which diverse peoples use different meaning systems to interpret their world and respond to it. Chapter 7 mentions some of the research methods that these changes seem to license. It shows how the methods are already being used by those doing research on language diversity and education.

CONCLUSION: LANGUAGE IN EDUCATION

Teachers, like researchers, are becoming more aware of the interpretative nature of social life. In their work, they are beginning to recognize the unique interpretations of meaning that their students bring with them into schools, because the realization is growing in education that discursive experiences shape each one of us differently, including individuals positioned inside diversities that are already distinct. Instead of accepting language as the mere vehicle through which the world is interpreted, teachers are beginning to see language and discourses of all kinds as the building blocks of the social world and as the 'substance' that shapes the human brain itself.

Inevitably, these developments are touching every aspect of education, because in schools language is the medium of instruction, it is the content of instruction, and it provides the pedagogical means by which that instruction is realized. Every outcome that schools try to achieve depends on the language ability of students: Students need high level skills in apprehending language; they also need to acquire the concepts at the heart of the curriculum that are expressed in language, or in other sign systems; and they need to make sense of the complex uses of language that teachers and texts employ in the process of passing on that curriculum knowledge. Constant, experience-based, discursive opportunities are central to these outcomes (Corson, 1998, 1999). Each new, experience-based encounter with the environment that a person has, builds on the embodied history of previous encounters. So children, and adults too, are continually renegotiating their subject positions and their identities within multiple and competing discourses.

More than all of this, beyond school, the life chances of students are determined by their ability to interact critically with the discourses around them, while still avoiding the temptation to be seduced by the disempowering messages those discourses often contain. The discourse surrounding children teaches them who they are, what their place is in the world, and what they need to do to become autonomous and valuable citizens. If they are unable to interact with those discourses with critical insight, they will be less autonomous and will likely become a burden to others. Language, critically acquired, is potentially empowering for people, as they constantly build on previous encounters with the world in their unique search for meaning and value.

DISCUSSION STARTERS

1. One of the central claims of positivist philosophers is that reality consists essentially in what is available to the senses. Do you agree or disagree with this? Why or why not? When might positivist approaches be adequate for describing human behaviour? Can you say why it is that a certain 'plausibility' exists in the findings of positivist researchers, as analyses of social life?

2. Human beings are capable of giving accounts of their own lives, and of their relationships with others. Why is this so important in distinguishing social research from other forms of scientific research?

3. Why does the deeper penetration into the social world allowed by interpretative methods also mean a loss in objectivity, precision and conclusiveness? How can this loss be justified? Is there any message in this for the accountability methods that employers often use to test their staff; or for the assessment and evaluation practices used in schools?

4. Describe two or three 'language games' that you play in. Are you always comfortable about being 'in' them? How do you react when the priorities of different language games overlap, or if they contradict one another? Do the different theories you develop about the world depend on the language game you are operating within?

5. Based on your own experiences, describe a few situations where people misinterpreted non-verbal signs in social settings? What caused these misinterpretations? Is the idea of 'rules of use' helpful in explaining misinterpretations? What is it about cultural differences exactly that affects the way different people interpret signs?

6. "Every verbal or non-verbal exchange in schools assumes some background knowledge that is expressed in signs whose rules of use are only partially shared". Explain this statement in your own words? How true is it? What does it mean for teacher practice? What does it mean for the practice of educational research?

7. What does 'being objective in interpreting the social world' really mean? Is it possible to be objective when dealing with other people who are socially or culturally different? Is it possible to be objective when doing research, or when teaching?

8. Based on your own experience of schools as a student or a teacher, what did those schools do to help students learn to interact critically with the discourses around them? What did they do to help students become critically autonomous and contributing citizens?

2

Language, Power, and Social Justice in Education

I don't know what they're saying. They could be saying anything, swearing at me, whatever. So it's a loss of control, power, that kind of stuff. And that's when their teacher's back gets up.

—*Ryan (1999, p. 175)*

In its first half, this chapter looks at language and power; and then at language and social justice in its second half. The chapter ends by bringing these two discussions together, suggesting how the great imbalances in power that language diversity tends to create in educational settings can be leavened in ways that maximize the distribution of social justice.

POWER AND LANGUAGE IN EDUCATION

For most everyday human purposes, power is exerted through verbal channels: Language is the vehicle for identifying, manipulating, and changing power relations between people. In this section, I point to the ways that education and the discourse practices that it authorizes can routinely repress, dominate, and disempower diverse groups whose practices differ from the norms that it establishes. I begin with some of the links between discourse and power, focusing on education, which often gives power to its own favoured norms of discourse, and so risks creating discrimination and injustice for the many who favour other discourses.

As mentioned already in chapter 1, 'discourse' for me refers to the full range of meaning-filled events and practices that we encounter in life. Discourse covers all the sign systems, including those that are not usually regarded as part of natural language itself. Again, "to be able to think is to be a skilled user of these sign systems, that is, to be capable of managing them correctly" (Harré & Gillett, 1994, p. 49).

Michel Foucault's views on the links between power and discourse have become influential: Rather than a privilege that an individual person possesses, power is a network of relations constantly in tension and ever-present in discursive activity. It is exercised through the production, accumulation, and functioning of various discourses. Discourse here is the fickle, uncontrollable 'object' of human conflict, although no-one is outside it completely, or sufficiently independent of discourses to manage them effectively. The conflicts that take place, however, over and around discourse, can be one-sided if the balance of power consistently favours some groups over others. So the study of power is best located at the point where the dominating activities of the powerful are played out in real and effective practices. For Foucault (1972, 1977, 1980), the development of particular forms of language meets the needs of the powerful but, as often as not, it meets those needs without any direct exercise of discursive influence by the powerful. Relevant to other points made here (including discussion in chap. 3–6), Foucault also speaks of the 'disciplining of discourse' (1984b): the way people (teachers for example), who are positioned by complex discourses that they themselves have had little hand in shaping, decide who has the right to talk and be listened to in discursive sites.

Even concepts that are at the heart of this book, like different 'ethnic groups', 'language varieties', and 'cultures' are constructed through the use of discourse in social situations. This means that these are only approximate descriptions of the lived realities and identities of people. In other words, people struggle over the way these expressions are used to refer to themselves: they resist their use, they embrace their use, or they modify their use. When we apply these labels to real people, in situations where important issues are at stake, we always have to confirm that the people themselves agree that these expressions can be used to refer to them. This means that for us as individuals, identity is a personal possession that we prefer to 'choose' for ourselves, not something that we receive at the hands of others. Nevertheless, people do make assumptions about other people's identities all the time, using whatever evidence is available to them.

Identity, Hegemony, and Cultural Background

Although a person's cultural background and language are very personal possessions, there are obvious similarities between people in these areas. Social distance (or closeness) between people is maintained by many things: by aspects of social structure; by the opportunities for interaction that people have; by constraints on behaviour; and by many other sociocultural processes and factors. All these things help change the meaning and the value of a person's presentation of self when he or she moves from context to context. In any setting, the discourses of social structure interact with people's social behaviour and with their social location, to add or sub-

tract shades of meaning or significance. So what people say, and the way in which
it is said, is heavily influenced by factors outside the individual. For others, our
identity is socially constructed, and it changes as we move from place to place,
sometimes in contradictory ways that position us differently with respect to powerful discourses.

Our perceptions of ourselves and our identities also change from place to place,
as the discourses we encounter give us different messages. And this is an important
factor in the way that power works. People have images of themselves and of their
roles that make them conform to different influences in their social environments.
Antonio Gramsci (1948/1966) highlights this non-coercive aspect of power, comparing it with the more obvious coercive forms of power. His concept of 'hegemony' describes how people agree to do things under the pressure of invisible
cultural power. In modern societies, power is based on wide-ranging agreements
of this kind. This non-coercive power penetrates consciousness itself, so that the
dominated become accomplices in their own domination.

Clearly, there is always pressure to trim and shape our identities to the context
we are in. Furthermore, this kind of hegemony is reinforced from both sides of the
power relationship: In their behaviour in any given context, the less powerful tend
to adhere to the norms created by powerful others who may be distant from them in
time and place. They do this while not always recognizing that they are being 'voluntarily coerced'. For instance, research on gendered relationships often uncovers
hegemony at work. Elinor Ochs and Carolyn Taylor (1995) look at family discussions that occur during mealtimes. They find that mothers commonly create forms
of interaction in which fathers become the arbiters of all the family's conduct. The
women set up the men as primary receivers of children's messages, and then implicitly agree to the males becoming the evaluators of other family members'
thoughts, actions, and feelings. In response to the historic images they have of
themselves, the fathers often turn these discussions into arenas where the mothers
become handy examples of incompetence for the children to observe and learn
from. This is hegemony at work, a notion that Frederick Erickson (1996) spells out
a little more fully:

> Hegemonic practices are routine actions and unexamined beliefs that are consonant
> with the cultural system of meaning and ontology within which it makes sense to take
> certain actions, entirely without malevolent intent, that nonetheless systematically
> limit the life chances of members of stigmatized groups. Were it not for the regularity
> of hegemonic practices, resistance by the stigmatized would not be necessary. (p. 45)

There seem to be psychological pressures from both sides of the power equation
that help the powerful by converting coercive forms of power into what is seen instead as legitimate authority (Wrong, 1979). Another example of this appears in
sociolinguistic studies. William Labov (1972a) found that stigmatized features of
speech are judged most harshly by the same people whose speech most exhibits
those features. This, too, is hegemony at work, and it allows formal organizations

like schools to feel more legitimate when they stigmatize different features of speech, non-standard varieties, languages, or other aspects of people's identities.

In fact, this working out of hegemony is nowhere more evident than in the restrictive cultural environments that most schools create for children from diverse backgrounds. Jim Cummins (1996) sees these schools as places where children who are different in some educationally relevant way are unable to 'negotiate their own identities'. They begin to lose their identity as human beings, before they ever gain it. For him, real change in the education of culturally diverse students means a shift from coercive to collaborative relations of power. Teachers need to re-define their roles and the types of structures at work in schools. These are the things that determine the micro-interactions that go on between educators, students, and communities. However, they are never neutral. Either they contribute to the disempowerment of culturally diverse students and their communities; or they enable teachers, students, and communities to challenge the operation of unwanted power structures.

No doubt most teachers do their best to promote fairness, and they certainly give the impression that they recognise diverse identities. Yet the professional roles they fill, as active members of a social institution, tend to put great limits on the actions of teachers, often against their will. This is also hegemony at work. Like any social institution with a long history, formal education is intolerant of any type of diversity that it has never recognised. And formal education is able to give free rein to this intolerance, even while it hides the relations that underlie its power, and even while it passes on a reality that can be highly partisan.

Systemic Bias in Educational Discourse

When it is in our interests to do so, people can easily rationalize and call this reasoning. We can distort through language and call this creative and original description. And we can repress others through language and call this 'being helpful' (Edelman, 1984). But we can also make this process go the other way and have it take more emancipatory directions. Norman Fairclough (1985, 1995) provides some examples of this that are relevant to the work of schools. He presents four descriptions of young people whose families, schools, and communities see them as misfits. They are thought of as 'incorrigible'; 'defiant'; 'lacking in responsibility'; and 'delinquent'. But Fairclough says these four expressions could be drastically re-worded, so that the same young people are seen differently: 'irrepressible' (incorrigible); 'debunking' (defiant); 'refusing to be sucked in by society' (lacking in responsibility); and 'spirited' (delinquent).

Probably neither wording really captures reality, since each reality depends on the viewpoint of the speaker, which in turn is shaped by the discourses that position that speaker, as was argued in chapter 1. In Fairclough's example, both wordings are loaded in some way. To some extent at least, they are distortions of reality. And if these distortions of different people's discursive 'realities' can happen within a single language, how distorted must the 'namings' of English appear to those raised in a very different culture who are also positioned by its very different language. North American Indian languages, for example, differ in important ways from English. The Indian languages use more verbs and verb phrases, while English relies more on the use of nouns and adjectives (Ross, 1996). One important thing about verbs is that they suggest that people are not one thing or another forever. In contrast, nouns and adjectives tend to create stereotypes in people's minds. For instance, in an Indian language, a person guilty of some crime could not be labelled easily as 'a criminal' or 'a recidivist'. Yet in English, people are labelled every day and the labels become naturalized. These labels win acceptance as neutral codes. And this happens in our schools as a routine activity, when professionals designate some children as 'gifted', 'visible minorities', 'learning disabled', or in a range of other ways.

Teachers often do this kind of labelling when they set out the limits of their working interests. Murray Edelman (1984) notes that professionals in schools often engage in rationalization, distortion, and repression in their discourse. Professionals even see these practices as part of their work, because an important part of it is to define the status of the clients of education: the 'underachiever'; the 'retarded'; the 'discipline problems'; the 'dropout'. By doing this, teachers define their own status in relation to their students. Up to a point, they also justify the work they do. In fact, they use special terms as labels in an exercise of power that would have much less significance if the terms were used by non-teachers. But in the hands of the empowered professionals, performing their roles, the terms become tools of power that can shape students' destinies. In this way, schools unwittingly help to reproduce inequalities between groups and between individuals.

Discourse, the School, and Sociocultural Reproduction

Schools play a key role in 'social and cultural reproduction'. This phrase is a shorthand way of referring to the process by which the features and attributes of a society or culture are passed on largely intact from one generation to another. Clearly, discourse itself is the key to reproducing the conventions of cultures and societies. We learn how to perform even the most simple conventional act, such as giving our names to new acquaintances, by observing how others do it, by using and listening to those others as models, and by noting the reactions of others to our performance and changing our behaviour accordingly. In this process of learning everyday conventional acts, each of us is a teacher, as well as a learner. In the signs and symbols that we use, we provide models to others and we learn from the signs and symbols used by others at different times.

Schools are places where most of a culture's dominant discourses are passed around and passed on. Michael Apple (1982) lists some of the major social functions that schools have: They select and certify a workforce; they maintain group privilege, by taking the form and content of the dominant culture and defining it as legitimate knowledge to be passed on; they help re-create a dominant culture; they legitimate new knowledge, new classes, and strata of social personnel. In short, for Apple, schools allocate people and legitimate knowledge, or legitimate people and allocate knowledge. As a result, formal education looks after the interests of some more privileged social groups better than it looks after the interests of some other sociocultural groups. Although doing all these things is not the purpose of schools, it is everywhere their function.

A central thinker in this area is the French anthropologist, Pierre Bourdieu (1966, 1981, 1984), whose work helps us understand several aspects of language, education and diversity. He sees the culture of the school as a creation of the dominant culture, whose practices are re-invented and perpetuated through education. As part of this reproduction process, some cultural conventions acquire a special status. So the owners of these things acquire status as well. And when these valued conventions and traditions are passed on to their offspring, the social advantages are passed on with them. Bourdieu is interested in this handing on of valued social attributes, and the handing on of social and cultural power that goes with it. He also talks about the modes of apprehension that people acquire through their own up-bringing that dispose them to see the world in certain ways, notably in ways familiar to them from within their own class or cultural position. These sets of dispositions seem to be linked to the language games or conceptual frameworks that I discussed in chapter 1. Although they do not control our thinking in any final way, they do dispose us to place more value on certain meaning systems rather than others, partly because those systems of signs are the most familiar to us.

To help explain the links between education and reproduction, Bourdieu presents 'culture' metaphorically as an 'economic system'. His phrase 'cultural capital' describes the advantages that people acquire as a part of their life experiences, their peer group contacts, and their family backgrounds. He lists some of these things: 'good taste', 'style', certain kinds of knowledge, abilities, and presentation of self. He also speaks of 'symbolic capital' which is the image of respectability, worthiness, and dignified authority that people acquire throughout their lives, often by devoting themselves painstakingly to maintaining and elaborating their personal reputations. As discussion in chapter 6 suggests, this symbolic capital is available to both men and women; but in traditional settings, this was the only kind of capital that women could readily accumulate. And simply by accumulating it, they added to the capital of their menfolk.

Most relevant to my theme in this book, Bourdieu also speaks of people possessing 'linguistic capital', which is the most important part of the cultural heritage. For Bourdieu, linguistic capital is more than the competence to produce grammatically well-formed expressions and forms of language. It also includes the ability to use appropriate norms for language use and to produce the right expressions at the right time for a particular 'linguistic market'. In any stratified society, variations in vocabulary, syntax, and accent are socially marked, so that even a basic interaction between people gives evidence of the social structure to which individuals belong. For example, to many people from Philadelphia, a change in one aspect of a single vowel in an utterance is enough to make a White speaker sound Black, and a Black speaker sound White (Fasold, 1990).

In Bourdieu's view, people in possession of 'appropriate' linguistic capital in any context are more favourably placed than others to exploit the situation. This setting of unequal linguistic power is affected in two ways:

- most profit or advantage comes from a use of modes of expression that are the least equally distributed
- the readiness of minority language or non-standard speakers to stigmatize their own variety means that they often condemn themselves to silence in public settings for fear of offending norms that they themselves sanction

Accordingly, using Bourdieu's metaphor, there are many linguistic markets in which rare or high status forms bring profit to the user, and where non-standard or low-status language use has a limited value, because it is not viewed from within the dominant modes of apprehension that dispose influential people to award it value. To such people, for example, a non-standard variety's different 'rules' of use seem inappropriate within that marketplace, unless someone contests the prevailing rules and modifies them in some way. As a result, children from non-dominant backgrounds are often silent within those 'markets', or they are forced to withdraw from taking part in them. And teachers in schools everywhere are very familiar with responses like these, especially from students of diversity.

Bourdieu argues that while the cultural or linguistic capital that is valued in schools is not equally available to children from different backgrounds, schools, as upper middle class institutions, still operate as if all children had equal access to it. By basing their assessments of school success and failure and their award of certificates and qualifications on children's possession of this high status capital, which is unequally available, schools act in such a way as to reproduce the social arrangements that are favourable to some social groups, but unfavourable to others. In this way, the value of the dominant cultural capital that is passed to the next generation, is reinforced yet again. This complex social process is described by Bourdieu as the application of 'symbolic power' by dominant social groups, who inflict 'symbolic violence' in this way upon non-dominant groups.

Elsewhere, I discuss the role of 'high status vocabulary use' as a tool for discriminating between students in the academic marketplace (Corson, 1995b, 1999). There is much evidence that vocabulary diversity is the most consistent marker of proficiency used throughout education; and I argue that the example this offers strongly supports Bourdieu's ideas. Just the motivated readiness that some people have to use high status vocabulary can allow them to exploit formal educational settings to their own advantage, even though this advantage comes mainly from the accumulated discourses of their relatively privileged upbringing. In other words—returning to the discussion in chapter 1—it is discursive relations outside education that 'position' people through their vocabularies.

As a result, some people are prepared by their comfortable grasp of powerful signs and sign systems for easy entry into lifetime prospects of relative privilege and educational success, while others find entry more difficult. Often, those others come from groups disempowered by things to do with their social class, race, gender, or cultural positioning. I argue that education fails to take account of the fact that many children's discursive relations, before and outside schools, are inconsistent with the kinds of lexico-semantic demands that schools and their high-status culture of literacy place upon them, often unnecessarily. Partly, as a result of this, many English-as-a-first language and English-as-a-second language students, from some cultural, linguistic and social backgrounds, are almost guaranteed to fail in the middle levels of present-day education, before they have a chance to show that they can succeed.

Again, for Bourdieu, people in possession of 'appropriate' linguistic capital in any context are more favourably placed to exploit the system of differences that exists. I return to this idea at many places in this book, relating it to non-standard varieties, different discourse norms, and non-dominant languages. Bourdieu's idea has become influential in educational debate, as it has gradually become clearer that the cultural capital that upper middle class institutions like schools place value on, is often different from the cultural capital valued by people in their own communities, and in other social spaces. Indeed, the kinds of language valued in schools really throws doors open for those who possess it. For example, students who speak the standard French that is more highly valued in Ontario's francophone schools than the vernacular Franco-Ontarian variety, are able to position themselves better in the dominant market, and so improve their life chances (Heller, 1999). For them, language is more than a democratic means for interacting with the world: it is a commodity, and a mechanism of social selection.

Diverse sociocultural groups do have their own highly valued sets of linguistic and cultural capital, but these can be quite different from the capital valued in schools. Despite this, schools still operate as if all children had equal access to the capital valued in formal education. As a result, they reproduce arrangements that are favourable to some and unfavourable to other groups, by basing their assessments of success on children's possession of this cultural capital, although it is unequally available. Moreover, the value of the school's form of cultural capital, passed to the next generation, is reinforced yet again, unless schools begin to value other forms of capital. Meanwhile, those whose cultural capital is not valued by schools find that their own capital is simply left out of the reproduction process. Over time, it begins to fade. And to that extent their sociocultural group begins to lose its cohesion, its solidarity, and its identity, unless its members have other avenues for passing on their capital, outside of formal education.

Yet most people still believe that schools are rather neutral in the way they do all this. Because of the way hegemony works, even the members of marginal groups are disposed to accept all this as 'the way things must be' in education. If their children do not succeed in schools, those treated unfairly by the institution of education still come to believe that their children's failure results from the children's natural inability: their lack of giftedness. They wrongly accept that the educational selection process is a fair one based on objective educational criteria. How does this happen?

Four points stand out in Bourdieu's discussion of the role of schools in reproduction. These points link schools with the actions of parents and pupils themselves (after Harker, 1990, pp. 89ff):

- knowing the lower success rate of children from marginalized backgrounds, and interpreting the discourses of schools as best they can, the marginalized students adjust their expectations downwards; and these lower expectations become part of the way these students look at the world
- when students from marginalized backgrounds do experience some success in schooling, their parents often make choices on their behalf that keep them away from the same kinds of opportunities that similarly endowed children from more dominant backgrounds are urged to grasp
- schools recognize those who play the game of schooling and who acknowledge the legitimacy of schools in offering that recognition, which means that the slanted criteria schools use to judge success are supported, because students and parents agree to submit to those criteria
- school qualifications lose their value if too many people gain access to them; so schools begin to place more value on other factors, especially the cultural capital prized and possessed by dominant groups, such as style, presentation of self, and the motivated use of high status language

In summary, then, the school passes on training and information which can only be fully received by those who have had the culturally and linguistically appropriate training that the school itself does not give. Again, all groups do have cultural capital of their own, but it is not always the same kind of capital that is recognized and valued in education. When we move from one cultural context to another, things that count as high status cultural capital change. Linguistically different children, seen from the context of this book, begin to feel lost in a school where the dominant varieties of the dominant language, and all their institutionalized discourse norms, permeate everything and define everything that matters.

Toward Some Resolution

Clearly, the way to resolve this unjust situation that affects education in every country, is for schools and school systems to acknowledge and address the different kinds of language diversity they contain. Later in this chapter, I suggest an approach to social justice that gives attention to the voices of non-dominant and minority groups. But there is another factor hard at work silencing voices of diversity, which needs considering first. It is a by-product of the so-called postmodern condition itself.

One of the main features of postmodernity is a trend away from centralization and toward diversity and devolution of control. In this new world, many more voices are being raised, including the voices of those who were once dispossessed. And these voices are bringing a surprisingly different range of messages, to educational policy makers and practitioners alike. These messages eloquently express human values that were once silenced by dominant ideologies and belief systems. Yet, in hearing these new voices now appearing at local levels, powerful forces beyond the local are still ignoring the messages that they raise. This is especially true of education, and it is true of education for diversity in particular. In many places, central authorities have become more remote and overbearing, rather than less so. Even the trend toward devolving control to local schools has led to injustices on a grand scale in many countries.

Part of the problem, as I suggest elsewhere (Corson, 1998), is that present-day education almost everywhere in the English-speaking world is set firmly within capitalist social relations. Seen on so grand a scale, this tight coupling of capitalism with all aspects of social life is a relatively recent development. This is because the pure free-market economic arrangements that are so essential to capitalism were limited in their effects as long as capitalism was kept a little separate from government:

> For forty years after the early 1930s the intellectual supporters of pure free-market economics were an isolated minority, apart from businessmen whose perspective always makes it difficult to recognize the best interests of their system as a whole, in proportion as it concentrates their minds on the best interests of their particular firm or industry. (Hobsbawm, 1989, p. 334)

All this has changed in recent decades. Even government itself has been captured in many places by free-market views that are far less restrained than those that formerly applied. Many present-day politicians and the intellectuals who advise them tend to believe that for governments to succeed, the whole world is best viewed as a business, and is best interpreted in business terms. As a result, citizens living in societies where this ideology is dominant, are forced to live their lives within the ideology, whether they want to or not. This is because public policy and the world itself are saturated by the ideology.

In this limited and limiting world view, the dominant metaphor is that all human beings inhabit a marketplace where the quality of something is decided according to the price it can fetch, rather than according to any intrinsic and real qualities it might have. Borrowing Bourdieu's metaphor, this is tantamount to saying that the only cultural capital that matters is the capital that has the highest prestige, as if social prestige were the only indicator of real value in the marketplace. Moreover, this trend is having a harmful impact on human social relations themselves, especially on the bonds that exist between people. These bonds today are valued more often by the quick standards of economic transactions than by the more lasting ties of culture or class. In turn, the unfortunate effect of all this is to project a respect for 'sameness' onto the social world, rather than a respect for the actual diversity that the social world contains, especially—in the context of this book—the actual diversity of language varieties and norms of use that exist alongside one another in single social spaces.

In spite of appearances to the contrary, then, these capitalist social relations are the most assimilationary cultural and linguistic forces that the world has ever seen. This means that any diversity in provisions that the new diverse voices are winning, is being taken away by the pressure towards assimilation that capitalism creates. In addition, this paradox occurs because capitalist social relations are also prospering under the new freedoms and the open message systems that are part of the postmodern condition. So what does all this mean for language diversity and education?

On the one hand, in this new world of postmodernity, the voices speaking out for language diversity are certainly being heard at last. But on the other hand, non-dominant varieties or norms have little value in the marketplace of that new world. As a consequence, wherever the values and interests of schools are linked tightly into that marketplace, students from linguistically diverse backgrounds find that their language interests are still missing from education. And paradoxically, even while they are being marked out in education by their linguistic differences, the same students find that forces of hegemony are hard at work pressuring them to keep silent, and to conceal their linguistic differences during formal education.

Not surprisingly, linguistically diverse students still feel anonymous and distant from the school's goals. And they feel powerless in the face of this anonymity. The remoteness from the school of their families and communities worsens these feelings of alienation. So rather than a route to freedom and self-fulfilment, the world of the school is still a place of daunting obstacles for many linguistically different students. Fortunately, teachers in some places are beginning at last to recognize the injustices inherent in this state of affairs (Corson, 1998). They are beginning to wrestle with these issues, whose resolution seems to depend on having a clearer conception of social justice and education.

SOCIAL JUSTICE AND LANGUAGE IN EDUCATION

In this section and the next, I will try to offer a clear and accessible social justice framework for making decisions in education about language policies and practices. I will begin by sketching the strengths and weaknesses of the rather individualist approach to social justice offered by John Rawls whose social justice ideas have been very influential over recent generations in the US and elsewhere. Then I will contrast that approach with a 'critically real' approach to judging social justice which is more respectful of minority group interests, and more closely linked to the way the world actually is.

A critically real approach to social justice recognizes that diversity is part of the reality of the human condition; language diversity no less than other forms of diversity. Because human groups and individuals have distinctly different language interests, those differences often need to be addressed in different ways in public policy if social justice is to be served.

Social Justice

Social justice has much to do with ideas about legitimacy, about fairness and impartiality, about welfare and mutual advantage, and about political and social consensus. Justice itself relates to the way that benefits and burdens are distributed, and is usually said to exist when people receive that to which they are entitled (Barry, 1989).

While uncertain about what 'justice' might be, most would agree with Rawls (1972) that justice is the first virtue of social institutions, in much the same way as truth is the first virtue of systems of thought. But a problem with Rawls' own account of social justice is its concentration on the justice needs of individuals, to the exclusion of the justice needs of groups. This creates serious problems when thinking about the fair treatment of language diversity issues in education. So I outline these here.

Rawls (1972, 1980, 1993) sees the individual as the starting point for any discussion about the criteria for a just society. My sketch of this account follows, suggesting some of its weaknesses. Later discussion will include a more recent conception that modifies Rawls' stark individualism. This other approach recognizes that people are inevitably positioned and shaped by the social and the cultural, so that a conception of individualism that ignores that fact is an impoverished one. It misses seeing the way people really are.

I argue that considerable room must be left for this critically real account in any discussion of social justice and language, if we are to give sufficient recognition to that most obvious feature of language itself: its essential role in allowing and promoting communicative interaction between social groups of two or more people.

My general point, then, in opposition to a starkly individualist account of justice, is this: If our aim is to provide language arrangements in education and society that are just ones, while also considering the rightful needs of human individuals, then we must inevitably consider the needs of the group at the same time as the individual, since language in its literal sense is a feature of human collectivities. A language is a set of social conventions having value and point only when it develops over time from the interactional and communicative needs of social groups. As a social institution itself, a language is not just an instrumental convenience made available by chance to the individuals who acquire it. Rather, as chapter 1 argues, it is the very means by which individual human beings are socialized and from which they develop a consciousness of themselves and their world. This consciousness is a direct and unique reflection of the culture that comprises the many social, ethnic, class, or gender groups who share the language.

In promoting social justice in language matters then, there is little that can be done for the individual that does not begin with the group at the same time. And speakers of minority language varieties are no less 'language groups' than the different groups of majority language speakers who live in a given setting.

The Rawls Account of Social Justice and Some Other Accounts

The basic idea to which Rawls is committed is also a cornerstone of ethics: that no individual can be treated as the means to the ends of society. Working from this, he sees social justice as the content of an agreement that rational people would reach under conditions that do not allow for bargaining power to be translated into advantage. In other words, social justice decisions need to be made in an impartial way by decision-makers who do not benefit unreasonably themselves from choosing as they do.

For example, on Rawls' account, any proponents of 'English Only' policies in the United States, would still have to support those policies even if they, as the proponents, were going to be disadvantaged by them (for instance, in the way that Hispanic speakers would be disadvantaged). The policy makers would try to work out what arrangements ought to exist, and do this in a context freed from their own self-interest and bias. In other words, they would decide what was just, after detaching themselves from their own interests, and while adopting a standpoint of strict impartiality. Rawls calls this attempt at detachment a 'veil of ignorance'.

One of the earliest statements of this impartial approach to justice is the New Testament's 'Golden Rule', which advises us to do unto others as we would have them do unto us. Indeed, most of the world's religions have a similar injunction, some predating the New Testament. Yet even this cornerstone of beneficence from the world's scriptures has a dark underside, as George Bernard Shaw cautions: Don't do to others as you would have them do to you; their tastes might be different (1903). This is a wry twist to the Rule, but there is more than humour in this rider from Shaw. He reminds us that we cannot easily see the world from the point of view of most other people, because they are 'positioned' very differently from ourselves. So we cannot easily make well-informed and fair decisions on behalf of those others, in anything like the neat way that Rawls envisions.

In other words, it is usually very difficult to determine in advance what fair treatment would be, in any given context, if one is not a participant in the discursive practices of the context and knowledgeable about all the cultural and historical influences that shape that context and position people within it. This is especially so in matters of language policy, where it is not easy to create a context freed of self-interest and bias, because each of us is burdened with the bias of the language varieties that we already possess, and few can be neutral in judging the interests of their own language variety's speakers against the speakers of language varieties that are not their own. We cannot step outside the interests that our socialization into a language variety creates for us, because it is these very interests, and the similar interests of those who share our language, that we feel ourselves obliged to defend, even through the use of the same language. We cannot escape our social positioning for long, if at all.

Indeed, Rawls' conception of the person seems 'unreal' because it sets the individual aside from the social being. Furby (1986) and Sandel (1982) argue that the individual person in Rawls' account lacks human sociality. Even in Rawls' (1993) later modifications of the theory, it is hard to escape the conclusion that individual agents all display the attitudes and beliefs of 'men in modern market societies', in a consistent and exclusive way. In other words, his agents are like Rawls himself. Moreover, he admits the practical limitations of his "well-ordered society," because it needs to be "a closed system" that has "no significant relations to other societies" (1980, p. 526). This implies, of course, a society with no significant relations with other language speakers, where everyone has broadly the same goals, values, interests, and world-view.

For language policy issues, these are very problematic aspects of this theory of justice because, as I have argued, language is a creation of social beings and has a value for the individual largely in social interaction. Even the private language in which much of our thinking is conducted is fuelled by social exchanges: To a very real extent our capacity to think itself depends on the many previous dialogues in which we have engaged. Again, our discursive positioning shapes our consciousness and our identity.

So the sense of the collective being, who is produced and produces him or herself through interaction within and across groups in a society or culture, is missing from Rawls. Nor does his early work focus on the institutional relations that are part of the social being, and which underlie economic classes (Nielsen, 1978; I. Young, 1981). Instead, he seems to see class inequality, and therefore cultural, gender, and linguistic inequality, as inevitable structures, even in his ideal human social system.

As an example, an 'English Only' policy is the kind of decision that Rawls' approach to social justice should be able to discourage. Yet, if applied to social practice, the Rawls' approach would actually sanction 'English Only' policies in many contexts. As mentioned, Rawls works from a first principle rather like the Golden Rule, but this first principle of his avoids the rider that Shaw adds to that Rule. It avoids the fact that decision makers cannot see the world from the point of view of those who are very different from themselves and who do not enjoy the same privileged language position. In the United States, for example, the Latino population's well-being is almost exclusively in the hands of English-speaking monolinguals who "have little or no understanding of the condition of bilingualism and little sympathy for the problems encountered by immigrant populations" (Valdés, 1997, p. 25).

In contrast to Rawls, internationally prominent liberal accounts of social justice that have been advanced recently in Canada have tried to incorporate a more collectivist ethic. Charles Taylor (1992) believes that a society with strong collectivist goals can still be liberal if it is capable of respecting diversity, especially diversity that includes those who might not share its common goals. For Taylor, the political search by Quebec for recognition of its distinctness as a society within Canada, for instance, is a collective goal that can be allowed to over-ride individual rights under certain circumstances. Taylor further suggests that the "rigidities of procedural liberalism may rapidly become impractical in tomorrow's world" (1992, p. 61).

As critics of liberalism often observe, however, "what defines liberalism is its disregard for the context of choice, for the way that choices are situated in cultural communities" (Kymlicka, 1989, p. 206). This usually translates into an active hostility by liberals to minority rights, so that "schemes which single out minority cultures for special measures," like bilingual education programs, seem "irremediably unjust, a disguise for creating or maintaining racial or ethnic privilege" (1989, p. 4). As a liberal theorist himself, Will Kymlicka tries to rehabilitate liberalism as it is commonly interpreted, especially by addressing its failure to respond to people's strong intuitions about the importance of cultural membership. In doing so, he also re-examines and questions the moral ontology of liberalism itself—its individualism, and its taken-for-granted, naive, and uncritical egalitarianism. He argues that membership of a cultural or linguistic community has to be a relevant criterion for distributing the benefits and burdens which are the concern of a liberal theory of justice.

In this chapter's final section, I recommend a critically real approach to social justice that recognizes diversity as part of the reality of the human condition—language diversity no less than other forms of diversity. Because human groups and individuals have distinctly different language interests, those differences often need to be addressed in different ways in public and educational policy, for social justice to be served.

LANGUAGE, POWER, AND SOCIAL JUSTICE

Critical Realism: An Emancipatory Conception of Social Justice

The prominent British philosopher of science, Roy Bhaskar, calls his emancipatory conception of discovery 'critical realism' (Bhaskar, 1986; Corson, 1997). Unlike Rawls' conception, this one sees the needs of different groups as quite different needs that arise from different group interests, and which often require different forms of treatment. In other words, to treat people equally and fairly, we do not treat them as if they were all the same, or even potentially the same.

Critical realism is an ontology: it asks, 'what are the most basic things that exist in the social world; what are the things that need to be recognized in the search for justice, or in the search for knowledge about anything?' Bhaskar shows that the most basic evidence we can have about the social world is the reasons and accounts that given people offer to describe the things in their world that they value, or the things that oppress them. This is always our 'prima facie' evidence, although as evidence it still needs to be confirmed and supported by other forms of evidence.

For example, decision makers creating a school's policies and practices, would need to consult the reasons and accounts of participants with interests at stake in the decision, and use this as the starting point for their policymaking. Teachers and administrators would do this early in the process, and they would keep on doing it at every stage. In fact, the policy makers themselves would tend to change. The actual decision makers would be different people, as the policy comes closer to local settings, because they would need to be in touch with the reality of those settings and the reality of people positioned within them. This would imply a rather ordered, devolutionary approach to policy making.

Briefly, this means devolving real decision-making power to those who are actually in touch with the things that oppress them, or with the things that they value. For example, in multilingual settings, this decision-making might include the following stages of increased devolution:

• first, a use of consultation at a wider system level (attending to the interests of those with a stake in the issue) to draw up any norms that could operate as principles across the system to increase the scope for optional use of any single minority language alongside English, and also alongside other minority languages

• second, a use of consultation in devolved local settings to establish more local norms for allotting status to minority languages, critically accepting the norms already identified at system level as a necessary starting point, and making use of any grounds for compatibility that follow from both sets of norms

• third, a use (as often as necessary) of consultation in decision making within increasingly devolved local settings, establishing sub-norms where needed to determine compatibility; and eventually, if necessary, compromising on incompatible issues

Throughout this process, compatible interests shared by language minority groups would provide the material for constructing over-riding norms, while incompatible interests become the subject of compromise at more local levels (state, community, district, school, grade-level, classroom, individual student).

To make this work, the first norms, or principles, for policy makers to decide are those that apply at whole system level. Below are some suggested principles for use in minority language policy making in education at district, state or national levels (Corson & Lemay, 1996). To meet the type of diversity found in multilingual settings, like the United States or Canada, three policy principles would seem necessary:

- The *first* policy principle guarantees the right of children to be educated wherever possible in the same variety of language that is learned at home or is valued most by them. For instance, young speakers of Spanish or French as first languages would be taught using their first language as the vehicle of instruction for most of the school day.
- When the first policy principle cannot be met, the *second* principle guarantees the right of children to attend a school that shows full respect for the language variety that is learned at home or valued most by them, including respect for its role in preserving important ethnic, traditional, social, gender, or religious values and interests. In other words, use of the minority language variety would be encouraged and valued in every school context, even while it is not used as the vehicle of instruction. (For an extensive list of approaches to valuing minority languages in schools, see Corson, 1999.)
- The third policy principle guarantees the right of children to learn, to the highest level of proficiency possible, the standard language variety of wider communication used by the society as a whole. In other words, complete mastery of some regionally 'standardized' variety of English (or French in Quebec) would be a key goal of children's education.

Now this third principle also meets the main concerns of 'English Only' advocates in the United States and elsewhere, if I understand them correctly. Clearly it would be socially unjust if any student left school without mastery of the regionally 'standardized' variety of English sufficient to continue on to later stages of education, and sufficient to live happily and autonomously in their own country.

In a later chapter, I address the first principle more fully. The ethical justification for minority first-language maintenance comes from the reasons and accounts of relevant users of that minority language in the local context. If the local people do value first-language maintenance in schools, then, following a critically real approach, policy makers are ethically obliged to support the first principle; or at least the second principle, if local conditions of great linguistic pluralism make it impossible to support the first.

On the other hand, if local people want nothing more than access to English, policy makers are obliged to respect that view too, but only after they have engaged in community education to point out the likely negative consequences of following that policy. In other words, people need to be fairly informed of the academic and intellectual advantages of bilingual education that they would be denying their children. I review these in a later chapter too.

At the same time, in settings where many languages exist alongside one another, like parts of New York, Toronto, or Los Angeles, it might not be possible for more than a few schools to be organized to meet the first principle. In discussions of ethical decision-making, 'ought' always implies 'can'. This means that people are not obliged to do what they cannot reasonably do. Again, in these highly pluralist settings, the second principle becomes the second-best alternative for most schools.

Yet the second principle is hardly good enough for children from a broad range of different backgrounds. Clearly, as I argue in later chapters, just valuing the minority language does not go far enough for many students, such as the signing Deaf, or users of Native languages, or indeed children in general for whom loss of their minority first language would create academic difficulties. These children, and many others, will always need the support that the first policy principle offers.

CONCLUSION

Probably more than at any other time in history, people are now calling for changes in language 'status'. But these advocates are meeting resistance from the assimilationary tendency that is part of the postmodern social condition, and from the hegemonic nature of present-day schooling, which is still intolerant of any diversities that it has never sanctioned. A critically real account acknowledges the existence of diversity as something that can no longer be excluded from human affairs, and as something that cannot be excluded from decisions about social and educational policies and practices. This conception sees the needs of different groups as different needs. They arise from different group interests, and they often require forms of fair treatment that vary from group to group. Roy Bhaskar's ideas themselves are simple, although the philosophical argument behind them is a complex and compelling one.

Briefly again, Bhaskar shows that people's reasons and accounts are the most basic evidence available to us for deciding anything about the social world, because they tell us the things that are in people's minds about that world. So they help us explain the operation of the many social things that position people. On this account, decision makers consult the reasons and accounts of participants who are really in touch with the factors that oppress them, or with the structures in their lives that they value. They then use that as preliminary evidence in their decision-making. There are several complementary lines of action that schools themselves can take in treating language and social justice issues in education (Corson, 1999). Each of these types of social action can help foster the language awareness needed to see through distorting ideologies and hegemonic practices, and to approach the world in a more critically real way. None will guarantee an end to the conflict that multiple forms of oppression create in social settings, as discursive injustices continually interact and play off one another. Yet each of these types of social action combines respect for the good of the individual with respect for the good of the social group.

First, there is a need to create better patterns of communication within school organizations, in classrooms and in staffrooms: patterns that free participants to consider planned, rational, just, and consensual action in pursuit of their educational aims;.

Secondly, schools in many places are finding they need commonly agreed, local policies, negotiated with the community, for meeting the kinds of complex problems that are considered in this chapter: language policies on race and minority cultures, bilingualism, poverty, and disadvantage.

Thirdly, many suggest that children in schools need to acquire 'critical language awareness' (see van Lier & Corson, 1997) through a language curriculum that promotes social awareness of discourse, critical awareness of variety, and consciousness of and practice for change.

DISCUSSION STARTERS

1. "Identity is a personal possession that we prefer to 'choose' for ourselves, not something that we receive at the hands of others." Is this always true for you? In what circumstances does your preferred identity conflict with the identity others have for you? How do you feel when this happens? What steps do you take to resist that imposed identity?

2. Do you agree that discourse is at the heart of power and the exercise of power? Are there situations where power is exercised without sending a sign or a signal of some kind? To what extent are those situations independent of discourse?

3. "Professionals in schools often engage in rationalization, distortion, and repression in their discourse." How true is this of schools that you are familiar with? Can you give an example of each practice? Assuming that they are not deliberate practices, what can teachers do to change them?

4. List some everyday occasions when you agree to do things yourself under the invisible pressure of "hegemony." How do you feel about this when it happens? Do you ever resist that pressure? When and how?

5. Does the example of different active access by students to academic vocabulary, help reveal what Bourdieu means by cultural capital? Why is it helpful (or unhelpful)? What other examples of high status cultural capital unfairly affect students in elementary and high schools?

6. How far can schools go in accommodating the cultural capital of diverse groups? Are some schools better placed to do this than others? What makes them different?

7. Three principles were described for use in minority language policy making. Are school systems in your local area satisfying any or all of these principles successfully? What obstacles stand in the way of reform? How might these obstacles be removed?

8. What steps would you take to develop a new language policy for use in some educational institution or school? What are some of the power and social justice factors that you would need to take into account?

9. Think about an educational institution that you have personally experienced. Discuss its effectiveness in valuing and promoting linguistic diversity. How helpful have each of the following groups been in furthering that process: its teachers, its administrators, student body, and wider community?

10. Whose cultural capital are schools recognizing if they do not recognize the cultural capital of diverse groups? Can you be specific about this cultural capital, and about who benefits and who loses?

11. How does 'symbolic capital' relate to 'cultural capital'? Can linguistic capital be a part of a person's symbolic capital? Give some everyday examples of the three types.

3

Different Cultural
Discourse Norms

She was always stoppin' me, sayin' "that's not important enough"; and I hadn't hardly
started talking!
                                                                          —*Michaels (1981, p. 439)*

This chapter examines language injustices that can affect culturally different students, even those who speak English proficiently. Language theorists have long argued that many of the difficulties for culturally different children in mainstream
schools can be attributed to sociolinguistic interference (Hymes, 1971). As individuals, we develop 'co-occurrence expectations' and 'contextualization expectations' through our interactions with others. These expectations about context
clues, the structuring of attention, the regulation of talk or turn-taking, are often
culturally specific. When we have our expectations about these things upset by
subtle variations in the signs of culturally different others, then our ability and
willingness to participate in that context is often reduced (Gumperz, 1977). While
there are other, more obvious difficulties that arise for children, especially if they
use a different language variety, these other difficulties are made worse, because
teachers can easily overlook the more subtle differences in norms that children
bring to school and the impact these differences in linguistic capital can have on
school learning.

There is now much evidence about the discourse norms that culturally different people acquire from their socialization, norms that usually reflect quite different cultural values. Teachers can easily misinterpret different discourse norms
when they come across them, especially when the signs used by students are similar to familiar signs but carry different meanings. This is particularly the case if
teachers are unaware that culturally different children do have different ways of
interacting, and that the rules of use associated with these norms are just as consistent and regular as those used in the teachers' own cultural community. For ex-

ample, sometimes teachers see culturally different children as unresponsive or disruptive, if the students are unwilling to look at them during interaction. Sometimes too, they wrongly label culturally different children as slow learners if they have different norms for answering and asking questions; or different norms for putting their stories into words, like the African American student quoted at the beginning of this chapter.

In reality, what some see as slowness or lack of responsiveness from children in classrooms, is often very context-specific. In other words, it appears mainly in 'key classroom situations'. For example, children from indigenous backgrounds sometimes respond less willingly in certain activities: when they are singled out before the group, in some formal classroom context; when they have to raise their hands to show that they want to answer a question; or when their own responses are assessed publicly, in ways that conflict with their own cultural experiences. But these patterns do not come from some acute shyness that shows up in formal contexts, or from embarrassment in the presence of people from another culture. Rather, they come from broadly different childhood cultural experiences, based on different cultural values, that give children discourse norms whose rules of use often seem inconsistent with the dominant norms of formal schooling. This chapter explores the research on these differences, and the way they affect classroom and school practices.

CULTURAL IDENTITY AND MISMATCHES IN DISCOURSE

The conceptual world of a culture includes many classificatory systems. Most of these are expressed or supported in the language of the culture. When the classificatory systems of two cultures come into contact, there is always some degree of mismatch. A simple example of this is the mismatch in colour coding observed between people from very different cultures. Although it remains the same real-world colour spectrum, different people divide that spectrum up differently. But there are other more subtle mismatches too, that occur away from the concrete, physical world. And many of these can lead to major intercultural misunderstandings. For example, mismatches in greeting styles; or in teasing behaviour can produce mistrust or a general unease, or even a sense of impending violence (McDonald, 1989). This kind of miscommunication can be disastrous, for instance, if heavily armed United Nations peacekeeping troops misinterpret the discourse norms of the inhabitants of a country they are policing. And more prosaically, in everyday educational contexts, these mismatches can have serious consequences for culturally different children.

The mismatches are more noticeable when they appear at a boundary between people that is already clear-cut. Often the rival classificatory system is treated ironically; it is portrayed as romantic, emotional, or comical. The humorous and caricatured ways in which the English and the French sometimes view one another and their cultures is an example of this. But when a minority population has been forced to become bicultural, through conquest, slavery, or through economic and political pressure, the differences between the two cultures can become a source of mutual misunderstanding. And while the differences and the way they are expressed might escape the notice of members of the dominant culture, they can be a continual source of oppression for the less powerful. Cultural identity becomes very important to people when their culture is under constant threat, especially when they feel themselves to be 'involuntary' minorities.

Voluntary and Involuntary Minorities

Discussing variations in rates of school success among culturally different communities, John Ogbu (1987) draws a useful distinction between 'involuntary' and 'voluntary' minority communities:

> The main factor differentiating the more successful from the less successful minorities appears to be the nature of the history, subordination, and exploitation of the minorities, and the nature of the minorities' own instrumental and expressive responses to their treatment, which enter into the process of their schooling. (p. 317)

Involuntary minorities are constrained by social, school, and classroom structures that denied them equal opportunity over many generations. Historically, they encountered a job ceiling in the world of work, inferior forms of education, and random racism in every sphere of living. Their cultural and linguistic capital has not been fully recognized in the institution of education, and their cultural interests have not been consulted by policy makers at system or school levels. In short, the members of these minorities have very good reasons for believing that they do not have an equal chance, when compared with members of the dominant group.

Most of the research on the discourse norms of involuntary minorities has concentrated on the African American and indigenous peoples of North America; or on aboriginal peoples elsewhere. Other involuntary minorities include francophone Canadians who inhabit ancestral territories outside francophone Quebec, or the Celtic-speaking peoples of Wales, Ireland, and Scotland, or the large, ancestral Hispanic populations in the south-west of the United States. Also, Black South Africans, living under apartheid, shared many of the characteristics of involuntary minorities, although these various African peoples made up a large majority of their country's population. For this and other reasons, the label 'minorities' is one that I use cautiously. In this chapter, I use it only when discussing Ogbu's ideas.

Involuntary minorities also have 'secondary cultural differences' that develop as "a response to a contact situation, especially a contact situation involving the domination of one group by another" (Ogbu, 1987, p. 322). This domination occurs in a setting from which the involuntary minority cannot withdraw, because the setting is really their own ancestral home. As a result, with no chance of living their lives away from the all-intruding dominant culture, they see the differences between themselves and the dominant culture as insurmountable. Indeed, their own identity is largely defined by the intricate differences between the two cultures. So, paradoxically perhaps, just bridging those differences risks diminishing their identity as a people whose culture can exist nowhere else. After so long in contact with the dominant culture, the minority culture's existence is intertwined with it.

All this contrasts with the more straightforward influences that affect voluntary immigrant minorities. Immigrants have discourse norms and other cultural characteristics of their own too, which are regularly misinterpreted in school settings. But members of these communities see their own cultural differences as barriers that they need to overcome to achieve success in employment, education, or lifestyle. They are much more relaxed about adapting: about becoming bicultural. They know that their culture still exists elsewhere, largely unaffected by the new culture. Often, they look back on their former homelands as places of fewer opportunities, where education in many cases was even worse than the worst forms of schooling that they experience in their new country. And because their 'primary cultural differences' are so starkly recognizable, it is easier for voluntary minorities to adopt strategies to improve their academic success and their social adjustment.

But regardless of background, the moment voluntary or involuntary minority children enter schools, they are expected to learn and abide by the cultural norms of the school. Almost everywhere, these same norms of behaviour match the values and traditions of the dominant culture. As outlined in chapter 2, Bourdieu compellingly sets out the case in support of this point. And it is a point that Muriel Saville-Troike (1979) echoes in describing her own US educational system: For her, that system mainly prepares middle class children, from the dominant culture, to take part in their own culture.

DIVERSE CULTURAL VALUES AND DISCOURSE NORMS

Many studies report mismatches between the discourse norms of culturally different children, and the norms favoured in schools and classrooms. Often these studies appear in rather inaccessible sources. And because they usually deal with relatively small cultural groups, in single countries, their relevance to other settings can be overlooked. This section draws together many of these studies. It compiles evidence about subtle differences in discourse norms and values that rarely appears in the professional training curriculum of teachers. As a result, that evidence still falls outside the taken-for-granted reality of professional practice in mainstream classrooms.

Discussion in chapter 4 is relevant here too. It looks at sociocultural differences in the way that literacy is viewed and used. Often culturally different students approach literacy activities in ways that are inconsistent with school norms, but still

quite consistent with their own cultural norms. The evidence confirms that because of this difference, teachers can and do make incorrect assessments of their
students' ability, which is more likely to occur when the distance between the
teacher's culture and the child's is greater. Different cultural values are playing an
important role here, because the discourse norms that different peoples use are cultural signs that have their rules of use buried deep within cultural values. In their
turn, though, cultural values are really shared interpretations of culturally significant discourses, including the discourse norms that manifest them.

This means that discourse norms are often much more than arbitrary habits that
people acquire in their socialization. Rather, each can convey a subtle meaning of
its own, whose rules of use can reflect core values of a culture.

For example, the Northern Athabaskan culture of sub-Arctic America main-
tains an ancient cultural value that has no close equivalent in the dominant culture
(Scollon & Scollon, 1979, 1981). The people there show an unusually high level of
respect for the personal world views of others. And this key value of theirs seems to
translate into Athabaskan norms for language behaviour. It shows up in child socialization practices, and in the narrative tradition of the people. In practice, it
means that individuals are always entitled to make their own sense of any situation,
without others enforcing their perspective. Consequently, in any given interaction,
Athabaskan participants engage in a great deal of negotiation, so their
interactional preference is for non-focused settings, with few pressures of time and
space, and where personal differences in world view can be negotiated. Clearly
too, there are implications for the education of Athabaskan children in this unusual
cultural value; and in the discourse norms that link with it.

There seems a simple relationship between the idea of 'a discourse norm' and
the idea of 'a cultural value'. A cultural value is an attitude or an interest that people in a group cherish for its own sake; or perhaps they cherish it instrumentally, as
something needed to maintain the group itself. A cultural value is something that
outsiders need to know about, if they are going to interact with a cultural group in
some relevant way. As mentioned already in chapter 2, giving fair treatment to different people means consulting them about their values, and taking those values
into account in decisions taken. It does not necessarily mean learning their discourse norms, or even sharing their values, because this might take a lifetime of interaction with them. Although a discourse norm is a sign that has its rules of use
rooted in the culture's values, occasionally the relevant cultural values will fade,
yet the discourse norms will live on as culturally different ways of behaving. More
often, however, the survival of distinct discourse norms signals the survival of important cultural values.

Another example comes from the ancestral Hispanic communities in the
south-west United States. The characteristic value of 'cariño' reflects an ethic of
closeness and responsibility (Cazden, 1988). And this cultural value often translates into norms for language use, notably in the discourse practices observed
when Hispanic teachers and their pupils interact. Typically, these teachers avoid

public forms of praise. Instead, they show approval with a quiet smile, and perhaps an encouraging nod. Probably people from other European backgrounds can identify with this value more readily than they can with the Athabaskan example above, because the Hispanic culture is part of the fabric of European civilization. But these days, descendants of Europeans who live in North America and elsewhere, are making contact with different peoples whose cultural roots are well removed from European cultures. So they are meeting cultural values well removed from their own norms. What follows is an attempt to describe some of these different values, although my discussion only hints at the many different forms that this key feature of human diversity can take.

Different Cultural Values and Education

In many Polynesian cultures, including the Samoan and the Hawaiian cultures, it is not customary for individuals to set themselves above other group members in status or in public achievement, unless the group allots that status first. Regardless of people's achievements in the wider world, the act of setting themselves above others, without some prior consent from the group, infringes a complex cultural value. This basic Polynesian value is only partially captured in European values of egalitarianism, modesty, community, and humility. But it shows up in many norms of language use. For example, Polynesians are often reluctant to reveal achievement, in case it is interpreted as conceit. They tend to avoid boasting, and they express deference to the group as the true source of their success. For many Polynesians, to infringe this value would bring great shame on themselves.

And children who bring this value into European-style classrooms are likely to display discourse norms that differ somewhat from other children's.

Sometimes cultural values are similar across quite different cultures, and lead to similar discourse norms. For example, there are many similarities between traditional Aboriginal Australian values about learning and schooling, and Maori values, even though the various Aboriginal and the Polynesian sets of cultures are not contiguous in any historical sense. One account of 'what Aboriginal Australians want from education' includes the following five 'sets of educational values' (Christie, 1988, pp. 5–19):

1. attention to the harmony and unity of Aboriginal life: individual achievement which ignores the meaningfulness of the Aboriginal group is not wanted
2. preserving continuity with the past, the land, and the people: progress is only good if it bolsters Aboriginal identity
3. valuing things done in response to the total physical and social environment
4. valuing personal independence, with no coercion and manipulation: unconditional acceptance of everyone
5. interference by White educators is the problem, not the solution

None of these points would be out of place in a Maori philosophy of schooling, either. In particular, point 5 reiterates a basic purpose in the creation and operation of monocultural Maori elementary schools in New Zealand.

The organizational arrangements of these *Kura Kaupapa Maori* aim to exclude functional interference in the schools by non-Maori New Zealanders, and to lessen the influence of non-Maori cultural forces. Similar aims lie behind the more recent creation of *Kula Kaiapuni* in Hawaii (Warner, 1999). However, this policy is not some form of incipient separatism by these two Polynesian peoples, because any children are free to attend their schools if they want to have an education shaped by Polynesian rather than by European values. This exclusion of non-Polynesian influences is linked with the people's desire to work out what is basic to the integrity of their cultures; and to re-create what was lost of the cultures' values through their century of enforced contact with European cultures. This underpins a desire, shared by many indigenous peoples, to control their own schools, their own school systems, and their own affairs more generally (Corson, 1998).

In points 1 and 2 above, we see a clear emphasis on bonding together: bonding with one another, with the culture, and with the environment. This key value permeates ideas seen as important in most, if not all, indigenous cultures. In Canada, for instance, Sullivan and his colleagues (1991) outline the differences in cultural values they experienced working with Algonquin, Cree, Mik'maq, and Mohawk aboriginal bands. They report that the European educator's ways of structuring educational contexts often contradict the cultural ways of knowing for many aboriginal students, who see ideas and things much more *holistically.* The very notion of deliberately narrowing and fragmenting a field of vision can be quite alien to the aboriginal way of thinking. Academic disciplines, for example, invite students to narrow and fragment their fields of vision in this way. When those disciplines address a single topic, like 'the mind', students are asked to pull it out of its broad background of discourses and consider it within some singular language game. And this can be foreign to their experiences and their preferences.

This holistic and cooperative relationship with the universe runs throughout the Maori view of language and learning too. The aim in Maori learning is the achievement of excellence, and the mastery of one's total self and the physical environment through a balanced curriculum. Maori ways of thinking and responding to experience are more concerned with the whole, than with the part. Ideally, then, the best school curriculum is holistic, with weak boundaries between fields of knowledge, and few obstacles preventing people from learning in their own way, in their own time, at their own pace, and throughout life.

When these values translate into school practices, very different things occur. Subject boundaries reduce or disappear; anyone who has knowledge teaches; schools are open outside normal hours; and teachers become facilitators rather than instructors. The boundary between school and community also falls away: The extended family and community become more involved; students get opportunities to learn alongside people with skills, interacting more with the real experts and less with a textbook. Classrooms and schools also have an atmosphere that promotes a sense of belonging, a family feeling of physical closeness, where each student is given personal attention, praise, encouragement, and the daily experience of success and accomplishment. High regard is paid to differences in learning style, but learning is still a cooperative exercise, with children, teachers, parents, and community all involved. Oral language interaction, adult-to-child and child-to-child, becomes the central pedagogy of the school. The older children assist and care for their younger relatives. Competitive individualism and individual gain give way to collaboration, cooperation, and group benefit. And this relative absence of competition shapes the methods of evaluation that are desirable. Again, great care is taken to avoid embarrassment in moments of student failure and to discourage conceit in moments of success.

Many of these Polynesian school values complement many other educational values favoured by Aboriginal Australian people. I continue this numbered list of different 'values' here, taking the ones below from another source (Brandl, 1983, pp. 32–37). Later, in the next section, I suggest how these values show up as signs in the discourse norms of students:

6. making a mistake is worse than admitting ignorance
7. learning by doing, not learning to do
8. the importance of experience in learning
9. the centrality of cooperative learning
10. competition only to catch up, not to excel
11. talking and learning related to the whole culture, not just to isolated bits of it
12. reinforcing cultural learning: what it means to be Aboriginal
13. allowing children to explore everything
14. mapping space and the environment differently

Cultural Values Translated into Discourse Norms

All these different values about learning translate in complex ways into discourse norms. Not surprisingly, these norms are also close to the norms valued in schools run by indigenous peoples. But when the same norms show up in dominant culture classrooms, teachers are not always ready for them. So they tend to misinterpret the messages the signs are sending.

There is clear evidence for this in the following list of speech acts used by Aboriginal Australian students in conventional classrooms (Malcolm, 1979, 1982):

(a) empty bidding in response to teacher questions, followed by silence
(b) declined replying, after a direct elicitation from the teacher
(c) deferred replying to a question, after a longer than normal pause
(d) shadowed replying to a question, in the shadow of the next speaker
(e) unsolicited replying

Clearly, these discourse norms differ from those sanctioned in mainstream schooling. Many conventionally trained teachers would see these different norms of interaction as signs of disruption or ill-discipline. Yet they relate directly to home and community values, and also to some of the valued learning emphases listed in the previous section. For example, (b) and (c) reflect point 4: ('personal independence, with no coercion and manipulation: unconditional acceptance of everyone') while (a), (b) and (d) reflect point 6 ('making a mistake is worse than admitting ignorance').

What is evidenced here, in Courtney Cazden's (1988) apt phrases, are "ethnic differences" becoming "ethnic borders" (p. 75). And perhaps these are rather impermeable boundaries for some. As I suggest later, these borders are not easily crossed by teachers in schools that are structured as they are at present. The strength of those borders, and the size of the obstacle that culturally different children face in mainstream schools, depends on the distance between the capital valued in the school itself, and the capital that the children acquire in their home communities. Different discourse norms are symbols in people's linguistic capital, which for Bourdieu is the most important part of the cultural heritage.

THE EFFECTS OF DOMINANT DISCOURSE NORMS:
TEACHERS AND CLASSROOMS

Although the educational changes that follow from all this are yet to make a major impact on teachers in mainstream classrooms, there is much supporting evidence from classroom research to spur on changes. Indeed, not all the evidence is recent.

A generation ago, on the Warm Springs reservation in Oregon, Susan Philips (1972, 1983) looked at children from several Native American tribes, both early and late in their elementary school careers. She reports that in their homes and communities, the children learn socially appropriate norms, for paying attention and regulating talk encounters, that are quite distinctive from those learned by European-American middle class children. Moreover, they are distinctive from the norms used in classroom interaction, yet they are never really taken into account in school planning. She says that this incompatibility makes it much more difficult for the children concerned to understand the key verbal exchanges that are the main part of regular classroom interactions.

A focus of Philips' interest is the way that humans use verbal and visual cues, as signs to designate whom they are addressing or attending to in language. This can vary in many ways, and across cultures: For instance, listeners often vary in the way they focus their eyes and their ears. In some cultures, it is customary to show attention by looking at the speaker, and in others by looking away, perhaps at the ground. Similarly, speakers vary in the way they recognize who is paying attention: People looking away in a conversation or in a classroom event, can appear uninterested, while for others, staring can seem rude. As a result, people from one culture might not recognize when people from another culture are addressing or receiving them. These are only a few examples, but there are many other signs for attention structuring, and for regulating talk: messages sent by varying the dialect used, by speaking more loudly or more softly, by using general rather than focused forms of address, or by showing hesitation in response to questions, as in the example from Malcolm cited above.

These differences are not confined to aboriginal students. In the United States, as Philips observes, children from other cultural groups, like African Americans and Hispanics, often appear unwilling to participate in official classroom interaction. Yet, the same children still show great interest in interacting informally with their peers, and they are very proficient at it. Meanwhile, many teachers seem less ready to integrate the talk of children from these groups into the sequential structure of official classroom talk. More often, they reprimand their students for what may appear to be inappropriate behavior: not paying attention, talking out of turn, or failing to talk at the right time. Philips (1983) says that "even where teachers are well intentioned, the results are similar," because the culturally different students' efforts to communicate "are often incomprehensible to the teacher and cannot be assimilated into the framework within which the teacher operates" (p. 129).

So, while the students themselves are marked down for not understanding the messages of the school, it is really teachers who seem to be lacking in understanding. Teachers struggle to apply norms based on school-approved ways of behaving, to students whose norms they often know little about. The school's norms are accepted uncritically. More seriously, teachers tend to make other critical judgments based on the evidence of student norms. A teacher in Philips' (1983) study, for instance, describes the Indian children's approach to interaction as 'inconsistent' (p. 113). Rather than seeing them as users of different norms, she tends to see the signs they display as disrespectful, misbehaved, and uninvolved. There are apparent confusions from the children's perspective too: They talk less often in official classroom interaction, and they respond less often to direct teacher questions. Their responses to teacher questions more often are seen as inappropriate. Additionally, their questions about the teacher's instructions reveal doubts about their own comprehension.

Again, Phillips observes that the Indian children convey attention in different ways, and so they are misrecognized as inattentive on occasions, even when they are not. But they do pay less attention than other children, spending more time interacting with their classmates, often in the good-natured 'teasing' behaviour common among indigenous cultures. Meanwhile, in the unfamiliar territory of the classroom, the Indian children take the initiative as speakers less often, they interrupt others less often to 'get the floor', and their talk is more evenly distributed among their fellows, regardless of academic ability. Not surprisingly, all these norms match the discourse norms found in the adult Warm Springs Indian communities. For example, one of the characteristics of face-to-face interaction among the adult Indians is that there is much more of it than among European-Americans.

The Warm Springs Indians spend more time with others; and as individuals they rarely live alone. They usually do things together, even things that might take only a single person to do. And talk is a common accompaniment to all these work and recreational activities.

All these features are common ones too in contemporary Polynesian communities, or among indigenous Australians who maintain traditional ways of life. And these richly interactive environments are steeped in values of community, cooperation, and collectivity. For instance, traditional Australians living in the vast, open spaces of their tribal lands, often sit close together, with many people of all ages interacting in a space no bigger than a large room in a house. Similarly, for Maori people the tribal meeting house and its surroundings are the focus of community life. On many occasions throughout the year, all the adults and children come together to talk, eat, and sleep in a communal environment.

The constant socialization that goes on in these communal environments inevitably produces different norms of interaction among children. These contrast with the discourse norms of children raised elsewhere in nuclear families, who live in relative isolation from non-family members, and who are surrounded by diversions, such as books and television sets, that require less human interaction. They also contrast with the norms favoured in classrooms, where a single, much older person almost always has the floor, where silent reading is common, and where strict no-talking rules obtain.

There are other contrasts too. While all the informal interaction that goes on in these traditional cultures is intense and continuous, there are fewer opportunities for individual children or for young adults to give formal verbal presentations. As a result, they often seem less motivated to perform publicly as individuals in mainstream school contexts and less motivated to use language that moves away from the everyday and the personal. For example, Jim Ryan (1992, 1994) notes the differences between the discourses used in many North American aboriginal communities, and the discourses used at senior levels of education. The authentic community discourse is much more personal, and tied more closely to the context of interaction itself. In contrast, the school's discourse is more abstract, decontextualized, and far more impersonal. Ryan concludes that these discontinuities between community and school present difficulties for some aboriginal students, even those working at senior-levels of education.

At the same time, when opportunities for verbal presentation do arise in traditional communities, as Philips (1983) notes, great stress is laid on economy of speech, on personal control, and on showing evidence that careful thought has been given to what is said. And it is unusual for young adults to get these opportunities. For example, in the Polynesian case cited earlier, those who put themselves forward in this setting, can be seen as pretentious and bold, so less value is placed on their contributions. Rarely do people without status ascribed by the group itself speak at ceremonies, or talk in a formal capacity on behalf of the group. Children do learn to participate singly in collective performances, but their efforts are part of the whole, and they are perceived as such.

All this contrasts with classrooms, where the presence of a single teacher as the sole authority figure and regulator of talk, is alien for many socially and culturally different children. Often, in their own communities, they are not oriented towards a single adult's authority, and they are not accustomed to competing with one another in discourse for one adult's attention. But there are deeper issues at work too, issues that are hardly touched upon in research. Again the evidence comes from some of the oldest cultures in the world, cultures whose ancient values and customs are still preserved in the discourse norms of their members.

Unique Ways of Organizing Discourse in Culture and School

In his work with Aboriginal Australian children, Malcolm (1994) highlights gross discontinuities in world view and discourse norms that exist. He works from Hymes' (1971) point about diverse sociocultural groups: "For one group, rules of speaking will be heavily bound to setting; for another primarily to participants; for a third, perhaps to topic" (p. 66). The children in Malcolm's later studies exhibit a culturally specific way of organizing their discourse that is not shared at all by teachers in mainstream classrooms, or by non-Aboriginals in other mainstream settings like a law-court or a government department. In fact, some narrative forms used by Aboriginals simply do not exist within the communicative competence of other speakers. As a result, when traditional Aboriginals use English to reconstruct the world they share with English-speakers, they often use the resources of English in a quite distinct way.

Specifically, the Aboriginal children in Malcolm's studies use narratives that are spatially rather than temporally related. Their narratives are constructed according to the movements of personalities from setting to setting, moving and stopping, then moving and stopping again. And these norms reflect long-standing customs and values that are key aspects of the ceremonial lives of Aborigines. So these moving and stopping narratives offer a deep-seated, cultural, organizing principle that lends the people's lives meanings that go far beyond the understanding of outsiders. Moreover, the way they do all this in their talk links English-speaking Aboriginal people with other Aborigines quite removed in space and time, to well before the arrival of the European colonisers. It links extant Aboriginal cultures and peoples with their pre-contact past. But when placed within a teacher-defined communication frame, the same Aboriginal children lose control of their discourse. That unique and ancient organizing principle is removed from the context; and some other school principle replaces it. Sometimes this is based on the special narratives favoured by Europeans, where speakers create a setting, raise a problem, and then bring the story to a close by resolving the problem in an entertaining or surprising way. Meanwhile, the teachers of these children have no idea how to set up conditions that would allow their students to communicate in ways that might reveal their competence.

This example of differences in cultural discourse norms might seem extreme. The indigenous children's ways of organizing their discourse seem uniquely strange to those looking from outside their ancient culture. But are their ways as strange as the peculiar norms that teachers insist upon when working formally with children? Much of the language behaviour considered normal in classrooms no doubt seems a strange form of oppression to many human beings, regardless of their background or age. Few parents would willingly submit to the discursive indignities that are routinely inflicted on their children in classrooms, yet they allow those practices to reproduce themselves over the generations. What is surprising, perhaps, is that so few children actually resist the strange, hegemonic practices they meet in school. Rather than resisting in classrooms—by showing excessive 'shyness', 'reticence', 'slowness', 'non-inquisitiveness' or 'disruptiveness'—socioculturally different children are often acting in ways that seem quite suitable to them under the strange circumstances that confront them.

KEY SITUATIONS AND CLASSROOM INTERACTION

The idea of 'key situation' comes from the work of two ethnographers of communication (Erickson,1975; Gumperz,1976). While living in complex, stratified societies, people encounter certain key 'gatekeeping' situations that are prerequisites for entering occupations, or for admission to advanced educational agencies, or for receiving official services. Because of social and cultural differences in discourse norms, some are favoured in these key settings, while others are denied the same ready access to social opportunities. Again, using Bourdieu's (1981) idea, some sociocultural groups bring a different form of linguistic capital to key situations or fields. If their capital is not valued in that setting, this disadvantages them.

Formal educational contexts are filled with key situations of this kind. Students have to display their knowledge in many communicative settings, and they are evaluated on the basis of that display, with little regard for the cultural values that lie behind the different discourse norms used. Again the school-approved discourses are taken-for-granted. Quite wrongly, they are recognized as 'value-neutral', while the norms brought in from elsewhere are misrecognized as signalling rules of use associated with negative values. For example, as mentioned already, the Athabaskan people place high value on the integrity of people's individual world views, so discourse norms in their culture favour the kinds of interaction where extensive, non-focused negotiation can take place. Everyone can make a distinctive contribution to these negotiations, working things out for themselves. But in mainstream classrooms, there are many 'key situations' where that special Athabaskan value and its norms seem out of place.

Scollon and Scollon (1981, 1984) note that the public school is a time-constrained, crowded, modernizing, bureaucratic institution. By placing its main stress on academic literacy only, the school creates focused key situations that contrast sharply with the non-focused situations more familiar to members of the Athabaskan culture. So their children often meet a paradox in acquiring academic literacy. Their own set of discourse norms is very different from those needed for school-type literacy, which means that in order to read and write, they cannot readily write 'as Athabaskans', and about Athabaskan things. In many key situations in school, they have to give up their own sense of the situation and their right to negotiate its meaning, even though the fact that they possess this right has been communicated to them since infancy as an important cultural value. Scollon and Scollon believe that Athabaskan children see this as a surrender of their cultural identity and their right to make sense of their own world. But again, in responding to the signs they display as students, their teachers often regard them as incompetent, insecure, hostile, and lacking in understanding.

Researchers have given extensive attention to several key situations. They have observed participant structures within particular speech events, and they have identified cultural differences in discourse norms in these key settings, showing how the differences often lead to unfair educational outcomes. Participation in structured activities, like 'sharing time' and 'storytelling', requires 'linguistic' knowledge but also pragmatic knowledge. While the former is recognizable in surface-level features of language, like vocabulary and syntax, teachers sometimes assume that children share the appropriate pragmatic signs when they do not.

Storytelling

Although storytelling is a basic narrative form, the usual surface features of the story can vary from culture to culture (Holmes, 1998; Taylor & Matsuda, 1988). What a storyteller's audience considers a proper norm for interaction can vary. In some cultures, audience participation is expected, and it is often necessary. In others, little or no audience involvement is the norm. And in some cultures, stories have a serial form and go on with no end. For example, in the Arapaho Indian culture, a good story is one that continues for night after night. So children from this culture sometimes tell stories in school that seem to be going nowhere in particular (Delpit, 1995).

One factor in these differences is the degree to which a given culture is more oral in its orientation to the world, or more literate. This seems to signal differences in narrative approaches, so that children from a more orally oriented culture are more likely to want to help a storyteller tell the story. Others are more prepared just to sit and listen. While everyone, given adequate exposure to joining in, can adapt his or her language use to perform at any point on an oral or literate continuum, people's cultural values and socialization will influence their decisions about which orientation is a comfortable way of interacting with the world.

For example, Polynesian children often tell stories that bring others in the classroom right into the events of the story. As well as making them participants in the action, they even hand the narration of the story over to these others for some of the time. But this can be threatening to culturally different teachers, and to other pupils who are not used to it. Of course, very young children are not free agents in choosing their narrative styles. And there is no single way to tell stories. We begin with the rules for storytelling that are favoured within the language games of our upbringing. Again, this is a form of linguistic capital, and the closer the practices of those sign systems are to the models of storytelling valued in classrooms, the more rewarding the school will tend to be.

Frequent exposure to books and literacy in early childhood gives children a preference for narrative modes more like the ones valued most in the school. Heath and Branscombe (1986) distinguish the narrative styles found in books from those found in comics, on television, or in routine conversations. Books force people to focus on saying what things are and what they mean, which develops skills that are critical for meeting the formal demands of schooling. This is not to say that children with less exposure to books outside school are less ready to use narratives than other children. Rather, what it means is the narrative forms they do use could be very different from the narratives used by children who are exposed to book reading.

From a continuum of different narrative types, each social or cultural group is likely to select only a few combinations of available types. For instance, Heath and Branscombe (1986) identify four broad categories of narrative: they list recounts, accounts, eventcasts, and stories. Within each, there are variations whose selection is affected by the type of power relations in the storytelling context, and by the rules for narrating things favoured in the narrator's own culture. For example, in some cultures the narration of stories is solely an adult function, dignified by its association with the role of elders in the community. Children here might listen to many stories in their early lives, but never get to narrate them, or develop much skill in doing so. So, quite possibly, the norms linked to the activity of storytelling will have to be acquired for the first time in schools.

'Sharing Time'

Many studies examine the different discourse norms that African American children tend to use in school and community (see chap. 4). Sarah Michaels (1981) looks at the key classroom activity of 'sharing time', which Philips (1983) also refers to as "show and tell": a participant structure that teachers rarely use with Warm Springs Indian children, because the students are reluctant to take part in this public activity, even in the senior years of schooling.

Consistent with earlier studies on the same topic, Michaels reports that the African American children in her study, especially the girls, use a 'topic associating' or episodic style. Here a series of personal anecdotes makes up the discourse, often linked only by 'and'. The point or theme of these strings is not made explicit to the listener; and each string's relevance to the topic can seem obscure to the teacher because the presentation has no end, middle, or any clear beginning. Similar findings are reported from classrooms where Canadian First Nations students take part in sharing time activities (Lindsay, 1992). And again, the mismatches affect teacher-child interactions, to the disadvantage of the culturally different children.

Nevertheless, further analysis by Michaels shows these episodic strings are quite coherently focussed. Moreover, she argues that this kind of discourse has other attributes that give it an independent narrative status. For example, it is rhythmically chunked, with pauses, holding pitches, and vowel lengthening to mark bridge-points between different anecdotes. At the same time, it is not marked by a use of sharp rising and falling contours. And this difference from the classroom norm seems to contribute to cross-cultural misunderstandings. One of the teachers in Michaels' study is more successful when she works with European-American children, who use a topic-centered style. The shared sense of topic and the synchronized exchanges enable the teacher and students to collaborate in producing a coherent account, even when describing a complex event. In her questions, this teacher provides an 'adult-like' model of literate discourse, encouraging precision, clarity, and explicitness in what seems an oral preparation for literacy. In contrast, when working with the African American children, the same teacher has trouble seeing the point of their narratives, and predicting the speaker's direction. She mistimes questions and makes inappropriate interruptions that disorient the children, while herding them towards an oral rehearsal of the norms for school-type literacy. Her own strategic aim tends to make her intolerant of the students' norms, and this seriously disadvantages the children themselves.

Young children engaging in dialogue with powerful adults like teachers almost always accept the discourse on the adult's terms. And all adults engage in 'strategic' communication with children. Usually there is some other purpose behind an adult's discourse with children, and the talk is only instrumental to achieving that end. When teachers are bent on reaching some curriculum or personal goal through their interactions, the imbalance in the power relationship gives many children a distorted view of the purposes of language. They can develop perceptions of their own powerlessness in school which reinforce their sense of powerlessness outside the school. Many girls, for example, are routinely disempowered in this way. School experiences can finish off a long process of discursively distorted socialization for young women from some cultural or social class positions. They go on to accept roles that they perceive as their lot in life, because most of the structural narratives they have encountered leave them with no alternative. I return to this point in chapter 6.

Michaels and Cazden (1986) extend Michaels' (1981) original study of "sharing time." These two deliberately sought out highly esteemed teachers, expecting some improvement on the earlier findings. But again, all the children's narratives favouring a topic-associating style are perceived more negatively by teachers than the topic-centered narratives. And the less-favoured narratives are used more often by African American children, in every classroom studied, and particularly by the girls. Again too, the teachers' responses to these narrative styles are similar to those in the earlier study. They are firmly based on adult notions of how literate discourse should be. As Bourdieu would predict, each teacher assumes that the children understand how to give an account that matches the unspoken model in the teacher's mind. Moreover, other commentators who are not African Americans and who look at the same evidence, are more likely to value the episodic accounts negatively. They are also more likely to make pessimistic forecasts about the children concerned (Cazden, 1988) than are African American teacher graduates. Accordingly, because Michaels and Cazden find even excellent teachers have difficulties in interactive collaboration with African American children, they conclude that the problems are not due to simple teacher incompetence or lack of good will. Rather, the teachers are simply unaware of these differences in norms.

Again, Frederick Erickson's study (1984) of discourse structures among adolescent African Americans reveals a system of discourse far removed from the literate style of linear sequencing valued in academic interactions. Instead, the logic and systematic coherence of the exchange is organized by audience/speaker interaction, and by the consistent application of quite public, aesthetic criteria for persuasion, often based on prosodic devices. Theirs is a sophisticated rhetorical style, no doubt admired and valued by younger children and adults alike in their own speech communities, whose aim is to involve the audience, not just inform them (Gee, 1997; Nichols, 1989). So values of community are cherished in interactions like these, linking them with other African American values that shape norms and show up in mainstream classroom events, often to the disadvantage of the users.

It seems that culturally different children are disadvantaged at two points by their distance from the norms accepted in schools. They are disadvantaged in the key situation itself, where they do not use the norms favoured by teachers. And later, they are disadvantaged in their literacy work, where they rely on different kinds of cohesive devices to provide the explicit connections thought desirable for formal academic writing. It is well understood now that readiness to use and apply the literate discourse style favoured in the school is not evenly distributed across different class and cultural fractions.

Access to the School's Literate Discourse Style

In becoming literate, adults and children pass through a sequence of cognitive, linguistic, and social adjustments that are rather like those passed through to communicate across cultural boundaries. In particular, there is growing evidence to suggest that many speakers' oral styles are not readily translatable into the expository written mode demanded by the school.

Shirley Heath (1983) examines the ways of 'taking' from printed material that young children learn from their home setting. Sometimes these ways of taking are inconsistent with the patterns expected in schools. These patterns established in the home leave many children unconnected with the traditionally assigned rewards that come from literacy: job preparation, social mobility, intellectual creativity, and information access. As a result, the motivation for reading and writing is different and literacy has different meanings which correspond with variations in its modes, functions, and uses. In particular, the academic usefulness of these skills is not enough to motivate their mastery. Heath argues that each community's ways of taking from the printed word, and their ways of using this knowledge, are interdependent with the ways children learn to talk through their interactions with parents and family.

Heath finds that mainstream, school-oriented children in their pre-school home setting receive three things: all the habits needed for asking and receiving 'what' explanations; experience of selectively attending to items of written text; and appropriate interaction styles for displaying a knowledge of their literate orientation to the environment in speech. She says that these acquisitions are finely tuned through recurrent exposure to activities of reinforcement in the home which routinely create knowledge that can be applied in school-acceptable ways. In contrast are children who come from homes without books and with few reading activities of any kind, but where there are explicit rewards for displays of language that show correspondence in function, style, configuration, and positioning between two different things or situations. These children are used to being asked for reason-explanations, rather than what-explanations. While they are not taught the names of attributes and events, they are familiar with group literacy events in which several people negotiate the meaning of a written text. And when these children go to school, they meet unfamiliar what-explanations. For instance, they are often asked to identify items by name which have only a flat, two-dimensional appearance on a printed page. Also, when presented with the usual achievement tests, they score in the lower levels if they have not changed their behaviour in the meantime.

It seems that the printed word and the ways of taking meaning from it, have little place in the world enjoyed by Heath's second group of children, even though they do have diverging orientations to the world that can be highly desirable in formal educational settings. For instance, their skills in linking two events or situations metaphorically are rarely tapped in schools; and by revealing these skills they make teachers think that they have difficulty thinking in straight lines, not unlike the African American girls in the sharing time setting. These lateral skills are not asked of them until later stages of schooling, but by the time they are required in the curriculum, the children have often missed the foundation literacy learning needed to support the presentation of their skills in school-acceptable ways.

Even children from families who strongly adhere to the dominant culture can have a different orientation towards language and school learning. Caroline Zinsser (1986) examines children whose early life contacts with literacy and school discourse are largely through fundamentalist Bible school training, which on its own gives them a very limited orientation to the printed and spoken word. For these children the sacred text, and the catechistic forms of speech that focus on that text, provide a guide to daily behaviour and a means to personal salvation which is authoritative and absolute. They have few options about what they are allowed to do with the Bible text; they cannot easily contrast it with other texts; they cannot select or reorder the material; they cannot ask 'what if' questions and fantasize about the outcome; and they cannot doubt and question the author's views. Zinsser argues that these early experiences with written texts give many young children an orientation to literacy, to learning, and to discourse itself which is very different from that valued in mainstream schools.

Similarly Heath (1986) describes a third group of children from families who followed fundamentalist practices in the home. These children were often criticized by mainstream teachers for their lack of imagination, their laconic answers, and for too rarely asking questions or extending ideas imaginatively. As Heath says, these children have different ways of 'taking' their literacy: They have not seen their parents take information into their value systems from written materials, or use their literacy skills to take part in institutions beyond their own community group. Instead, these children often possess well developed skills in labelling, learning under direction, and following the textbook. Summarizing her findings, Heath says that "in each society, certain kinds of childhood participation in literacy events may precede others" and "the ways of taking employed in the school may in turn build directly on the preschool development, may require substantial adaptation on the part of the children, or may even run directly counter to aspects of the community's pattern" (1982, p. 70).

It seems that access to a literate discourse style is not the same for all children. From studies of Appalachian and of African American, inner-city children there is evidence too that the different type of literate discourse found in basal readers provides greater problems of discontinuity than other forms of children's literature; and that the rather odd patterns of the basal readers are imitated in teachers' talk in ways that doubly disadvantage some children (DeStefano, 1991). Basal readers contain many anomalous discourse patterns, as do the forms of interaction found in high school classrooms, which are removed in style and meaning from interactions in the everyday world (Edwards & Westgate, 1994). Some students are clearly advantaged in bringing a style of discoursing that is closer to the demands of the school. This means that less learning is needed by some, and more by others. But when the teacher's style contrasts too much with the student's, this severely hinders interaction. Frequent interruptions become necessary in formal activities. The student's true abilities are misjudged. And misinterpretation becomes a commonplace, especially in the kinds of key situation discussed here.

Group Reading Narration

Other researchers seek better instructional practices for teaching reading, and better ways of organizing classrooms and motivating culturally different students. One study examines the socialization of Hawaiian Polynesian children at home, and also their lives at school (Vogt, Jordan & Tharp, 1987). In Hawaiian schools, as elsewhere, those who are not middle class by family background, and not fully acculturated to the dominant European-American culture, are likely to do less well in academic contexts. This research identifies several useful strategies for teaching reading to these children. These strategies seem more compatible with the children's lived culture outside the school.

For example, in adapting the classroom to better suit the students, the researchers relax the usual stress on high rates of teacher praise directed at individuals. They replace it with more indirect praise, or with a form of praise addressed to the group as a whole. They do this because in the community itself, the children work in groups where individuals are rarely singled out for praise. The researchers also put more stress on reading for meaning, by using comprehension lessons in preference to drilling in skills. And they group the children vertically, to create settings where the more advanced students are able to assist the less advanced, as is more common during informal learning in their home communities

A single key situation is the researchers' focus. This approach to group reading narration is modelled on a communication strategy used in the Hawaiian community itself, called 'talk story'. When used naturally in cultural settings, this narrative form has some distinctive features, like overlapping speech, voluntary turn-taking, co-narration in a form similar to responsive reading, and joint construction of the story, using speech that resembles chanting. When this strategy is adapted to the classroom to replace the regular pattern for group teaching of reading, the students seem liberated by the change. They begin to contribute more freely in a speech style that is more familiar to them. The teachers begin to adapt their own responses to match the more natural styles of the children. Instead of isolating individual students for correction and interaction, the teachers relate to them more as a group. Gradually, the teachers begin to see the Polynesian children more favourably and, eventually these new reading structures replace the old methods used in the formal curriculum.

Later, the same researchers try to implement a similar innovative program with Navajo children at Rough Rock in Arizona (Vogt, Jordan, & Tharp, 1987). But in this setting, the results are rather disappointing. The use of vertical grouping promotes little peer tutoring among the Navajo children, although it is more successful when tried out later with smaller, same-sex groups. This style of interaction seems consistent with the separation of the sexes that is common in the Navajo culture. And like the Hawaiian children, the Navajo students seem comfortable responding to questions directed to the group, but uncomfortable chopping a story into small segments. Instead, they prefer stories presented as complete units. So while the Hawaiian program is useful for working with children from the Polynesian culture;, it does not work as well with the Navajo.

Other differences also emerge from this research. The Navajo children tend to speak longer than the Polynesian. They volunteer their own questions and offer opinions that are not linked as much to other contributions, although the opinions are more complex and fully developed. So the Navajo are demanding great respect for their own expressed interpretations of the world, and they seem to get this respect from one another. It appears that differences between the Polynesian and the Navajo cultures in their discourse norms and expectations for learning affect the program's success in different ways. In explaining this, Cazden (1988) remarks that the cultural contrasts between the Hawaiian and the Navajo are probably extreme. Interestingly, though, the Navajo culture is historically related to the Athabaskan cultures of sub-Arctic North America. I have heard people from Dene communities in northern Canada, located a thousand miles from Arizona, remark on the linguistic similarities between their own languages and the Navajo. And it would seem that these historically related cultures also share a similar cultural value. They display unusual respect for individual differences in world view, and this respect survives in non-focused patterns of interaction in their similar discourse norms.

THE POWER OF CLASSROOM CONTEXT
AND TEACHER PRACTICES

As the evidence confirms, children from a broad range of backgrounds all tend to respond less readily in certain classroom activities. Indeed, the pattern seems a common one that extends beyond indigenous children, to other socioculturally different children too. So it would be wrong to say that all these groups of children are unusual in their discourse norms. Rather, the unusual thing is the demand that teachers in classrooms continue to place on children, asking them to perform in ways that formal education itself has established to suit its own purposes without making much reference to the norms used by different groups of students. And these different patterns derive not from reticence or shyness in institutional contexts , but from broadly different patterns of childrearing, sign systems, and cultural values that produce discourse norms inconsistent with the hegemonic practices of formal schooling. Commonly, the pressures to conform to those school-ordained practices silence children. And this silence seems to express complex cultural values that are nowhere more evident than in whole-class teacher-pupil interaction.

Alison Jones (1987) reports a study of fifteen year old girls in mixed ability classes in a New Zealand secondary school. Although born in New Zealand, these Pacific Island students tend to speak and are spoken to much less in these classes than their European-New Zealand classmates. The Polynesian girls avoid eye contact with the teacher. They are reluctant to speak up; and they tend to mutter more often. The same girls say that they are unwilling to take part in the verbal competition of whole class interactions because of their fear of being singled out. They mention the cultural value of ma (shame) which makes them feel uncomfortable at the centre of attention. In response, the teachers react sensitively to the discomfort that their questioning causes the girls. But while they reduce the public demands made on these Polynesian children, they offer them no alternative pedagogies. As a result, the education offered in these classrooms rewards the display of school-approved discourse norms, reproducing successful patterns in those who have the cultural capital to copy them. At the same time, the school actively penalizes the discourse norms of culturally different children in such a way as to reproduce again the very patterns that it penalizes. So the practices used by the teachers seem to be the source of the problem, and also the means for removing it.

Elsewhere, comparable practices are observed. In their ancestral Australian homeland, one important feature of Milingimbi yolngu discourse norms is that for them it is socially acceptable to ignore questions. Michael Christie (1985) notes that this group of people rarely use hypothetical questions in the same way that European Australians do, to clarify and explain. So their children find it confusing to answer teacher questions when they sense that the teacher already knows the answers. Similarly in Canada, Martha Crago (1992) compares norms in the homes of Inuktitut-speaking Inuit children with the norms they meet with non-Inuit second language teachers of French and English. She reports very significant differences. For example, unlike the classroom teachers, Inuit parents do not normally ask children to reveal knowledge about things that the parents already know. And when learning in their own communities, Inuit children more often take the role of spectators, observing and listening, rather than answering questions like those asked in schools. But none of the non-Inuit teachers is aware of these differences. They create learning settings where limited responses are given to the young children's vocalizations, even though this is contrary to what the Inuit children expect. Later, when asked to comment on the language strengths of their pupils, the teachers wrongly conclude that as many as 30% of the children have language disabilities, because they do not talk in class.

Other evidence suggests that psychological reluctance does exist, but that it belongs to teachers, not students. Many teachers seem unable to promote extended interactions with culturally different children, even when they have no trouble mounting extended interactions with other children (Cazden, 1990). There are strong indications that regular classroom teachers are unskilled in creating conditions to facilitate interactions with culturally different children. This is suggested in a study of Panjabi new entrant children in Britain (Biggs & Edwards, 1991). On the one hand, there are no differences in the patterns of interaction initiated by the Panjabi children themselves with their teachers. But there are significant differences in the patterns of interaction initiated by teachers. While the children seek the teachers' advice and assistance like other children, the teachers spend far less quality time interacting with them. The researchers argue that because different amounts of time and different kinds of teacher interaction are linked with different groups of children, then any reluctance must lie with the teachers.

Indeed, if these moments of teacher reluctance continue throughout a whole school day, and then on throughout children's careers in classrooms, then some groups of culturally different children inevitably have much less contact with the subject matter of the curriculum, and with school learning itself. Cazden (1990) mentions that by missing four teaching opportunities each school morning, culturally different pupils could miss out on as many as 300 teaching interactions over a school term.

CHANGING EDUCATIONAL PRACTICES

In an ideal world, teachers would understand the cultural values of all the culturally different children they were working with. To interpret the child's discourse norms, and react appropriately, the culture of the child needs to be in the mind of the teacher. So perhaps the Hispanic example, early in this chapter, points the way here. The value of 'cariño', reflecting an ethic of closeness and responsibility, is one that many Hispanic teachers share with their students; and they can appreciate one another's discourse norms more readily, as a result. Again ideally, teachers or consultants are needed who share the children's culture and understand its values and norms sufficiently well to pass that cultural knowledge on to their colleagues. Certainly this matches the tenet from critical realism discussed in chapter 2: that we begin with the expressed reasons and accounts of the same people whose values are at stake.

But in all the many places where great student diversity is the norm rather than the exception, little of this is possible. In the present-day world of schools, most teachers have to work in settings where many different cultures and languages congregate in the same classroom. So what can the majority of teachers do to improve their practices in the face of different discourse norms? What can they do to make those practices fairer? There are some styles of control and interaction that can help children from any background feel more comfortable. Cazden (1988) distinguishes between two styles which she calls 'personalization' and 'privatization'.

Teacher Control and Interaction Styles

'Privatization' is a strategy for minimizing 'face threatening situations'. This works when teachers avoid calling on children for public and competitive displays of what they do not know, and instead correct them individually where necessary, and in private. And this seems a good teaching practice for use with children everywhere. Perhaps education in general would benefit if privatization were more widely used, because the practice of correcting students in public, only to make a teaching point for the rest of the class, can easily strike at children's self-esteem. No matter how carefully teachers handle it, the children are being used as a means to the teacher's ends.

In contrast, the strategy of 'personalization' is aimed less at eliminating 'face threatening situations' and more at reducing their negative effect. By using simple courtesies, like those that adults use in polite relations with one another, teachers can meet difficult disciplinary or instructional tasks with fewer negative results. Cazden suggests the use of affectionate forms of address, diminutives, and, in particular, phrases that show respect for the rights and dignity of the children. Teachers can borrow discourse norms, showing respect and courtesy, that they know are welcomed between adults and children in the different culture. When used well, this personalized style also reveals a teacher's awareness of the world of the children, their families, and their homes.

Cazden also believes that teachers bring about more effective change when they focus on classroom situations, rather than directly on cultural differences. For example, skilled teachers of young children are often good at providing 'individualization of instruction' in the new entrant classroom. In this approach, the teacher moves from one child to another, dealing quickly with learning problems. But this can be threatening if children are not accustomed to one-on-one interactions with adults outside the home. Young Polynesian children, for example, are quite used to interacting with adults informally, but sometimes they are more relaxed working with an adult in a group, rather than in an individual setting.

In small group learning contexts, teachers can still personalize their teaching; and they can extend students' conversations by using the resources of several speakers. Here Cazden (1990) recommends the use of 'wait-time': When a teacher waits for three seconds or more, before responding to a student's utterance, the student speaks longer and in more detail; and this allows the teacher to reply at length. Also, in choosing a topic for talk with very young children, Cazden suggests three types of topic:

• those specific to the local culture
• those specific to individual children
• those that are familiar to the teacher and the child

In fact, shared experiences provide the best basis for interaction with children at any age and from any culture. Clearly the nature of these 'experiences' will change across cultural settings: Once again the culture of the child has to be in the mind of the teacher. And the nature of the experiences that can be shared changes, as children grow older. For example, teachers working with the very young need to know about past events in the children's lives; they need to have shared some concrete experiences with the children for them to talk about together, and so expand their learning. Teachers working with older students try to get inside the more abstract ideas in their students' minds, that represent their developing theories about the world. Once informed in this way, teachers use this shared experience as a basis for interaction.

At the same time, none of the suggestions above will resolve the problems of structure and power that constrain culturally different children in schools, as they try to renegotiate and construct their identities within multiple and competing discourses. The above suggestions might make the teacher's life a little easier, and cause the child a little less discomfort, but the unjust structural effects of schools will continue as long as teachers are unaware of the lived realities of their students. The nub of the problem, according to Malcolm (1994), is that professionals in schools know very little about the knowledge culturally different children bring to classrooms. He raises three 'matters of significance' for teachers:

- teachers need to know that discourse structure is related to world view and that culturally different children may be operating according to organizing principles different from the teachers, who need to learn those norms if education is to be 'two-way' across cultural differences
- teachers need to know that culturally different children may be attending to different elements of the situation from those that interest the teacher (for example, teachers may be focussed on stopping, when it is the continuous movement that holds the attention of the children)
- teachers need to recognize the different ways culturally different children use narrative to construct meaning and identity, because these narratives will often be functionally significant in the children's communities and tied closely to the children's identities and self-esteem

Clearly, giving fair classroom treatment to culturally different children can be a delicate balancing act for teachers. Some suggest that successful teachers are those who achieve a 'balance of rights', by trading their control over participation structures; and that less effective teachers try to maintain conventional norms, only to pay a price in student disaffection and loss of control over lesson content (Au & Mason, 1983). Although the approaches in the next couple of paragraphs might not work in all classrooms, they do suggest a process of thinking that is valuable in making classrooms more compatible with the diverse backgrounds of children.

Oral Language Activities

As with all students, there is wide agreement that oral language activities, promoting purposeful and motivated dialogue, are a priority for classroom work with culturally different students, as with all others. For example, Crago (1992) recommends much greater use of cooperative learning approaches for Inuit students, because peer-oriented talk is an important part of first language learning in the Inuit culture. She also warns that the kind of cooperative approaches found in teacher textbooks needs modifying to accommodate the exact cultural repertoire of the students. Ryan (1994) suggests strategies for older students to use when exploring and critiquing aspects of language-in-use. These include opportunities to work alongside an experienced person on a complex task, where the novice can use, practice, and develop the discourses of schooling by weaving everyday concepts and language into the academic discourses of education.

If applied in classrooms, all these suggestions would open the door to new forms of academic discourse, particularly at more senior school levels. Certain 'ways of talking' are still seen as unsuitable for 'proper' participation in some subject areas. For instance, in the high school science classroom, students and teachers usually avoid the following forms of discourse (Lemke, 1990):

- colloquial language
- figurative language
- emotional, colourful, or value-laden words
- hyperboles and exaggerations
- stories
- humour
- references to individual human beings and their actions

Instead, students and teachers in science, and elsewhere too in the formal curriculum, aim for a more impersonal and expository style of talk, even though this tends to exclude many students from participation, especially students whose life experiences of talk have been quite different.

Some change in the accepted school norms seems necessary here. New approaches that respect children's discourse rights would modify some of the norms of the school just to suit the students, rather than always expecting the students to change their norms to suit the school. Two North American researchers, for example, report that, by relaxing the demand for formal language use in science classrooms, students can be brought more readily inside academic meaning systems (Ballenger, 1997; Tiede, 1996).

The two studies are based on records of immigrant students doing science activities while using their own first languages. In both, the students manage to stay 'on task' in their academic topics. Yet they do this while talking in much the same way as they would at home, or in the playground. This prompts one teacher to allow more of this informal type of talk into his classroom, because it seems a good way to get the students to take part. These students usually say very little in lessons, but under their teacher's more relaxed classroom approach, their own private discourses begin to make contact with the discourses of science. And these different ways of talking begin to bump up against one another. As a result, the classroom talk becomes more authentic for the students, as multiple perspectives from the teacher and the students come into contact, and as the academic culture melds with the students' own culture and their discourse norms.

As Bakhtin (1975/1981) says, when people make a new discourse their own, they populate it with their own intentions and purposes. So it is no surprise that relatively few students ever penetrate far into the academic discourses of schooling when they are never encouraged to do this. Indeed, this seems a special problem for classrooms in English-speaking countries, where the pressure to use a formal style of language in academic subjects is often more traditional than necessary. It is also interesting that both these North American studies were looking at ESL students working in their own first languages, because many ESL speakers seem so affected by the traditional norms of discourse required in regular science classrooms that they are left with only two unattractive choices: either use the formal style with embarrassing clumsiness; or remain silent. In other words, for many students, the idea of relating to the language games of science in their colloquial and informal language seems out of the question.

These researchers are raising fundamental issues about the type of discourse made available in classrooms. In fact, the use of oral discourse in classrooms has become one of the most dynamic and thriving areas for research and practice in education (Davies & Corson, 1997). This seems true for first-language education, for ESL programs, and for other second-language contexts. Moreover, this research also points to the dangers of excessive teacher control of talk in classrooms, where students' preferred discourse norms are ignored or trampled on. For example, in question-and-answer whole-class sessions, speakers' rights are usually distributed so unequally that students have few opportunities for any sustained interaction that might allow them to put new conceptual signs to use, or even learn their uses. At the same time, the one-sided claims that teachers make, and which students must accept uncritically when drawn into these interrogation sessions, often mean that the classroom is little more than a site of intellectual indoctrination (Chouliaraki, 1996; R. E. Young, 1992). Also it seems that teachers and students differ markedly in their beliefs about the role of 'silence' in classrooms (Jaworski & Sachdev, 1998). And sometimes teacher preferences about classroom interaction are upheld through a specious ideology of 'respect' which means that children either have to follow the teacher's authorized norms, or not talk at all (Heller, 1999).

Recognizing these sorts of constraints, many students are turned off academic work, and remain hostile to it for much of their lives. From the research on classroom talk, several conclusions seem to follow relevant to secondary school students (Corson, 1995b):

- high school classroom interactions are often removed in norms and meaning from interactions in the everyday world
- the formality, strangeness, and abstractness of academic words contributes a great deal to the 'other-worldliness' of classroom language

- to master the unusual patterns of signs used in academic language games, students need wide opportunities to engage in the kind of talk that uses the patterns
- but over-formal uses of discourse norms discourages students from engaging in that talk, and from bringing their own meanings and theories, expressed in their own informal language, to the curriculum
- so to engage in that talk, students need the freedom to couch the specialist signs in their own colloquial language, using their own norms of interaction

What does all this mean for the role of the teacher? Does increased, oral language use by students make teachers less necessary? The difference between what students can do on their own in using language, and what they can do with the help of an older or more experienced language user, working closely with them, is still very important. It makes the teacher indispensable in formal education. In fact, the informal 'scaffolding' that the teacher's dialogue and discourse norms provide is the most basic kind of assistance that academic learning can get. Talk and display by a teacher, working with a class or large group, is very necessary for giving initial access to academic meanings and to the special discourse norms used to communicate them. But for most students, it gives little more than this.

It is the later use of dialogue that gives the necessary elaboration. This talk can be with classmates, or even with friends or family outside the class. It provides the much more important series of reconceptualizations needed to master discourse norms and rules of word use across different contexts, and across the many subtle changes in sense that words and other signs have when they appear in different texts. So group work, or some other dialogue activity, needs to follow the initial conceptualization to add the more important benefits that come when quality language input is followed by quality output. And in these less formal settings, the students' own discourse norms can have a free rein.

CONCLUSION

Here, I take up a key problem that many teachers meet in multi-ethnic classrooms: How to respond to the multiple differences in discourse norms that they often face. Again, some teachers are better placed than others to do this. In some settings, studies have tried to help teachers specifically with this problem. For example, achieving classroom cultural compatibility was the objective of the Kamehameha program for Polynesian children in Hawaii. On the evidence of that program, Cathy Jordan (1985) says that achieving a comfortable environment does not mean reproducing the home culture in the class, because that would disadvantage children from other cultures in the same class. Instead, her aim is to translate relevant values into the classroom by using teaching methods that accommodate those values. For her, then, there are two things to do in this respect:

- find cultural features in the naturally occurring contexts outside schools that link with relevant forms of student behaviour inside schools
- rearrange classroom practices accordingly

Again, all this is much easier for teachers to do if they share the culture of the students. Elsewhere, Alice Eriks-Brophy and Martha Crago (1994) report on the quite natural transformation of mainstream classroom discourse that Inuit teachers and Inuit students achieve when working together. Here, all the participants introduce interaction patterns that are culturally congruent. By doing so, the teachers give status and recognition to the more traditional aboriginal values, reinforcing them for the Inuit children. In chapter 7, I discuss this study more fully, describing the methods that Eriks-Brophy and Crago use in their research. However, unlike the aboriginal teachers in that study, few are well positioned by their own discursive background to interpret and recognize the cultural values of many of the culturally different children they teach. And without that sort of understanding, most will continue to use a less congruent style: for much of the time, and with most of their students. So what can these more mainstream teachers do?

All the evidence presented in this chapter raises a social justice issue about the findings of the research itself. There is a risk of teachers stereotyping culturally different students according to the trends found in the norms of interaction for their group as a whole. To a certain extent, then, researchers are creating stereotypes themselves when they communicate their findings to teachers about discourse norms, as I have done in this chapter. This raises two questions that are hard to answer conclusively:

- is it better for teachers to note the differences found in research, then try to treat children as if the differences did not exist?
- is it better (or even possible) for teachers in multi-ethnic classrooms to adjust their own interaction styles somewhat to suit what they know about norms of interaction for different groups of children?

Again, my preference is to have more teachers from appropriate cultural backgrounds entering classrooms that cater for diverse students. However, this is an ideal that is far from being realized. And although every context and mix of students is a different one for dealing with these difficult issues, in general, the more knowledge teachers have about their students' likely discourse norms and cultural values, the more likely they are to make the right choices in interacting with them from moment to moment.

Of course, a most important thing teachers can do in this regard is to think about their own discourse norms, then ask themselves whether culturally different children are receiving unintended messages of domination, exclusion, or hostility from the way they interact with their students themselves.

DISCUSSION STARTERS

1. Think about the different ethnolinguistic groups that you encounter. Using the criteria presented on pages 38-39 in this chapter, which groups would you classify as "involuntary minorities" and which would you classify as "voluntary minorities"? How are the prospects of their children affected by that history?
2. Discuss the relationship between cultural values and discourse norms using some examples from your own experience. Which comes first: the norms or the values? Can we know? Does it matter?
3. "These norms are also close to the norms valued in schools run by indigenous peoples." Is there a case in this chapter's discussion to support separate schools or separate classrooms for culturally different children? Discuss the pros and cons of this case, relating your discussion to discourse norms and cultural values. Are there already schools in your region that pay special attention to a single group's values and norms?
4. "More often they reprimand their students for behaving inappropriately: by not paying attention; by talking out of turn; or by failing to talk at the right time." Do classroom discipline problems often have their origins in the misreading of different cultural norms? How often? What might reduce this miscommunication? What makes it worse?
5. Are there other "key situations" in schools where some children are *unfairly* favoured by the linguistic capital they bring from their home communities? Think about the full range of activities covered by the pedagogy, curriculum, evaluation, and administration practices of schools. What might be done to reduce the unfairness?
6. Academic literacy has evolved in certain ways to serve the purposes of literate societies. What discourse norms get valued in academic literacy? What norms are valued more lowly? How equally are these sets of norms distributed among people?
7. How do differences in discourse norms help maintain hegemonies beyond the school? From your own experience, can you list a few examples of injustice that go beyond the discussion in this chapter? To what extent is the school's right to value different discourse norms justified?
8. Look at the three recommendations made by Malcolm on page 60. How easy would it be for teachers to follow these? What obstacles would need to be overcome first? How would initial teacher education have to change to accommodate these recommendations?
9. How can teachers in culturally diverse classrooms adjust their own interaction styles to suit the norms of different groups of children? How far can they reasonably go? How far would you go?

4

Non-Standard Varieties

Britain's Prince Charles complains that American English is having a "very corrupting" influence on "proper English," which, through the darndest coincidence, happens to be the brand of English he speaks.

—*McFeatters (1995, p. A11)*

I can usually understand what Prince Charles says. What I don't always understand is why he says it! He might be interested in a little story from my family. When our eight-year-old daughter entered school in Toronto, she took with her a strong New Zealand-English accent, the legacy of five years living in that country. As a family we were dismayed to learn from our daughter that an experienced and respected teacher in the school mocked her accent, pretending not to understand what she said. In front of the class, he repeated her words out loud, substituting his own Toronto English accent in a censuring way. Other children began to follow the teacher's example outside the classroom, asking our daughter to say things, then mocking the result.

This insensitivity made her early weeks in a Canadian school much more difficult than they needed to be. Although she soon became settled and successful in the same school, it was clear that the non-standard variety she brought into the school initially affected her education most negatively. As a family, we decided not to intervene directly in her support, relying instead on her strong will and strong sense of identity to overcome this treatment. However, the episode made us think about the less privileged immigrants, refugees, and indigenous peoples who enter schools in Canada, bringing their own non-standard varieties of the country's two official languages. How much more difficult must it be for students already stigmatized by skin colour, nationality, or class background to cope with additional prejudices aimed at their language varieties?

This chapter uses the term *language variety* to cover any standard or non-standard form of a language, whether a geographical or social dialect, a patois, a creole, or some other code of a language. All these varieties are much more than different styles of language that are chosen only for affect. Most speakers of a language use a variety that differs in recognizable ways from the standard variety; none of these varieties is in any sense inherently inferior to the standard variety in grammar, accent, or phonology. At the same time, these sociocultural and geographical variations within a language are signalling matters of great importance to those who use them. Varieties serve valuable group identity functions for their speakers; they express interests that are closely linked to matters of self-respect and other psychological attributes. It follows that different language varieties deserve respect and recognition in education.

Nevertheless, in many settings the non-standard language of socially marginalized people is often used unjustly as a guide to their potential for achievement and even to their worth as human beings. This occurs in stratified societies where many variations in vocabulary, syntax, accent, and discourse style are socially marked, so that even a basic communicative exchange between individuals can suggest their place in the social structure. For instance, to people from Philadelphia, a change in one aspect of a single vowel in an utterance can be enough to make a White speaker sound Black and a Black speaker sound White (Fasold, 1990).

In any language community, including all monolingual societies, there is a range of language varieties that is used by closely knit social or ethnic groups. And these varieties are brought into the work of the school in one way or another. This myriad of language varieties exists everywhere in communities, without people having much awareness of them. In the United States, for instance, the debate over the use of Ebonics that began in the 1990s and which still has some life, suggests that considerable public confusion exists about language varieties, and what they really are. And the intensity of that debate confirms that bias against non-standard varieties of English is still prevalent in that country (Baugh, 1997a). Ebonics is a name given by some people to the many varieties of African American Vernacular English (AAVE) that retain traces of African languages in their form and structure. Because there are many rival views on the place these varieties should have in formal education, there is little consensus on what should be done. Later discussion illustrates this lack of consensus.

Clearly, following a critical realist account of social justice, more critical awareness of variety is badly needed, especially by people associated with education. Indeed, the power and justice issues involved here for schools are complex in the extreme. To give non-standard varieties the respect they deserve, as regular and systematic varieties of language that mean a great deal to their speakers, non-standard varieties need to be valued in schools, in much the same way as community languages other than English need valuing (see chapter 5). At the same time, non-standard varieties can rarely be used as the school's vehicle of instruction. In this chapter I discuss some of the reasons for this, but still leave open the possibility of devolving the policy decision to local contexts. That is to say, whatever non-standard varieties get valued in a school should be decided by informed locals, not by some agency unconnected with the context itself, and unfamiliar with the values and needs of the people who live there.

The chapter discusses language policies in its first section. In its second section, it suggests practices for teachers that might promote fairer treatment for users of non-standard varieties. I suggest ways of valuing non-standard varieties and giving students and teachers greater critical awareness of these varieties. This leads into a discussion of linguistic stereotyping, the need for greater levels of critical literacy among students, and more critical language awareness for both teachers and students, especially in settings where teachers are using the standard variety of the school while teaching non-standard language users.

NON-STANDARD VARIETIES AND EDUCATIONAL POLICY

Formal educational policies for the treatment of non-standard varieties in schools are conspicuous by their absence in most educational systems. Where they do exist, their net effect is usually to strengthen the position of the standard variety in formal education (see Poulson, Radmor, & Turner-Bisset, 1996). Yet, in any language community, including all monolingual societies, there is a range of non-standard varieties that is used by closely knit social or ethnic groups. These varieties are brought into the work of the school in one way or another. Children coming from these backgrounds may possess two or more varieties that they use in their everyday language; perhaps one variety is used in the home, another in the peer group, and a third in the school. Largely as a result of the school's influence, this last variety may come to be very close to the standard variety.

At the same time, many children arrive in schools with little or no contact with the more standard variety used as the language of formal education. Often these children are penalized for having a language variety that is different from the high status linguistic capital of the school. So the absence of formal policies that give explicit respect to non-standard varieties actually creates a tacit form of language policy that legitimizes the standard variety, creating a paradoxical situation for non-standard language users: As Bourdieu might argue, they come to believe that non-possession of the standard variety is no excuse for not using it.

In this section, I examine the roots of the common prejudices that exist about non-standard varieties and suggest policy directions that schools and school systems might take in softening this form of linguistic discrimination that affects non-standard users everywhere.

Early Developments

In language, there is a constant dynamism at work, even in the more standard varieties of English, although few people notice its constancy. Because infants arrive in a
language system that is already fully developed and functioning, there is a tendency
for us to see language as something stable and natural. People often see language as
something unaffected by social forces, struggles, and historical events, even though
different language varieties exist solely because of historical events. They come
from different patterns of behaviour, especially differences in access to power and
differences in people's language experiences. Typically, non-standard varieties are
associated with the powerless, rather than the powerful; but as my personal anecdote
above shows, even the children of affluent people can face discrimination if they use
a geographical variety that differs from a dominant local one.

In fact, the history of prejudice against the users of non-standard varieties of a
dominant language is probably as old as the history of language itself. It is certain
that the Ancient Greeks used the evidence of different Greek dialects as a way of
stereotyping other Greeks. Indeed, their wars with one another tended to be fought
by armies allied by dialect, despite the fact that all the Greek city states just used
different varieties of the same language. At the same time, foreigners living as immigrants in ancient Athens were often the target of public mockery for the different regional varieties of Greek that they brought with them or for the different
social varieties that they developed while learning Attic Greek as a second language. Aristophanes, the comic playwright, regularly drew his humour from poking fun at different dialects, in much the same way as modern music hall
performers and less sophisticated television comedians still do. Linguists today
are more cautious about using the word 'dialect' because of the negative associa-
tions it tends to have. Many find it more logical to use the word 'variety,' because
every type of language is a variety. Even a standard language is little more than a
variety with a polished reputation, although I hasten to add that the language history that built that standard variety's reputation is often a glorious one.

"Speech is a mirror to the soul: As a people speak, so are they." This harsh judgment, made by the playwright Publilius Cyrus in the Roman world, did not die with
that world. This prejudice against the non-standard varieties of marginalized
groups continues today. In some places it is supported by official policies. For example, over several centuries in France, the Académie Française has directed its
efforts towards maintaining the 'purity' of the French standard variety. And this
State policy has a direct impact on French schooling. Claudine Dannequin (1987)
describes very young students, who are non-standard speakers of French, as 'les
enfants baîllonnés': as children who are gagged in their own classrooms. Through
its purifying practices, the Académie has lent institutional support in French education to what I call an 'ideology of correctness' which affects languages and
schools on every continent, creating problems for speakers who do not use the
standard variety of their language.

In South America, for instance, standard Spanish and Portuguese varieties are highly valued in schools (Bortoni-Ricardo, 1985; Telles, 1996), but always with negative consequences for the speakers of kindred varieties who are asked to accept the distorted view that certain varieties of their languages are more 'correct' than others. Also, in eastern and central Europe, national or other dominant varieties, especially varieties of German, receive special recognition in schools while local varieties are ignored (Ammon, 1972; Oevermann, 1972; Pollack, 1973; Wodak, 1975; Wodak & de Cillia, 1995). Finally, in many different places, the speakers of aboriginal languages develop new varieties to facilitate communication with the users of more dominant languages, yet no room is found for these different codes in schools (Harris & Devlin, 1997; Khubchandani, 1997).

The role of the State has been central in maintaining an ideology of correctness. It is governments that legitimize a particular form of language by making it obligatory on official occasions and also in official settings, like schools, public administration, and political institutions. This prestigious form of language, as Bourdieu (1981) points out, then becomes the 'legitimate language' against which all other linguistic practices are measured, including especially the practices sanctioned in schools. In their turn, professionals in schools, who are empowered by the authority of their ascribed positions, follow the lead offered by the State and make certain language choices on behalf of their students. They feel justified in making these choices for reasons that I discuss later in this chapter. Although the professionals are almost always aware that their activities here are discriminatory, they feel this practice of discriminating against certain language varieties in favour of others, is far less blameworthy than discriminating on grounds of race or gender, because it is possible in principle for people to change the way they speak. Moreover, schools have traditionally given most of their attention to 'improving' the language of their pupils, because the very purpose of schools was always caught up in that activity. As a result, the power the State has to legitimize certain norms of language receives much of its practical impact in the power of schools to mandate those norms.

Similar practices are put in place by nation states almost everywhere, notably in England where researchers, out of deference to men like Prince Charles, still count the incidence of 'non-standard features' in people's speech (Hudson & Holmes, 1995) or in their writing (Williamson & Hardman, 1997). There seems to be a rough consensus among linguists in England about what the 'standard' really is, even though, as later discussion here suggests, this is more an ideological issue than a linguistic one. Is it really possible to identify the exact linguistic elements of a language variety? For example, in the case of non-standard varieties of English in England, is it the vocabulary that matters, or the accent, or the grammar, or the use of Americanisms, of archaisms, or loan words from other languages? Even just asking what these principles of selection should be, is an ideological question that betrays bias of some kind. So rather than the features of a language variety being so significant, it is often just the very idea of a language variety that is important to its users. Those who argue for 'standard English' in England, like Prince Charles, have certain aspects of their identities caught up in what they see as the standard. And as Monica Heller (Personal Communication) suggests, French speakers all think they 'know' what constitutes *le bon français* but they constantly get into fights over whether specific French forms are good examples of it or not.

In the wider societies of the English-speaking world, this ideology of correctness has been declining in recent decades (Herriman & Burnaby, 1996), especially in those countries where non-standard varieties have never been stigmatized or socially marked to the degree that they are in England. Nevertheless, discrimination against a range of non-standard varieties is too easily disguised in other places too, even in a country like Canada that prides itself on its reputation for linguistic tolerance. Intolerance towards other language varieties can increase for some people when the varietal differences lead to genuine miscommunication between speakers; and this is more common in high immigrant-receiving countries like Canada, Australia, and the US. Again like Prince Charles, people inconvenienced by this cross-varietal miscommunication sometimes have an ideal language variety in their own minds that is remarkably close to the one they use themselves, and quite unlike the one that other speakers use.

All this is made possible because of the human tendency to take language for granted. An ideology of correctness in language use is maintained by the common-sense prejudices of human beings themselves, the most difficult prejudices for education to overcome. Bourdieu (1984) describes a related trait that is especially characteristic of teachers: "the tendency to hyper-correction, a vigilance which overshoots the mark for fear of falling short and pounces on linguistic incorrectness, in oneself and others" (p. 331). He sees this tendency as a particular trait of the *petit-bourgeois,* the lower middle classes, as they seek to cement their status within the dominant classes of a society. Historically, schools have supported this ideology of correctness, because it seems to offer an objective benchmark to support the credentialism that formal education has as one of its functions. In other words, schools find it easier and fairer to give special status to some dominant language variety or other, partly because this simplifies the task of ranking and sorting students. As a result, this distortion of linguistic reality becomes a function of schooling, although it is certainly not its purpose. And because some children start out in schools with more of the valued linguistic resource than others, and are consistently rewarded for its possession, an injustice results for the many who arrive in schools with less of the standard variety.

For the latter, the 'standard' variety valued in schools represents more than just a convention. It is the model of excellence against which their own varieties are measured; it is deemed 'correct', while their own varieties are less correct. In the company of their friends and associates, they find they may have to rationalize the use of their own non-standard variety. They sometimes do this by ironicizing its features, in much the same way as they poke fun at the features of the standard variety in some contexts. Indeed, in order to explain away major differences in language use, people sometimes pillory variations in the language use of others; they describe differences that exist as poor or sloppy speech, arising from the speaker's ignorance, laziness, lack of education, or even perversity. These prejudiced notions, circulated in the discourse of language communities, reproduce the ideology of correctness and make the facts of the matter seem contrary to commonsense. But the facts are rather more straightforward: We all make a great many errors in our language use at times, especially when speaking informally or in a hurry. However the 'errors' that people perceive in the language of others (who are usually from slightly different sociocultural groups) are not necessarily errors at all. Rather, they are often evidence for the existence of a different variety of the language, a variety which preserves its features as systematically and regularly as any language variety.

Early Contributions to the Non-Standard Debate

Three theorists contributed most to recent debate on the place of non-standard varieties in educational policy and practice: Pierre Bourdieu, Basil Bernstein, and William Labov (Corson, 1995b). Bourdieu's early experiences as an ethnographer, in francophone parts of North Africa inform his later work and his conclusions. As set out already in chapter 2, Bourdieu (1981) argues that all forms of power that impose meanings in such a way as to legitimate those meanings and conceal the relations that underlie the exercise of power itself, add their own specifically symbolic force to those relations of power. In this way, dominant ideas reinforce the power of the same forces that exercise it. He sees the culture of education as a creation of the dominant culture, which is a culture that automatically works to sanction its own language varieties.

Bourdieu's ideas here rest not on some notion of linguistic deficit that can be linked in turn to levels of syntactic or verbal complexity of utterances. Rather he argues from the different types of relations that different sociocultural groups have with their sociocultural backgrounds, relations which are themselves embedded in different sets of dispositions and attitudes towards the material world and towards other people. His phrase 'cultural capital' describes those culturally esteemed advantages that people acquire as a part of their life experiences. And his 'linguistic capital' is the key part of that cultural heritage. But this is much more than the competence to produce grammatically well formed expressions and language forms. It also includes the ability to utilize appropriate norms for language use, including the language variety and style considered 'appropriate' in a given setting, and to produce the 'right' expression at the right time for a particular context of situation.

Bourdieu argues that while the linguistic capital that is valued in education is not equally available to people from different backgrounds, education everywhere still operates as if everyone had equal access to it. By basing its assessments of success and failure on people's possession of this high status capital, education reproduces the sociocultural arrangements that create the situation in the first place. And the members of some sociocultural groups come to believe that their educational failure, rather than coming from their lowly esteemed sociocultural status, results from their natural inability: their lack of giftedness. They wrongly come to believe that social and cultural factors are somehow neutralized in the educational selection process, and that the process itself is a fair one, based on objective educational criteria.

Bernstein's position is similar to Bourdieu's, and he likewise offers a complex sociological and philosophical argument. Like Bourdieu too, his theories have been misinterpreted by some who take pieces out of the theories and critique them away from their original meaning system. In fact, Bernstein's early work seemed to lend itself very well to this kind of misinterpretation, and it had a quite unhelpful impact on educational debates. Yet he says that his project was always a clear one: He was trying to show how people from different class positions differ in the ways that they categorize and conceptually order the world. And it is only within this essentially sociological theory that he became concerned with language. His interest in contexts, meaning systems, and the different orientations to the world that go with them, encouraged him to look for linguistic evidence of these differences. And this led to the famous misunderstanding that he has been at pains to correct:

> What is at stake is not the issue of the intrinsic nature of different varieties of language but different modalities of privileged meanings, practices and social relations which act selectively upon shared linguistic resources ... Educational failure (official pedagogic failure) is a complex function of the official transmission system of the school and the local acquisition process of the family/peer group/community. (1990, p. 114)

So, this position seems very close to Bourdieu's. As far as non-standard varieties are concerned, the linguistic evidence that Bernstein and his associates gathered was used only illustratively to present his central idea of 'code': "a regulative principle, tacitly acquired, which selects and integrates relevant meanings, forms of realizations, and evoking contexts" (1990, p. 101). Although he says this concern with standard and non-standard varieties of language was only an incidental interest at most, his work attracted the ire of linguists, in particular. Linguists tend to believe, as a logical principle, that all languages and language varieties are equal. Because he seemed to offer evidence of 'inequality between varieties', Bernstein earned the hostility of linguists who found their rallying point in the work of the American descriptive linguist, Labov.

Labov's studies comparing Black American and Puerto Rican vernaculars of English, and other varieties (1966, 1972a), offered many original insights. In particular, he found that people from different sociocultural backgrounds speak different kinds of English that in all important respects deviate systematically and regularly from each other. His findings helped overturn the common stereotype that these and many other varieties are misuses of the standard language. Rather, he was able to show that non-standard varieties have their own norms and rules of use. Accordingly they deserve respect and valuation, although the institution of education itself, as a standard and routine practice, disvalues varieties that are very different from the dominant norm.

Labov (1972b) successfully argued that there is no real basis for attributing poor performance to the grammatical and phonological characteristics of any non-standard variety of English. At the same time, the status of vocabulary in his account was left open. He explicitly allowed that certain key aspects of words and their meanings, including mastery of the very different morphosemantic features of Latinate words in English, could be critical attainments for educational success. As mentioned in chapter 2, studies of the lexico-semantic range of adolescents from different sociocultural and language backgrounds, suggest that Labov's guardedness on the matter of vocabulary was justified (Corson, 1995b). Clearly, educational experience, and language experience itself, are vital factors in shaping lexico-semantic range, and through it access to the cultural meaning systems that schools try to disseminate.

Labov's studies also suggested that conflict between the norms of the wider society and those of local communities of non-standard speakers, produced a heightening of local non-standard features, to express solidarity or resistance to the mainstream culture (Edwards, 1997). Labov was also among the protagonists in a celebrated court case that took place in Ann Arbor, Michigan. As part of its judgment in favour of parents, the court required teachers to take a course of professional development in sociolinguistics (Labov, 1982), and the precedent offered has affected teacher education programs in other U.S. states (Lanehart, 1998). In the legal case itself, the parents of African American children had brought an action against a school, alleging that their children were failing because they were wrongly labelled 'educationally disabled' solely on the basis of their use of an African American non-standard variety in answering tests. These tests have since been shown to be biased against African Americans. In response, the court ruled that the language variety used by the children, in itself, was in no sense an obstacle to their success. Rather, the expectations of pupil success that teachers held, based on their stereotypes about that variety, led the school as a whole to misperceive the children's real potential, thus causing them to fail. The children were deemed to be deficient in educational potential because their language variety was wrongly assessed as deficient in the context of the school. Generalizing on this point, much of the blame for misjudgments of this kind is due to simple ignorance among people about the range of regular varieties that can and do co-exist in a single linguistic space.

Linking the Non-Standard Debate to Policy Practice

The work of language-in-education theorists (Barnes, Britton & Rosen, 1969; Britton, 1970; Rosen & Rosen, 1973), coupled with Labov's findings, prompted official recognition of the need to give fairer treatment to non-standard varieties in education. This is best evidenced in the Bullock Report (Department of Education and Science, 1975), a policy document for England and Wales that recommended schools begin to value whatever language variety children bring with them, while adding to it, in every case, those other forms, functions, styles, and registers that are necessary acquisitions for educated people to make. This watershed report prompted a search for ways to make teachers more aware of their own prejudices about non-standard varieties and more aware of the range of varieties that do co-exist in monolingual societies. More recently, the idea emerged that students and teachers need to become much more *critically aware* of language varieties, especially of their role in activating prejudices and stereotypes.

Yet, most policy recommendations offered about the difficult issue of valuing non-standard varieties in the classroom, are either statements about what not to do, or statements that side-step the issue entirely. For example, the Kingman Report into the Teaching of English in England and Wales (Department of Education and Science, 1988), placed a proper stress on 'historical and geographical variation' but curiously ignored social and cultural variation, perhaps in the vain hope that these latter varieties of English would disappear if they were ignored. And schools almost everywhere still place little value on non-standard varieties; they uncritically uphold the ideology of correctness. Moreover, beginning and experienced teachers admit that they deliberately exclude non-standard varieties from their classrooms as a routine practice (see Blair, 1986, for Canada and Australia; Telles, 1996, for Brazil; Smitherman, 1992, for the United States.

As a result, children who use non-standard varieties still tend to see the standard variety valued in schools as the model of excellence against which their own varieties are measured. This readiness to stigmatize their own varieties means that as children and later as adults, they often condemn themselves to silence in public settings for fear of offending norms that work against them in ways that they themselves sanction. Using Bourdieu's (1981) metaphor, there are many linguistic markets in which some people assign a limited value to their own speech. They are either silent within those 'markets' or they withdraw from them. And in the middle and upper levels of education, both these responses from children of low-income or socially marginalized backgrounds are common.

So what should the policy be? Can school systems justify maintaining a ubiquitous but largely tacit policy that gives high status only to some standard variety? If so, can the unfairness for students who are non-standard users be softened in some way? Many do argue for a guaranteed central place for the standard variety in education. It is also clear that teachers themselves tend to agree that all children should have access to standard forms of the language (Poulson, Radmor & Turner-Bisset, 1996). In fact, most teachers rarely associate the standard variety with any particularly privileged section of society. For them, it is no more than the standard language of the school, whose actual mastery is a correlate of school success. While people disagree about how this mastery of the standard variety might be provided, the standard increasingly gets preference not because of its 'correctness' but because of what many see as its more general 'appropriateness'.

Christopher Winch (1989) distinguishes criteria of 'appropriateness' in language use from the criteria of 'correctness' that firm rules provide. In defending the use of the standard variety for teaching purposes, school policy makers have a better case, according to Winch, if they argue from the appropriateness of the standard variety, across a wide range of contexts, rather than from its correctness. On the other hand, Norman Fairclough (1992) asks teachers and others to think carefully about what they really mean when they use this word 'appropriateness' to discuss the respective place of standard and non-standard varieties in schools. He sees the idea of 'appropriateness' itself as only a compromise that allows the standard variety to maintain its position of prestige, thus confusing sociolinguistic reality with ideology. In the United States, Rosina Lippi-Green (1997) has a similar view. She points out that appropriacy arguments rationalize the process by which low-status, non-standard varieties are both acknowledged and rejected simultaneously.

My own view is that the topic of language variety needs to be explored in classrooms with the same intensity and focus as issues of class, race, culture and gender. In the same way as critically aware teachers tend to disdain school and classroom practices based on narrow class, racial, cultural, or gendered norms, the same teachers need to question policies and practices that privilege one language variety and its users ahead of other varieties and their users. At the same time, schools in local contexts still have to get on with the job of teaching a language-based curriculum that uses some language variety as its main pedagogical vehicle. The choice of some standard variety, or (much more rarely) a non-standard variety, is very largely determined for teachers by the practices they inherit from their pedagogical predecessors, and by the policy decisions of their political masters. Often, at most, they can only work to reform systemic injustices in language policies by nudging them in more socially just directions, in their own local contexts. I suggest some ways of doing this below.

While a policy argument based on claims of correctness would always seem to fail, the appropriateness argument has a little more logical support, and in most contexts is supported by justice claims, as well as on the following more pragmatic grounds: A standard variety of a language that is widely used, provides a more effective means of communication across contexts than non-standard varieties. It is far more acceptable from a practical viewpoint, in that it meets the acquired interests and expectations of many groups, rather than just the interests of its more particular speakers. There are other practical advantages too, identified by Winch (1989) and by Gramsci (1948/1966). If the standard variety is associated historically with the written language, access to it is empowering for individuals in the acquisition of literacy. If it has traditionally been the language of higher and technical education, access to it can give easier access to the technical registers of scientific and academic discourse. And if that standard variety is both a national and an international variety, access to it is empowering in all those contexts where it provides a medium of communication across national boundaries. We need to note, however, that different international varieties of English are appearing all the time (Pakir, 1997), and every one of these would be heard as a non-standard variety if used in countries where English is the dominant language. In fact, the internationally standard variety of a language seems to be little more than its written version. And even this variety will vary orthographically, semantically, and increasingly syntactically too (as in the case of the written variety of English now in use in North America).

But if the standard variety of a language is a necessary acquisition for 'educated' speakers of that language to make, because its possession meets the objective interests of speakers as individuals and as a group, what is to be done about the rights of non-standard speakers in schools and about the objective sociolinguistic fact that non-standard varieties exist in everyone's world? I believe that the difficulty can be minimized by taking the language policy that the Bullock Report (Department of Education and Science, 1975) recommends much further, by adding a necessary rider to its recommendation: For the 'valuing' of language diversity to really count, it needs to be carried out in a genuinely *critical* context. In other words, all children need to become critically aware of the social and historical factors that have combined to make one variety of the language more appropriate in contexts resonant with power and prestige, while allotting non-standard varieties a status of appropriateness only in marginalized contexts. Clearly for this to happen, school systems need policies of professional development that promote much greater teacher awareness of language diversity.

Valuing non-standard varieties is not an easy thing for people to do, especially if they are only vaguely aware that non-standard varieties exist. For teachers, it may be contrary to a professional lifetime of tacit prejudice against non-standard varieties, a form of prejudice that endures, as in my daughter's case, even when the differences between their own varieties and those of students present few difficulties of mutual comprehension (Edwards, 1997). Clearly, the attitudes of teachers themselves are important variables here. Helping school staff members become clearer about the risks of stereotyping children is an early step that needs to be taken at whole school and system level, so staff can support one another in making the necessary changes in attitude. The Ann Arbor experience offers a lead that policy makers at system level might consider: In-service education of practitioners in the sociolinguistics of schooling would certainly be helpful in identifying prejudices and ending the undesirable practices that result from them. Assessment policies are also a key area for attention.

Assessment Policies

Ralph Fasold (1990) reviews work on the importance of the non-standard/standard issue in language testing procedures. Others too have identified different forms of bias in IQ tests (Smitherman, 1977; Wolfram, 1991). Clearly, test developers do not use criteria of 'appropriateness' as benchmarks when putting together their instruments. Instead, they routinely use standards of 'correctness' in language, which are impossible to support on justice grounds because these test norms, based uncritically on the standard variety, will always count against non-standard users. This seems to follow inevitably from the fact that non-standard varieties are systematically and regularly different from the standard variety. Even when non-standard speakers have wide access to the standard variety, their possession of two varieties can mean that they have to draw on an intricate and ambiguous web of suppositions in correcting their own written texts. Fasold argues that there are similar difficulties for non-standard users in reading and answering a language test using the standard variety:

- non-standard speakers cannot rely on what 'sounds right', because what sounds right will sometimes be non-standard and so will be wrong in the context
- non-standard speakers cannot always rely on a 'sounds right so it must be wrong' strategy, because in most cases this will be misleading too
- while standard speakers also have instances of confusion between formal and informal uses of the standard variety (i.e. 'may' versus 'can'), non-standard speakers have many more instances of these differences to remember, and so many more of them to get wrong

These ambiguities significantly affect scores recorded on language tests. To counteract this, various assessment policy alternatives are possible in testing the language of non-standard speakers. The best alternative might be for test administrators always to use tests compiled by sociolinguistically competent designers. But while this policy might already be widespread, it is more difficult to ensure that sociolinguistically competent people actually use language tests in schools.

Recent approaches to assessing second language competence also seem relevant to first language assessments in contexts where there are users of non-standard varieties (Clapham & Corson, 1997). Instead of measuring the more visible and highly recurring features of language, like pronunciation patterns, vocabulary use, and grammatical usages, other aspects of second language learning now attract more attention. Performing a thorough observation of 'language in use' is now a common basis for assessment. When this form of 'communicative proficiency assessment' complements or replaces traditional language testing, the role of norms, statistics, and inflexible criteria of correctness lessens. The 'norm' for all children becomes a measure of observed proficiency in communicating meaning, set against an individual assessment of their potential for development. Ethnographic methods are called for here, especially participant observation in naturalistic settings where the children's language use is not inhibited by unfavourable expectations about the interaction. Labov's early work (1966, 1972b) found that individual African American children in the United States revealed a high level of verbal productivity and creativity when the research context was changed from a formal to an informal one that was more consistent with the interactional settings the children themselves were used to. In creating a school-wide environment where non-standard varieties are really valued, there is much that schools and teachers could borrow from Labov's early findings.

RESEARCH ON NON-STANDARD VARIETIES
IN NORTH AMERICAN CLASSROOMS

Almost everywhere, classroom-related work on non-standard varieties is still in its infancy (Christian & Wolfram, 1989; Wolfram, 1993). It is made more difficult by the almost limitless range of varieties that do exist, by their local nature, and by the fact that speakers vary their use of varieties in response to the multiple and competing discourses they encounter. For example, early Canadian interests spanned four broad sets of different varieties: non-standard varieties of French in minority francophone settings; non-standard varieties of English in majority anglophone settings; non-standard varieties of English or French used by aboriginal peoples; and non-standard varieties of immigrant and refugee languages used in heritage language programs (Corson & Lemay, 1996). Much of this early work in Canada, and elsewhere too, had its roots in the Bullock Report and the responses made by curriculum practitioners and theorists to that report's recommendations.

Meanwhile, the United States has had a long history of linguistic research on African American Vernacular English (AAVE). John and Angela Rickford (1995) review the three decades of that research. They conclude that only the first decade, from 1964–1974, was strongly oriented to educational concerns. At that time, the focus of research was on finding better methods for teaching reading and language arts generally to AAVE students who lived in inner-city areas. Since that time, the only major issues touching directly on education were the Ann Arbor trial, discussed above, and the rather different use of discourse norms by some AAVE speakers, already discussed in chapter 3. Other studies in the United States analyze educational policies for non-standard varieties. These studies critique attempts in different constituencies to outlaw various non-standard varieties from schools and classrooms (Lippi-Green, 1997), attempts that extend from official pronunciation and accent tests inflicted on prospective teachers in New York and California as late as the 1970s, to the evidence of strong and enduring public prejudices against teachers who have accents different from the school-approved norm.

In the late twentieth century, the Ebonics debate briefly captured public attention in the United States, so I give a summary of some of the relevant views here. The term 'Ebonics' was coined by Robert Williams in 1973 as a name for Black English. While there are a range of definitions of the term that sometimes contradict each other (Baugh, 2000), Williams (as cited in Woodford, 1997) defined Ebonics as:

> the linguistic and paralinguistic features which on a concentric continuum represent the communicative competence of the West African, Caribbean, and United States slave descendants of African origin. It includes the various idioms, patois, argots, ideolects, and social dialects of black people, especially those who have been forced to adapt to colonial circumstances. (1997, p. 2)

This definition leapt into prominence in the language world in 1996, when the Oakland Board of Education in California suggested that Ebonics "is not a black dialect or any other dialect of English" (Baugh, 1997a, p. 113). The implication raised here was that Ebonics had many of the features of a distinct language. And some argued from this that the Board was entitled to extra funding made available by government for bilingual education programs. But as the Board's supporters were quick to point out, its goal here was not just to gain access to extra funding. Rather, its members were anxious to do something different to reverse the alarming failure rate of African American children in Oakland schools, where 71% of all students were designated as special education candidates. As Geneva Smitherman (1997) observes: "We should applaud their refusal to continue doing more of the same that has not worked in the past" (p. 29).

Whether the Board's claim was spurious or not has been fiercely debated. Different people's conclusions seem to turn on the different definitions of 'language' they choose to use, and the importance they pay to the complex questions of identity that underpin the debate. James Baldwin (1997), for instance, sees Black English as a language in its own right, because to see it as anything less would be to demean the identity of those who use it. In respect to identity at least, this point is consistent with Sonia Lanehart's (1998) observation that the issue of identity is always at stake when we talk about language, yet in discussions about Ebonics this issue is not recognized. Like Lanehart, John McWhorter (1997) regards Black English as a variety of English, because for him its surface-level features do not differ enough from the more standard variety of that language. Like Labov and those called by the court at Ann Arbor, McWhorter sees the problem of African American school failure as one of poverty, disadvantage, and racism, not one of language difference. As he argues, most children bring a different home language variety to school, and not all groups tend to fail.

So, McWhorter's position is perhaps close to that of Michele Foster (1997), who says "the reason that African American English has drawn such fire is not because it is inferior, but because it is spoken by Black people" (p. 11). Meanwhile, Jacquelyne Jackson (1997) sees Black English as the mother tongue of many students, to which the standard variety of English should be added as a second language (variety). Finally, Smitherman (1997) cites research from the 1970s confirming that an approach to reading instruction that began with Black English, and then moved on to a more standard variety, can produce great improvements in academic literacy levels. Her approach would preserve and enhance the Black English mother tongue, while adding to it the 'language of wider communication'.

Indeed, access to academic literacy seems a major concern of many contributors to this US debate. But additional insights and more recent education-focused research come from Canada, where various non-standard varieties of Canadian French are in use in communities where a more standard variety of French is the language of the school. So diverse are these non-standard varieties that researchers like Mougeon and Nadasdi (1998) wonder if the idea of 'speech community' is a valid one to use when referring to Franco-Ontarians who inhabit such a variety of social spaces. Rather than race, it is social class background and region of living that usually provide the key variables in Canada. Also, being more recent than the early dialect research carried out in US schools, the research in Canada is more ethnographically sophisticated. As a result, it is more revealing of the power and social justice forces that come into play in educational settings where different varieties of a language share the same social space.

Based on her studies of Franco-Ontarian students and their non-standard varieties of French, Monica Heller (1999) argues that the legitimizing ideology of French-language minority education is based on the collective identity authenticated through Canadian French, which is a set of vernacular varieties quite heavily influenced by English; yet it moves towards forms of social mobility that are legitimized through French language standardization. Drawing on data comparing an advanced-level French class, consisting mostly of middle class students, with a general level class, consisting mostly of working class students, Heller argues that the interests of middle class students coincide with those of the school, which is directed towards French language standardization. Bilingual student speakers of standard French collaborate with the school to their own advantage, by not challenging its norms. At the same time, school institutional processes marginalize working class students, along with their non-standard varieties of French. The students help this hegemonic process along by using their vernacular varieties, which are filled with English expressions and localisms, and by not using 'pure' French. "Ironically" Heller observes, "it can sometimes be easier for a middle-class child, who speaks little French outside school, to do well than for a monolingual speaker of vernacular Franco-Ontarian, Acadian, or Quebec French" (p. 148). Moreover, according to Heller (1997), the institutional power that brings all this about is further masked by legitimizing classroom ideologies:

> The authority of the teacher is maintained through an interactional order based on a sequential organization of turn-taking, which is institutionally legitimized though the notion of "respect" ("respect" means listening silently while others talk, and talking when invited to do so). This local interactional order permits teachers to control both the form and content of talk in ways which, among other things, allow them to reproduce institutional language norms (a preference for standard, monolingual-type French). (pp. 91–92)

The school's focus here then, is on transmitting and promoting 'le bon français', a policy that puts the interests of many users of Franco-Ontarian varieties at risk (for more on this, see chapter 7). Interestingly too, by choosing to use a standard or a non-standard variety of French, or even a variety of English, many students themselves manage to sustain, weaken, or resist the powerful forces they encounter in schools (Heller, 1995).

Heller (1995) also began to put ethnography to work as a teaching strategy, as some have done elsewhere (Cheshire & Edwards, 1993; Tannen, Kendall & Adger, 1997). She had three main reasons for doing this:

- partly to help Franco-Ontarian students learn about the ways their own varieties of French come into contact with more standard varieties
- partly to help them in their daily encounters with the dominant English language that surrounds them
- partly to build bridges between Franco-Ontarian students and the French-speaking immigrants and refugees arriving from parts of Africa, the Caribbean, the rest of Canada, or from France itself

In this ethnographic language awareness work, students were asked to discover the different ways French is used in settings outside their immediate experience; or they were asked to examine the relationship between situations and public modes of communication, like advertising; or they were encouraged to look at the history of local francophone communities, to see how imbalances in power over time affected their linguistic and social positioning. Chapter 6 looks at the situation for linguistic minorities, like the francophones of Ontario or the Spanish-speaking residents of southern California and New Mexico. And chapter 7 looks more closely at the research methods Heller used in these studies.

MAJOR ISSUES FOR TEACHING PRACTICE

Prejudices and Stereotypes: Professional Development

This is the key issue for teachers to address, because the evidence of language itself is central in confirming stereotypes and activating prejudices: Negative teacher attitudes towards the speech of culturally and socially different children undoubtedly affect teacher expectations that, in turn, affect pupil performance (J. Edwards, 1989). Indeed, a general and long-standing finding of research is that teachers' perceptions of children's non-standard speech produces negative expectations about the children's personalities, social backgrounds, and academic abilities (Giles, Hewstone, Ryan & Johnson, 1987). Studies suggest that although our awareness of this key injustice stretches back over at least a generation of research, in practice this has not lessened the injustice very much. In Britain, for example, there remain grave doubts about teachers' ability to be objective when formally assessing oral language ability at senior school level. Findings there reveal that students who are closer in usage to the standard variety favoured by the school, are rated much more favourably than non-standard speakers (Corson, 1993).

Perhaps the teachers' motives here can be inferred from my discussion so far in this chapter. It seems that they bring these stereotypes with them into the profession, only to have them reinforced there. For instance, Viv Edwards (1986) reports student-teacher evaluations of anonymous children's speech, where both the academic and the interest level of speakers of non-standard varieties was viewed less favourably. So, it seems reasonable to argue as follows: Since teachers typically come from lower middle class backgrounds, they are exposed to the many language games associated with those class positions. And as Bourdieu (1981) suggests, lower middle class people want to 'belong' to something that they perceive as 'better'. Clearly, the standard variety valued by the school offers a powerful symbol whose rules of use give very public evidence of that 'belonging to something better'. Moreover, by adopting the school's standard as their own, young teachers often have to modify or turn away from their own familiar variety, substituting a more 'educated' one for that acquired in their home speech community. Not surprisingly, after going through this often drastic process of language change, teachers tend to see it as anachronistic when they are asked to value the very thing they have often jettisoned from themselves. So in this respect, their practical actions in support of the standard seem far from malevolent. Rather, many teachers tend to believe that by supporting the standard variety in schools, and not valuing the non-standard, they are doing something motivated by democratic, professional, and even generous intentions.

Remarkably too, there is now much evidence that teacher attitudes to children's non-standard language use are more critical in judging the quality of language use than the children's actual language itself. There is even evidence to suggest that the stereotypes that beginning teachers from the majority culture hold about children from backgrounds of diversity causes them to 'hear' those children as non-standard in their language, regardless of how standard their speech actually is (Fasold, 1984). Yet, as I argued above, the perseverance of these negative stereotypes can rarely be blamed on simple ignorance among teachers about the range of varieties that can and do co-exist in a single linguistic space. Research confirms the perseverance of these stereotypes.

For example, new aboriginal varieties of English are appearing in North America and Australasia, as aboriginal peoples try to relate their own languages to English and French in Canada, or to English in the United States and Australia. Research carried out on both continents reveals the depths that teacher prejudices can reach (for the United States, see Rickford & Rickford, 1995). From a comparative study of 200 teachers in the Canadian province of Saskatchewan and the Australian state of Queensland, Blair (1986) concludes that older teachers with more experience tend to support a deficit model of non-standard language. In other words, unaware of more recent research findings, the older teachers believe that non-standard varieties are deficient in some way in the forms and structures that schools need. At the same time, younger teachers tend to support a difference model of non-standard language. In other words, more aware of the findings from research conducted in the last generation, they believe that non-standard varieties are simply different from the language that is presently valued in schools. Despite this, however, Blair reports that neither young nor older teachers are prepared to tolerate non-standard varieties from aboriginal students in their classrooms!

Trying to reverse this situation of systemic prejudice means asking teachers to operate at a level of professional development that many have not reached, and perhaps cannot reach without a great deal of one-to-one dialogic support and frequent modelling opportunities. Implementing practices that place more value on children's non-standard varieties clearly means major changes in teacher attitudes and in the choices of pedagogy that teachers make. So changing those attitudes requires a general level of professional development in a school's staff sufficient to make the necessary changes in attitude appear reasonable, realistic, and attainable. But for teachers already reluctant to worry about this issue, professional development has to be gradual and carefully scheduled. It could build on successful examples of practices introduced by respected colleagues in the school itself, or by others in neighbouring districts.

But it is the school's leaders, through their own discourse about non-standard varieties, who give activity of this kind the status that it requires, and who establish attitudes and values more consistent with the needs of students. Because teachers in general are very resistant to the evidence of discrimination in this area, a process of information-sharing followed by professional development activities is one way forward. As another starting point, there is a place for collaborative action research projects, conducted by willing teachers with one another, and then shared more widely. These could use observation studies or audio-visual media to examine whole class practices. Terri McCarty (1997) has a lot to say about teacher research methods like these, as does Joe Kincheloe (1991). Also a whole school plan or language policy, designed largely by teachers themselves (Corson, 1999), can set out the kind of teacher research that is needed, and the responsibilities and professional development activities that result. Curiously, though, changing teacher attitudes seems best achieved by changing teacher behaviour first. For example, Guskey (1986) offers three goals for the in-service training of teachers:

- changes in teachers' behaviour
- enhancement of student learning
- changes in teachers' attitudes and beliefs

Although these three goals might seem out of order, changing teachers' behaviour gets priority because this impacts directly on student success which, in turn, changes teachers' beliefs about their own behaviour.

For example, teachers are not easily convinced by research evidence that teaching practices almost everywhere are unfair to the users of non-standard varieties. But if the same teachers are encouraged by a school-wide plan of professional development to try some new techniques with their students, the school might reach the second and third goals above more easily: Student achievement would go up, and then teacher attitudes would begin to change. In the conclusion to this chapter, I list some practical guidelines for valuing varietal differences. And at the end of chapter 5, I provide some approaches schools can use to value any variety of language that differs from the school's main variety of instruction.

There is an obvious link here with all the other differences that exist in the student body: critical awareness of language varieties means teachers who are critically aware of all the many forms of diversity that confront them.

Practical Classroom Knowledge

When children are asked to listen to the standard variety in classrooms, this seems to create few practical problems for non-standard speakers. For all of their lives, most modern children have constant aural exposure to some version of a standard variety through their daily contacts with the mass media. While there can be occasional moments of incomprehension (Sato, 1989), these are probably no more serious than the incomprehension that two speakers of the same variety encounter in normal situations of interaction. Evidence also suggests that there are few practical difficulties for non-standard speakers in reading the standard variety. Joshua Fishman (1969) points to the high levels of literacy in the standard variety of their languages that non-standard speakers achieve in Japan, Germany, and Switzerland. In these countries, and in others like Norway, the majority of people speak non-standard varieties; and they do so with evident pride and with no negative educational consequences. Moreover, Labov (1972a) argues that the range of structures unique to AAVE could never account for the record of reading failure by AAVE users in inner-city schools.

Others in the United States are trying to use a non-standard variety of AAVE as a starting point for teaching reading (Rickford & Rickford, 1995). And they are finding interesting gender and other differences in the level of student acceptance of non-standard texts. Many more girls, for example, seem to prefer standard texts ahead of non-standard ones, which seems consistent with other research suggesting that female speech norms tend to be closer to the more prestigious forms (A. D. Edwards, 1997). As they introduce AAVE readers into classrooms, these US researchers are also encountering longstanding objections, coming from many parents and teachers, to the use of so-called 'dialect readers'

(Labov, 1994). African American parents and community leaders still tend to see a good education as one that disseminates the standard variety, even when they use the AAVE variety themselves. Once again, the largely unchallenged linguistic hegemony of education operates here on both sides of the power divide. Perhaps part of the problem is that there are many more than just one AAVE variety, and each is a dynamic code of language in its own right. As a result, texts written in a single variety can easily sound strange or even dated, if taken away from its proper context and time. If these reading textbooks are to be successful, then perhaps they will need to be purpose-written, in a locally relevant AAVE variety. And their use in the school will also need the support of local parents and teachers, informed about their use through a program of community education conducted by school authorities.

When children are asked to write in the standard variety, this can create certain difficulties that sometimes disadvantage non-standard users. This occurs even though non-standard varieties will typically have the standard variety as their written version. For example, there are several ways in which the use of a non-standard variety can influence a student's performance in writing standard English. The evidence appears in early studies of AAVE in the United States that trace non-standard features in writing back to their use in speech by the writer (Whiteman, 1981). Instances of direct interference are limited, but at the time these early studies were conducted, they seem to have been frequent. More recent studies, however, suggest these concerns are no longer as relevant.

From her longitudinal surveys of academic writing, Geneva Smitherman (1992) reaches two conclusions: The use of AAVE in writing has significantly declined since the late 1960s; and the use of AAVE does not presently affect scores received when assessors are rating specific writing tasks. She sees the latter as testimony to the various forces in the United States that have combined to sensitize teachers to non-standard varieties. Current teachers in the United States seem more willing to separate assessment of success in writing from attention to dialect-related features of grammar. Also, in a study of dialect interference in the writing of students in the Caribbean island-nation of St Lucia, Christopher Winch and John Gingell (1994) reach conclusions that seem to support Smitherman. At the very least, they say, the conventional wisdom that creole interference causes St Lucian children problems with their academic writing, needs careful re-examination. The most common errors that could be attributed to non-standard interference by dialect-speaking young people, in this former British colony, also appear in studies of students in Britain, and probably have rather different causes. There might be a stronger case to show that a non-standard variety interferes with students' ability to monitor and edit the standard use of verb forms, inflectional endings, spelling and punctuation. As mentioned, this seems to happen because usually a non-standard variety is the children's first language, so they cannot always depend on their knowledge of that variety to help them tell whether a piece of text is standard or not.

Fair treatment seems less likely, however, when teachers insist that students speak in the standard variety. Clearly attempts to force children to use the standard against their wishes, with all the correcting practices that that entails, will tend to devalue their non-standard varieties and the mark of identity that the varieties carry. Even students who are just reading aloud to teachers, using non-standard forms of accent and pronunciation, can be treated quite differently from those who read in the standard. In classroom instructional practices, the former tend to be corrected more often, and they also get less help with the kind of 'reading for meaning' that really matters (Tannen, Kendall & Adger, 1997).

In contrast, there are good results when non-standard varieties are adopted for spoken purposes in classrooms (V. Edwards, 1989). Indeed the results are good enough to suggest that, if really necessary at all, extension into the spoken standard variety, not replacement by it, is a better and fairer practice to pursue. Over their years of schooling, most non-standard speakers experience the standard variety in many contexts, and this promotes proficiency in the different varieties. In settings where more is possible, there are sensitive approaches for changing classroom practices in ways that extend children's language repertoire, while also developing their communicative and analytic competence (Mehan, 1984; Young, 1992). One view is that "if the teacher consistently uses the standard form while accepting student utterances" in the non-standard, then "students will gradually shift to using the standard in the school context" (Cummins, 1981, p. 35). And this view seems consistent with a general sociolinguistic principle that Labov offers (1971): whenever speakers of a non-dominant language system are in contact with a more dominant one, those speakers will gradually change their speech to accommodate the features of the more dominant system.

Moreover, it seems that older non-standard users in classrooms readily shift towards the standard variety in any case, whenever the lesson activity suggests the need for it (Tannen, Kendall, & Adger, 1997). What facilitates this shift is on-going interaction with those who already use the standard variety. And of course, the process works the other way, as well: Teachers who value the use of non-standard varieties for spoken purposes in their classrooms, gradually become proficient themselves and can offer a lesson to students about language change, and about the potential for changing power relationships. As Lanehart (1998) warns "no matter how many times teachers tell students their language is beautiful or quite acceptable at home with friends, it all goes for naught when it is paired with 'but in school we must use standard English' as a rebuke" (p. 129).

Some Other Relevant Research on Non-Standard Varieties

In line with Labov's early studies, Frederick Erickson (1984) reports that AAVE, like the other varieties discussed here, is a fully developed, internally coherent, and entirely effective system of language for use by its in-group members. But that variety's discourse structures also reveal a system far removed from the literate style of linear sequencing that is presently valued in educated discourse. Instead, as the discussion of key situations in chapter 3 indicates, the logic and systematic coherence of the discourse is organized by audience/speaker interaction and by the consistent application of public aesthetic criteria for persuasion, often based on prosodic devices. Perhaps a rider needs to be added to Erickson's conclusions, however. What he describes as a single variety is no doubt a great many varieties reaching across a broad continuum of variation, as do Canadian varieties of minority French. Diversity in language codes is much greater than the early linguistic researchers and their methods were ready to detect. Relatedly, Barbara Speicher and Seane McMahon (1992) report problems that the label 'Black English Vernacular' (BEV) had for the identities of some of its 'users'. It seems that the naming of this variety, like the naming of any variety, was a social construction of linguists and applied linguists. For the speakers themselves, it seems certain that this label suggested a view of their varieties that cast them together as if they were a monolithic linguistic group. But on the evidence, this view of African American varieties hardly seems to be shared by African Americans in general.

The patois used by many children in Britain of Caribbean origin is helpful in seeing this point. In fact, this patois is a continuum of codes which the children often range across, switching variety depending on the context (V. Edwards, 1986). And examples of code switching of this kind are to be found to some extent in every community where modern schools operate. They offer a different dimension of language variation. For instance, Hewitt (1989) identifies two kinds of Creole operating among Londoners of Caribbean descent in a single community: the relatively stable community language of the older generations of Caribbean immigrants; and a variety of the 'London-Jamaican' anti-language of the young. The former is a creatively developed community language, serving the normal range of everyday functions that community languages serve; the latter is a strategic and contextually variable use of Creole to mark race in the context of the daily anti-racist struggle that the adolescent users find themselves in. This form of Creole is similar in one respect to the varieties reported among African American youth because they serve a similar function (Erickson, 1996; Delpit, 1995): All the varieties used by these youth cultures are structured to heighten their contrast with other language codes.

Findings like these suggest that the range of diversity in language varieties is greater than most people realise. And the knowledge we can reasonably have about this range is highly local and context-specific. So sometimes it might be necessary for teachers to become aware of local differences that only they themselves are in a position to discover. Often too, these varieties are silenced in the normal, daily round of classroom events, and in the unique culture of power that schools create.

Non-Standard Varieties and Classroom Power

Discussing what she calls 'the culture of power' in classrooms, Lisa Delpit (1995) makes the following simple points:

1. issues of power are enacted in classrooms
2. there are codes or rules for participating in this power
3. the rules of the culture of power are a reflection of the rules of the culture of those who have power
4. if you are not already a participant in the culture of power, being told explicitly the rules of that culture makes acquiring power easier
5. those with power are frequently least aware of its existence.
6. those with less power are often most aware of its existence

Delpit's Points 1 to 5 here follow quite directly from the discussion of Bourdieu's and Foucault's work presented in chapter 2. And they seem quite consistent with that discussion. But on first encounter, her point 6 seems contrary to the way that hegemony usually works. For hegemony to do what it does, it has to be maintained from both sides of the power equation at the same time. In other words, relevant to this chapter's discussion, non-standard speakers tend to collaborate in their own disempowerment by seeing their own varieties in a negative way, which helps reinforce their disempowerment. Certainly, though, there is much more to the working out of hegemony in schools than just that. As Heller (1999) discovered in her work with Franco-Ontarians, a complex interplay of power forces is at work in schools. Sometimes students resist the power of the school, thwarting its influence or softening its effects by using forbidden varieties; and sometimes they collaborate with it, playing the school's game by using its language, but for their own ends. In some places, like the 'Capital High' in Washington DC that Signithia Fordham (1999) describes, African American students seem to invert the standard variety's role: They reinvent it as a peculiar vernacular that they use only between 9 a.m. and 3 p.m.

Indeed many teachers are familiar with the deliberate challenge that non-standard speaking adolescents can bring to the classroom's culture of power, and the evident pleasure this gives the young people themselves (Willis, 1977). And some teachers openly disapprove of non-standard usage, claiming that it undermines their legitimate authority. So, to that extent, Delpit is right to claim that those with little power are sometimes acutely aware of the power situation they are caught up in, even while not understanding its workings. To better interpret their position, students do need access to the codes or rules she mentions in her points 2, 3 and 4: the critical things that make acquiring power more easy. And they need to feel relaxed about asking how those rules were constructed in the first place, and questioning the discretionary influence the empowered have to construct and privilege different language forms.

Critical Language Awareness for Critical Awareness of Variety

Valuing the variety that students bring to school, while adding other varieties to it, involves careful classroom planning. James Lockhart (1991) offers a range of practices that he uses in his middle school, U.S. classroom, where children from different heritages share the experiences with him. Beginning with passages from literature and television using varieties of English that are distant from those represented in the classroom, Lockhart asks the students to identify any qualities of language that seem unusual to them. He explains to them that code-shifting is a practice almost all users of English engage in. Above all, he stresses the need for students to respect linguistic diversity. Delpit (1995) also suggests having groups of students create dictionaries of the standard and the non-standard varieties; or getting them to engage in role play activities, or puppet shows, or newscasters' presentations where they can 'get the feel' of using the standard variety without threat of correction. She also recommends students read books written in different varieties, or discuss how different cultural groups speak, or interview people who use different varieties. There are opportunities too for students to teach the teacher and other students about their variety, or to translate songs, poems, and stories into different varieties. Delpit's starting points are that the context should be nonthreatening, have a real purpose, and be intrinsically enjoyable. In this way, teachers can add other voices and discourses to the repertoire of discourses the students already possess, while always giving value to the language diversity they encounter.

Other work confirms that students in classrooms where their non-standard varieties are valued seem more engaged and less intimidated (Rickford & Rickford, 1995). And this parallels studies reported in chapter 3, where the use of children's prefered discourse norms leads to greater student engagement. But critical language awareness (CLA) asks teachers to go much further than any of this (Clark & Ivanic, 1997; Fairclough, 1992; Janks, 1997). CLA certainly asks teachers to value the varieties children bring to school. But as mentioned already, for that 'valuing' of varieties to really count, it needs to be carried out in a genuinely *critical* context where they become aware of the factors that make one variety of the language seem more 'appropriate' in some settings. Using Delpit's (1995) words, students need access to the codes or the rules for participating autonomously in those powerful contexts.

On the one hand, students need to be aware that their use of less prestigious forms and expressions will be judged unfavourably in many social settings, and might cause them to be disadvantaged as individuals in those contexts. Using a non-standard variety can be a real barrier to social success. But at the same time, in the interests of their own critical language awareness and their sense of identity, children need to know that non-standard language used regularly and systematically by people for their own purposes is not incorrect (or inappropriate). Perhaps children can be helped to grasp this difficult social paradox by some examples of language forms in English that are widely judged to be 'incorrect', but whose use is more frequent among language users even than the so-called correct versions.

Among other examples, Andersson and Trudgill (1990) cite the form "I done it" which is usually regarded as a mistaken form of "I did it". This happens despite the fact that "I did it" is normally used by no more than 30% of native speakers of English. The more common form "I done it" is regarded as mistaken usually because of the social background of those who tend to use it: Its users are rarely those with wealth, status, power, prestige, and education; and their lowly regarded linguistic capital is unfairly stigmatized by those in possession of high status capital, which includes the power to say whose language is right (or appropriate), and whose is wrong.

Andersson & Trudgill (1990) also offer a valuable instructional principle in this area: *while discrimination may result in many contexts from a use of forms like the above, which is reason enough to urge students to be aware of the stigma that may attach to them, students also need to be aware that by avoiding their use they are doing so for social reasons, and not for reasons of linguistic correctness.* Again children need to be aware of the social and historical factors that make one variety of the language more 'appropriate' in prestigious contexts, and others only in contexts at the margins of polite discourse. But there is much more to say about a critical language awareness curriculum, and it goes well beyond discussions of language variety (Corson, 1999).

Critical Literacy

In the face of the school's ideology of 'standard variety correctness', non-standard users often come to see their own varieties as things of lesser worth. Coupling this with the other signs of rejection often met in schools, they can lose interest in the very things the school has to offer, especially its academic literacy. Evidence here comes from the same population fraction that Heller studies in Canada. Serge Wagner (1991) also looks at Franco-Ontarian students. The incidence of illiteracy in this population is more than twice the Canadian average, which is an alarming statistic in a country the United Nations describes annually as the best place in the world to live, using educational outcomes as one of its criteria. Wagner explores some of the historical and structural factors that help make these linguistic minority children hostile to school-type literacy. He sees these factors manifested in two ways: first, in an 'illiteracy of oppression'; and then, in an 'illiteracy of resistance'.

The 'illiteracy of oppression' is the direct result of processes of assimilation into the majority anglophone culture that Ontario's education system promotes. These subtle pressures on students to conform to the dominant culture permeate dominant culture schools. They can lead to a gradual dilution of identity and a weakening of the means these linguistic minority group children have to resist assimilation. Passively, the children lose the motivation to learn what they cannot identify with. They fall victims to an 'illiteracy of oppression'.

In contrast, the 'illiteracy of resistance' is a more active thing. It is a subtle kind of minority revolt against the tyranny of majority culture schooling, especially the threat this schooling offers to the minority language and its culture. Typically this revolt is expressed in a desire by students to use spoken rather than the written language. In other words, they prefer to resist the literacy of oppression and to remain academically 'illiterate' rather than risk losing their minority language.

These two contrasting 'illiteracies' combine to produce three types of functional, academic illiteracy among this linguistic minority:

- some students become illiterate in both French and English
- some become only semi-literate in both
- some become illiterate in the minority French but literate in English

We can extend the scope of Wagner's work, away from linguistic minority students and towards other students who bring a different culture, a different identity, and a very different language variety into the work of the school. For instance, some students whose home language is an African American variety of English are known to resist academic literacy (Baugh, 1997b). And the reasons here link racial identity with language difference, as Erickson (1996) observes: The fear of 'acting white' in order to succeed in the work of high schools, prompts some adolescents to reject the schooled literacy that is served up to them. Indeed this would seem quite likely if that literacy is only presented in a standard variety that they scorn (Fordham, 1999). So these AAVE speakers find themselves caught up in an academic 'illiteracy of resistance'.

All this can happen despite the fact that the children come from homes rich in print materials where they are engaged in multiple uses of different kinds of literacy (Auerbach, 1997), whose acquisition is often influenced by significant others, like older siblings. Similar to Wagner's linguistic minorities, the reaction of children of diversity to academic literacy is often resistance to the pressures to conform to the unwanted standard varieties and literacies of the school. More than this, many children from non-dominant backgrounds find that just being 'successful' in education involves rejecting the social origins evidenced in their language varieties, so different are the literate and standardized academic practices of schools from much that the children themselves are familiar with or value (D. Smith, 1986). When these students look at educational success realistically, from their own social positions, that 'success' is out of reach for most of them. As a result:

- they quickly come to believe that there is little truth in the claim that school success will really lead to a better life for them

- they recognize that there is a ceiling on their achievements put there by social constraints that have little to do with being able to read and write
- they often conclude that to learn to read and write is to subordinate themselves to a game whose rules are set by a dominant social order that they themselves are forever excluded from

This is a large group of students in most high schools. These students need to find something else in their literacy education if it is to be motivating and relevant to their lives. If literacy's only purpose is to entice them into an academic culture that seems closed or unwelcoming to them (because of the apparent powerlessness of their own social position), then they may spend their school careers resisting literacy, just as James Moffett (1989) suggests:

> Looking at [literacy] as a means of transmitting our culture to our children, we give it priority in education, but recognizing the threat of its backfiring we make it so tiresome and personally unrewarding that youngsters don't want to do it on their own ... The net effect of this ambivalence is to give literacy with one hand and take it back with the other, in keeping with our contradictory wish for youngsters to learn to think but only about what we already have in mind for them. (p. 85)

Instead of these academic 'illiteracies', the literacy offered in present-day schools needs to be linked into students' lives and identities much more than it has traditionally been. It needs to slot into the cultural existences and language varieties that students value, not least by venturing beyond the conventional settings where literacy is housed. In other words, the common school practice of keeping most literacy events inside the private and silent domains of libraries, or in classrooms where no talking is often the rule, can set literacy apart from the reality of students' lives. Also, if academic literacy tasks have no real-world context attached to them, they will be less engaging for all children (Blake, 1998), but especially for those from marginalized backgrounds. Literacy's relevance to the lives of students can be made more explicit by relating it to the complex, contemporary worlds of work, discrimination, communication, and leisure that confront young people.

The demands of these new worlds are not served at all well by academic literacy on its own. In its place, literacy is taking on a much broader meaning that includes many different social and metaphorical literacies that broaden the narrow conception of functional literacy that was once seen as the chief output of schooling. By this I mean things like:

- computer literacy
- visual literacy
- media literacy
- technological literacy
- political literacy
- cultural literacy

For many educators, this more 'social view' of literacy also means a 'social view' of learning that is sensitive to context and all its social relations, especially the relations contracted between the teacher and the learner. In practice, this means moving some of the emphasis away from textbooks, written always in the standard variety, and more towards 'real' materials written in the vernacular of the students, integrating and drawn from these multiple types of literacy. As part of all this, family and community forms of literacy are gaining new importance in the school. These literacies, of the home and the neighbourhood, are getting acknowledged and respected as a necessary complement to academic forms of literacy (Auerbach, 1997), although not in any sense a substitute for them.

It would be a mistake to think that these social literacies could 'become' the new curriculum. That would be swinging the pendulum much too far. For example, students still need exposure to writers like Joseph Conrad, to see how English can be used with style and drama; and to understand that language deployed with style can enhance the use of any variety. But modern students need to know the reasons for that exposure. It is easy to put Conrad on the syllabus. But it is an act of professional brilliance to sell him to adolescents. Yet, the role of traditional forms of literacy is as important as it ever was. And ingenious teachers *are* finding new ways to communicate that importance, and to show its relevance to student lives (McGonigal, 1997).

All this helps create a very different kind of academic literacy. I agree with the many people who are presently saying that nothing less than radical, critical literacy will do, if we are to reverse the spiralling disenchantment with academic education that plagues most educational systems. This different kind of academic literacy would be 'critical' in three important ways: First, it would be something that young people could use for exploring, interpreting, and questioning their own real-world setting. Second, it would be an enabling device that allowed them to pry open and strip away the ideologies and other distortions that lurk in the many message systems that surround them. And third, it would be a ready tool for them to use in taking as much control of their own lives as they wanted. In short, this critical approach to literacy would equip children with 'literacy for active, autonomous, and democratic citizenship'.

There is much more to say on this topic than I am saying here (for instance, Agnihotri, 1997; Auerbach, 1997; Bigelow, Christensen, Karp, Miner & Peterson, 1994; Cummins & Sayers, 1995; Egbo, 1997; Hornberger & Skilton-Sylvester, in press; Luke, 1997; Street, 1997; Wagner, 1991). But working from these and other accounts, this is what a curriculum in critical literacy would look like for me (Corson, 1998). It would be:

- Grounded in the lives and identities of students: using and creating texts to probe the way their lives connect to the broader society and the way their lives are limited by that society

- Critical: asking who makes decisions? Who benefits? Who suffers? What alternatives are possible? How can change occur?
- Multicultural, multilingual, non-racist, non-sexist: a social justice literacy curriculum addressing the lives and experiences of every social group while valuing their languages and their language varieties
- Participatory and experience-based: focussed on creating and using texts that invite questions, collaborative problem-solving, new challenges, student research, and original decision-making
- Hopeful, joyful, kind, visionary: developed within a curriculum that presents learning experiences in ways that make students feel significant and cared about
- Outward-looking: supportive of literacy practices, varieties, and activities found in the students' own families and communities, and respectful of the community's knowledge about those practices
- Activist: using texts that reflect the diversity of people who have helped to improve the human condition, from all of a society's different cultures, language varieties, and social strata
- Academically rigorous: inspiring levels of academic performance in students far higher than those motivated or measured by grades or test scores
- Culturally sensitive and inclusive: using and creating texts that give insights into cultural circumstances and texts beyond the experience of most teachers themselves

Obviously this is a wish-list that does not begin to deal with the problems of implementing all these ideas in specific contexts. But to be consistent with the thrust of this book, this list and any other recommendations for practice that I make, have to be interpreted against the background of a real-world setting by people who are familiar with the rules of use in whatever language game they happen to be playing. And this is the key problem of educating people for any profession: Any generalizations that the compilers of wish-lists like this make, have to be set against a setting where the flux and flow of real-world obstacles and pressures can become apparent. Only then can wish-lists be made to work, usually by people quite removed from those who did the wishing.

CONCLUSION: FUTURE DIRECTIONS

The position of teachers in all this is critical. Yet, if we generalize from Blair's (1986) rather unhopeful finding about old and young teachers' attitudes to non-standard varieties, there seems very little that reforming activities can do to change the practices of today's teachers. Beyond the school-wide professional development programs already discussed, there are just too many teachers to mount the kind of extended dialogic process of individual teacher counselling and awareness-building that is needed. Joao Telles (1996) describes exactly this kind of shared reflective process, which he used as a teacher developer to foster greater critical awareness of variety in Brazil. Telles' use of critical dialogue, over an extended period, helped a single teacher in a Portuguese-speaking school to see how her own life history shaped the stereotypes she had about her own students, who came from non-standard speaking backgrounds. This teacher came to recognize the importance of language varieties in the construction of her students' identities. But opportunities for this kind of professional development work are few, and teachers are many. So probably the best place to begin is with the new generations of teachers found in teacher education itself. Blair (1986) provides some teacher education guidelines aimed at valuing varietal differences. In recommendations reminiscent of the Bullock Report, she says that teachers need to:

- learn to appreciate non-standard varieties as assets rather than hindrances in the acquisition of the standard (variety)
- extend the range of children's skills by showing them that in certain situations it is appropriate to use certain forms of language, while others suit other contexts
- teach the features of the standard (variety) that do not exist in the children's variety, looking at genuine communication needs rather than teaching isolated features artificially
- pay attention to differences in the rules of interaction between the children's community environment and in the more formal environments where the standard (variety) is used
- learn as much as possible about the children's cultural and linguistic traditions
- avoid testing procedures that favour the standard (variety) since these may not reveal genuine ability, only a knowledge of the standard (variety)

While there is everything to agree with in these suggestions, workers in critical language awareness would want to take teachers-in-training way beyond this point. They would want to acquaint beginning teachers with the political choices that linguistic inequality raises for education: Should teachers go no further than empowering students within the rules of established language games? Should they teach students to critique the rules of those games? Should they try to change the rules, in the interests of their students? Perhaps one way for beginning teachers to become critically aware of non-standard and standard issues, would be for them to study the critical practices of critical practitioners themselves: to look at other teachers who have managed to put themselves inside these issues, and then used that awareness to reconstruct the education they offer.

A major challenge for beginning teachers is to understand how language differences construct and reflect ideologies and power relations, especially through the work that teachers do themselves. Since teachers and teachers-in-training are forced by the archaic structures of formal education to follow rather conservative patterns of professional behaviour, it is difficult to see widespread change occurring rapidly. This is especially so since schools will always tend to accept that their job is to pass on the cultural heritage, including some or other standard version of the culture's language. Again the circle turns back fully to teacher education itself, and even beyond it, to the selection of those responsible for introducing teachers to their professional practice. For change to occur, it is certain that a more explicit and thorough discussion of questions of power and social justice, like those raised in chapter 2, needs to enter the curriculum of teacher education.

DISCUSSION STARTERS

1. Bourdieu talks about "the tendency to hyper-correction, a vigilance which overshoots the mark for fear of falling short and pounces on linguistic incorrectness, in oneself and others." Do teachers in your experience suffer from this tendency? If so, what causes it? Who are the victims of the practice? How justifiable is it?

2. Support for some standard variety of English, as the language of schooling, is sometimes based on criteria of correctness and sometimes on criteria of appropriateness. What are these criteria? Which would be more persuasive for teachers? For students? For parents and other community members?

3. "African American parents and community leaders still tend to see a good education as one that disseminates the standard variety, even when they use the AAVE variety themselves." How do you explain the persistence of this view? Should teachers and language experts try to change it? What could be done in practice?

4. A communicative proficiency assessment of language provides a measure of observed proficiency in communicating meaning, set against an individual assessment of each student's potential for development. How would you set up this participant observation in practice? How would you document and record your findings? How would you ensure the assessment was authentic and reliable?

5. Critical language awareness does make sense to most people. Yet most people continue to accept language as a given: as something that they are born into, and which exists in near final form before they exist. What problems does this raise for introducing CLA to the staff of a school? To its parents and other community members? How could teachers begin to overcome these problems?

6. Guskey suggests that changing teachers' behaviour gets priority because this impacts directly on student success which in turn changes teachers' beliefs about their own behaviour. Does this make sense to you? Supposing it does,

what sort of changes to pedagogy might lead teachers to see that many of their existing practices are unfair to the users of non-standard varieties?

7. The so-called 'Pygmalion effect' confirms that teacher expectations directly affect student performance in classrooms. What is your own experience of this phenomenon? How difficult would it be for teachers to overcome their biases against non-standard varieties? Are some teachers better placed to do this than others? In what ways?

8. The evidence suggests that the users of non-standard varieties have a much higher failure rate in school. Does this match your own experience? Can you offer examples? Do you know of exceptions? What other factors might explain these exceptions?

5

Bilingual and English as a Second Language Education

I heard crying in the infants' school as though a child had fallen and the voice came nearer and fell flat upon the air as a small girl came through the door and walked a couple of steps towards us … About her neck a piece of new cord, and from the cord, a board that hung to her shins and cut her as she walked … And the board dragged her down, for she was small, and the cord rasped the flesh on her neck, and there were marks upon her shins where the edge of the board had cut … Chalked on the board, in the fist of Mr Elijah Jonas-Sessions, "I must not speak Welsh in school" …

—*Llewellyn (1968, p. 267)*

Perhaps the most critical policy decision to be made in any school system is the choice of the language used as the medium of instruction for children. This chapter addresses the importance, on social justice grounds, of providing bilingual education to minority language students up to the middle years of childhood or, at the very least, the importance of providing education that fully respects children's minority first languages. It also discusses the range of best practices for teaching English as a Second Language (ESL), and for the education of established linguistic minorities, and the signing Deaf.

A helpful definition of bilingual education contrasts it sharply with ESL education. Bilingual education differs from ESL in important ways. Bilingual education uses a non-dominant language as the medium of instruction during some substantial part of the school day (Cummins & Corson, 1997). On this definition, true bilingual education is only rarely available in English-speaking countries, apart from the extensive French-English bilingual education found in some parts of Canada.

Although the US Bilingual Education Act seems to respond directly to the fact that the premature loss of minority students' first languages tends to inhibit their transition to learning the majority tongue, in practice the response of most schools and school districts in the United States has always been to treat language minority students in a deficit way with respect to English. In other words, because these students are perceived as lacking English, the typical policy response is to give them extra teaching in English (ESL), with a rapid transition expected to the use of English across the curriculum. This policy is close to the zero level of first language support sanctioned by the Unz Initiative in California. Indeed, for most of the history of schooling in all English-speaking countries, minority language children have not had the valuable start that bilingual education offers. In fact, whole communities have been made to feel ashamed of their first languages, as Richard Llewellyn (1968) so poignantly demonstrates in his above account.

This chapter looks at the fairness and educational effectiveness of these policies. It discusses the powerful intellectual and cultural benefits that come from maintaining young children's first languages in education: benefits that go well beyond those offered by ESL education. After looking at research on the cognitive advantages of becoming bilingual, the chapter presents evidence about the value of offering bilingual education more widely, asking whether schools for language minorities are better at doing what they do if they offer quality bilingual programs. Then, the chapter examines bilingual education programs at work in the dozens of countries where they operate successfully, including comparison studies in the United States and elsewhere.

The chapter will also look at situations where bilingual provisions are out of reach, because of the many different languages in use. Although the need for fair treatment continues in these settings, their linguistic complexity calls for imaginative and ingenious responses that try to provide the 'second-best arrangement' introduced in chapter 2. Schools in these settings try to value students' minority languages in other ways. There are many different ways to support and value minority first language development, even when the school does all its teaching in English. I present these in outline.

SOCIAL JUSTICE AND BILINGUAL EDUCATION

Harking back to discussions of social justice in chapters 2 and 4, I see a rough parallel between the position of minority language users in a community and the position of users of non-standard varieties of the dominant language. As Susan Gal (1988) puts it:

Sociolinguistic examples demonstrate that the mechanisms underlying the maintenance of a minority language sometimes match those supporting a persistent working
class vernacular. Indeed, this tension between dominant and oppositional code, and
the role of the dominant language as that *against which* the other is evaluated, are essential to the contextualized analysis of bilingual minorities. (p. 249)

Nevertheless, there are important sociological differences that distinguish
dominated social class groups from linguistic minorities. For example, most users
of a non-standard variety are similar to one another sociologically. In other words,
they tend to be members of certain social or racial strata or they inhabit some relatively isolated social space, like an inner-urban environment, or a remote rural region. But in the modern world, the same things apply only rarely to linguistic
minorities.

Today, different groups of speakers of a single minority language can extend
across the full range of social classes in a society. And the more affluent among
them are likely to be fully bilingual in both the dominant and the minority language. Furthermore, speakers of minority languages are often more dispersed geo-
graphically than the users of a non-standard variety. Although a chief factor that
supports the existence of a minority language is the opportunity it allows people to
communicate with family and neighbours, lack of contact with kindred speakers
can be offset by the bilingual proficiency that minority language users have to develop. Fluent bilinguals can keep their minority language for use in settings where
they feel comfortable about speaking it.

Moreover, many minority language users are distinguished from non-standard
speakers by the strong political links they form with fellow-speakers in order to ensure their minority voices are heard. In doing so, they often manage to resist complete dominance by the majority language, and to avoid linguistic assimilation. In
contrast, the working class speakers of non-standard varieties are usually without
much political power or social organization. Finally, the speakers of immigrant
minority languages often have economic links and family connections with people
in other countries who use the same language, especially links in the source country for their language. This can also offer elaborate means for resisting the influence of the dominant language.

When taken together, all these differences mean that the social justice
entitlements of minority language users are rather different from those I discussed
for non-standard speakers in chapter 4. At the same time, the kind of symbolic
domination that Bourdieu (1981) talks about, still seems to affect speakers of both
types of language variety, because the hegemony of dominant social traits is always a factor in society. Whether their varieties are non-standard versions of the
dominant language or quite different minority languages, there is a tendency for
people to give respect to prestigious language varieties, and to value their own varieties less in comparison. Indeed, Bourdieu is careful to include language minorities in his discussion of symbolic violence.

Language Minorities

Language policies are now receiving world-wide attention because of the great population shifts that occurred over the last two or three generations. These shifts highlight language issues that once went unnoticed, even in those countries where there were always significant language minorities. Reporting from his international studies, Churchill (1986) sees major changes everywhere in national attitudes to language minorities. He sees the most potent factor in this move to be the recent development of an international climate of opinion favouring the more open and tolerant treatment of minorities. Changes in international law and other structural arrangements have resulted (Hastings, 1997; Skutnabb-Kangas, 1997).

Broadly speaking there are three main types of language minorities in modern societies:

- *ancestral peoples,* including those aboriginal groups long-established in their native countries, like the Amerindians, the First Nations, and the Inuit in North America
- *established minorities,* including the more long-standing Spanish-speaking communities in the United States, the Acadian French in North America generally, or the Franco-Ontarian community in Ontario
- *new minorities,* including immigrants, refugees or asylum-seekers, foreign workers living semi-permanently in their new home, and expatriates serving in countries tied in a loose community

Classifying Minority Language Policies in Education

There are many ways of comparing and evaluating the treatment that language minorities receive in different countries. Churchill (1986) locates OECD countries at various points on an ascending ladder of six levels. His ranking is based on each country's policy response in recognizing minority language communities and in implementing suitable educational policies. The most basic level of development is when a country simply ignores the special educational needs of language minority groups, which is still a common response in parts of the Americas. But all OECD countries now have some policies reflecting at least the levels 1 or 2 in the list below; and all the major English-speaking countries are rather similar in their policies. In practice, this means language policies fall under one or more of the following three categories:

1. the existing policy sees the new language minority groups as lacking English, and the typical policy response is to provide extra teaching in English (ESL) with a rapid transition expected to a use of English

2. the existing policy sees the minority groups' need for English as also linked to
   family status, so an additional response is to provide special measures to help
   minority students to adjust to the majority society, such as aids, tutors, psy-
   chologists, social workers, career advisers, etc.
3. the existing policy sees the minority groups' need for English as linked to dis-
   parities in esteem between the group's culture and the majority culture, so additional policy responses include multicultural teaching programs for all
   children, sensitizing teachers to minority needs, and revising textbooks to
   eliminate racial stereotyping

With only rare exception and in very limited contexts, language policies for *immigrant* minorities in North America, Britain, and Australasia are located at one
or other of the three levels mentioned above. But elsewhere, especially in Northern Europe, fairer language policies do exist. These provide three more levels of
response:

4. the existing policy sees the premature loss of the minority language as inhib-
   iting transition to learning the majority tongue, so an additional response is to
   provide some study of the minority languages in schools, perhaps as a very
   early or occasional medium of transitional instruction
5. the existing policy sees the minority groups' languages threatened with ex-
   tinction as community languages if they are not supported, so the policy response is to provide the minority languages as media of instruction, usually
   exclusively in the early years of schooling
6. the existing policy sees the minority and majority languages having equal
   rights in society, with special support available for the less viable languages,
   so policy responses include: recognition of a minority language as an official
   language; separate educational institutions or school systems for language
   groups; opportunities for all children to learn both languages voluntarily; and
   support beyond educational systems.

Only a few of the very old bilingual or multilingual OECD states have reached
level 6. There is some ambiguity in other countries, like Canada where policies differ markedly across provincial boundaries and school districts. In general, only
francophone minorities outside Quebec and anglophone minorities inside Quebec
have rights approaching level 6 (see Burnaby, 1997; Corson & Lemay, 1996).

The US Bilingual Education Act legislation would seem to locate that country
firmly at level 4, although, excepting those places where two-way programs are
operating (see below), the responses of most schools and school districts seem to
be at a much lower level. So in practice, the United States is located at levels 1 or 2.
There seem major obstacles to producing much advance on this, given the fact that
English has been repeatedly fostered to create an 'American ethnicity'. Moreover,
exclusive English-only policies get much wider political support than in other

countries (see Ricento, 1997). In chapter 2, I discussed the 'English Only' movement which directly challenges the development of fairer bilingual education policies in the United States. But an equally potent if indirect opposition to language diversity is the on-going political campaign against immigration itself. That opposition is well organized and highly vocal.

For example, the Center for Immigration Studies in Washington is a non-profit organization dedicated to supporting stronger immigration controls. By construing Census Survey figures showing that the number of immigrants living in the country rose from under 10 million in 1970 to more than 26 million in 1998, the Center concludes that the overall characteristics of this immigrant pool are that they are poorer, less educated, and more inclined to receive welfare (Escobar, 1999). Pointedly, more than half of all immigrants living in the United States are Spanish-speaking, which means that one-sided assessments disseminated in this way are bound to smear the Hispanic community, and help dissuade them from using their languages. I say 'one-sided' because the official evidence about immigrants coming into Canada, essentially from the same source countries as those entering the US, is that they contribute disproportionately more to the country's economy, they are better educated than the Canadian average, they commit half the number of crimes, and they pay much more in taxes than they take out in benefits (Myths and facts of immigration, 1999).

Elsewhere, Australia is located at levels 4 or 5 on the evidence of its treatment of many users of aboriginal languages and some immigrant language users, although level 3 is perhaps closer to the actual practices in most States (see Clyne, 1997). New Zealand has begun to move towards the enrichment levels 5 and 6, but only for its ancestral Maori minority. In its language policies for immigrants, New Zealand is still located at levels 1 or 2 (see Watts, 1997). Its major Celtic areas apart, Britain has much in common with the United States. Britain is at level 3 in the attitudes to multiculturalism that curriculum specialists advocate, but it is only at level 1 in its treatment of immigrant minority language users. Immigrant community languages in Britain receive some recognition, but only in the very early stages of schooling to ease transition to English (see Rassool, 1997).

Transitional or Maintenance Bilingual Education

The bilingual education issue is complicated by sharp differences in the value placed on minority languages in the schooling process. The middle levels listed above in the development of minority language policies give the minority language an instrumental value in learning the majority language, while higher levels give it value for its own sake as well. Wallace Lambert (1975) saw the aims of schooling in respect to bilingualism falling into two distinct categories: 'additive bilingualism' when a second language is acquired with the expectation that the mother tongue will continue to be used; and 'subtractive bilingualism' when a dominant language is learned with the expectation that it will replace the mother tongue. The former is a 'maintenance' form of bilingual education, which sets out to use both languages as media of instruction for a significant portion of the school career. The latter is a 'transitional' form of bilingual schooling covering only the early years of schooling, with the dominant language taking over as the means of instruction after that.

An important social justice issue is at stake here, hinted at a generation ago by Barbara Horvath (1980) when she said that the United States Office of Civil Rights supports the maintenance approach, which is consistent with seeing cultural groups forming a broad mosaic across the nation, while the United States Office of Education supports the transitional approach, which is more consistent with seeing cultural groups eventually shedding their identity in the melting pot of the American nation. No doubt there were financial and rather backward-looking ideological considerations that informed the Office of Education's view, but today transitional bilingual education of the subtractive variety, is not a policy that can be readily supported on either pedagogical or justice grounds.

As discussion later in this chapter confirms, a radical change in attitude and approach to bilingual education accompanied the growth in information about the links between language, culture, identity, thinking prowess, and academic success. In many places, the transitional, subtractive bilingual education that the early research supported, has given way to enrichment and maintenance programs (Cummins & Corson, 1997). As the new evidence accumulated, beliefs about the effects of bilingualism on the individual changed, almost reversing themselves. In most of the early studies, the overwhelming trend in research supported the view that being bilingual had negative consequences for the individual. Minority language pupils' lower performance on verbal IQ tests, their poor academic performance in general, and their lack of adjustment in schooling were all linked in the research with their bilingualism. Some investigations even suggested that bilinguals were untrustworthy (Cummins, 1984).

In these early studies, variables other than the minority language itself were discounted. Little attention was paid to other aspects of high status cultural capital that minority language students did not possess. In other words, the research discounted the very things that minority language children tend not to bring to school, things that lead to the very inequalities in school performance that were measured but never explained by the tests of researchers. Indeed, purely linguistic factors, like the possession of the dominant language, or some variant of it, may be simply second or third order reflections of the social and cultural contexts of schooling. Stereotypes based on race, gender, class, religion, national origin, sexual orientation, and region of living all affect the judgments schools make about students. These things influence the way people process information. They create expectancies about others, and go on to create self-fulfilling prophecies. Moreover, discrimination varies not just between peoples, but also across different contexts for the same people.

For example, John Ogbu (1983) discusses the outcaste minority group in Japan, the buraku, who encounter school failure in Japanese schools, but who achieve on an equal footing with other Japanese students when they move to American schools. Again, Rudolph Troike (1981) offers the case of Finnish immigrants to Sweden who are viewed rather negatively there because they come from a former Swedish colony. In contrast, in Australia, the Finns rank more highly among immigrants because they are perceived as Scandinavians. So in Swedish schools, the Finns do poorly as a group, but in Australian schools they do rather well. Clearly certain things are at work here that have little to do with language itself. As Jim Cummins (1986) remarks, "widespread school failure does not occur in minority groups that are positively oriented towards both their own and the dominant culture, that do not perceive themselves as inferior to the dominant group, and that are not alienated from their own cultural values" (p. 22).

In the past, lacking these insights and in line with the ideology of the time, school systems were licensed by the research on bilingualism to force-feed the majority language to their minority language students. In English-speaking countries, if anything at all was done, transitional ESL programs became the standard solution to the minority language problem. And for all of the twentieth century, even the most progressive educational systems pursued this harmful policy, harming their own societies in the process. For example, a Toronto study of the problems of new Canadians in the 1960s and 1970s lamented the "implications of seeing the entire problem of immigrant adaptation as a language problem" so that "undue emphasis was laid on the teaching of the English language itself, with almost no appreciation of the cultural cost to the immigrant or to the greater Canadian society" (Masemann, 1984, p. 354). Commenting on the same study, Thomas Greenfield (1976) argued that policymakers approached second language programs "technocratically, with little concern for what they are to do," as long as they can convince themselves "that the programs are 'effective', acceptable to taxpayers, and good for children. Whether the programs meet any of these criteria is seldom known, for they rarely receive searching analysis in terms of their relationship to the language and cultural questions which so obviously beset Canadian society" (p. 112). Greenfield added that ESL alone may be a less efficient method pedagogically than teaching in two languages (p. 118).

There is a transparent ideology at work in the early bilingual research from 1910 to 1960. Responding to robust narratives of racism, and trying to remove the threat to social cohesion and national solidarity that widespread linguistic diversity was said to represent, efforts were made almost everywhere to replace minority languages with the dominant language or languages. And policy makers selectively preferred research evidence detailing the negative effects of bilingualism to justify established practices. Meanwhile, other studies, like those from George Sanchez (1934), were marginalized. Minority language speakers were blamed for possessing linguistic capital that had low status in the school, and that blame was supported by evidence traduced to justify this act of symbolic violence. Although recent studies no longer support this ideology, it is hardly absent from policy making in education.

The Social Justice Support for Each of the Six Levels

Levels 1 to 4 above are all based on the view that linguistic minorities should seek the same social outcomes and educational objectives as the majority. Levels 1 and 2 are clearly assimilative, in that the aim of the policies is for students to lose their minority language, along with its culture, in the short to medium term. Clearly policies like these are unjust because the minimal language rights of individuals are not guaranteed, and minority language children are expected to perform equally well in an educational setting without the linguistic wherewithal needed to compete on an equal footing.

Policies at levels 1 and 2 could once have been justified by selective reference to the pre-1960s research evidence about the negative effects of being bilingual. However, to support these policies in the modern world requires a deliberate marshalling of community prejudices. In some places, this kind of policy activity is rationalized and supported by narratives of racism that still circulate relatively unchecked in English-speaking countries that have minority language communities. This endemic racism can be traced back to many sources, but most have to do with ignorance and fear of cultures and languages that even today are little understood or valued by people from more dominant cultures. Other vague fears have their roots in prejudices that are particularly strong in places that were once the colonies of European countries.

Policies at levels 3 and 4 respond to the more recent research evidence that I discuss in later sections of this chapter. Level 3 recognizes the unjust effect of not valuing a child's culture; it develops approaches for placing more value on that culture. And level 4 recognizes the cognitive and linguistic effects of not supporting the minority first language; it develops approaches for using that language in transition to the dominant language. But neither level offers a completely fair response to the difficulties of minority language groups. Firstly, neither recognizes the culturally acquired interests of minority peoples that a critically real approach urges us to adopt, since they do not consult minority preferences about the maintenance and use of their languages as vehicles of instruction in schools. The need for transition to the majority tongue outweighs these other considerations. Secondly, neither level recognizes the linguistic capital that children bring to schools. Rather than receiving its proper intrinsic value, the children's minority language has only an instrumental value in level 4 as a means for learning the dominant language. Thirdly, the policies covered at both levels suppress the minority languages in ways consistent with Bourdieu's (1981) description of the workings of symbolic domination.

The fact that most schools in most OECD countries are operating under policies at levels 3 or 4 highlights the practical difficulties of pursuing the alternatives offered by later stages. The language situation in the US, Canada, and Australia is very complex. Australia, for instance, is a country where more than 100 community languages are in regular use, where 50 Aboriginal languages still survive, and where English is not the mother tongue of a very large minority of the population. In the face of this social and cultural complexity, Australian schools would be hard-pressed to maintain and develop the first languages of even a fraction of their minority pupils, because in that country, as in Canada, it is not customary for minority groups to congregate in single areas to quite the same degree as elsewhere. Each school, as a result, can have a sprinkling of many different minority language speakers. This means that, on the principle of 'ought implies can' introduced in chapter 2, many schools in these English-speaking countries cannot in fairness be held to account for not providing the enrichment policies at higher levels. At the same time, there are many schools in these countries, especially those serving large, remote, indigenous communities and other closely knit minority groups, that do have a clear obligation to provide first language maintenance and development.

Levels 5 and 6 involve objectives and outcomes that differ from the earlier levels. These are of a rather minor enrichment kind at level 5, which allows enhanced private use of the minority language and the higher esteem associated with it. But these objectives and outcomes become more substantial at level 6, where the minority language and culture have equal status in society with the majority culture, and where there is the added possibility of biculturalism and bilingualism. Only at these later levels are the values of a strictly monolingual society loosened. And only in these later stages is the value of 'additive bilingual education' recognized. At both these levels, there is emphasis on changing the school to suit the child, rather than changing the child to suit the school. Some attempt is made at level 5 to give value to the minority child's linguistic capital while, at level 6, the linguistic capital and the interests of the minority culture itself are given full recognition.

The rest of this chapter looks at the education of communities whose first or preferred language is a language other than English. I borrow material from two other publications (Corson, 1998, 1999). These language groups fall into four categories:

- immigrant students receiving bilingual education
- linguistic minorities who are not recent immigrants
- signing Deaf students
- immigrant students learning English as a second language

The next section looks at the education of immigrant (and refugee) children up to middle childhood. It concentrates on bilingual education, because most forms of bilingual education are aimed at younger children. Then the following section looks at the education of linguistic minorities who live permanently inside the borders of several English-speaking countries but who have cultures and languages that are different from the majority of the population. Often these minorities experience internal tensions based on class, gender and ethnicity in addition to tensions produced by contact with dominant groups. It will be clear to readers that these first two sections stress the point that 'talking about text' is the key practical activity of schooling. But a third section addresses the special needs of another linguistic minority: Deaf signing students, who 'talk about text' in another way. Then a final section concentrates on ESL education which is the more common provision for immigrant children at secondary or high school levels. This section also looks at some wider areas in the language curriculum, like media education and language awareness, that are relevant to all students.

THE BILINGUAL EDUCATION
OF IMMIGRANT CHILDREN UP TO MIDDLE CHILDHOOD

Curriculum theorists of a generation ago put together ideas that still shape the curriculum in every English-speaking country. James Moffett's (1968) book *Teaching the Universe of Discourse,* set the scene with the key idea that our ability to think depends on the many previous dialogues that we have taken part in. Research in a range of disciplines (see chapter 1) now confirms the accuracy of that key idea. It puts language and discourse at the very heart of education.

The same ideas drew people's attention to the fact that schools make too little use of students' own language, especially their informal and expressive talk and writing, as a learning resource in the classroom. And these ideas are just as applicable to the education of second language learners of English as they are to students of English as a first language. Specifically, the following four points have been supported widely in studies of the observed behaviours of students and teachers:

- language develops mainly through its purposeful use
- learning usually involves talking, writing, shaping, and moving
- learning usually occurs through talking, writing, shaping, and moving
- the use of discourse is basic to intellectual development

Here, as elsewhere in this book, 'discourse' refers to the full range of meaning-filled events and sign systems that we encounter in life; and the words of a language are the most common systems of signs that people meet. Although many systems of signs, inside and outside education, have shared meanings, words provide most of the important symbols for forming and refining thought.

Up to middle childhood, English-speaking students are rather similar in the words that they need and which they choose to learn. The basic Anglo-Saxon vocabulary of English serves most of their purposes. Later, however, things change. As discussion below indicates at more length, after 12 years children begin to acquire the shared meanings of tens of thousands of new words and the other signs that they need to succeed at higher levels of formal education (Corson, 1995b). Many students do not acquire enough of those shared meanings to succeed in senior education. This has little to do with innate ability and it has little to do with the present efforts of schools themselves. It happens because an adequate foundation for what schools demand from students, often unnecessarily, is not laid in many children's early life experiences.

Language Development and Early Childhood Education

It is no surprise, then, that *early* language development is the secret to intellectual growth, including later language development and educational success itself. So the most important foundation for any system of education is a strong and universally available system of early childhood education, beginning at around three years of age. Yet for all their wealth and educational commitment, many English-speaking constituencies still lack this provision, and their educational outcomes are inevitably lower than they could be.

We know that later attainment leaps when children have pre-school education. In fact, the huge benefits for later education of early childhood education are among the most widely attested findings in educational research. In answer to the question 'does early childhood education do any good?' a broad range of longitudinal studies in Europe and the United States followed children's careers throughout their schooling (Royal Commission on Learning in Ontario, 1995). They found these lasting beneficial effects for school leavers who have had early childhood education at three and four years:

- improved cognitive performance and achievement throughout education
- greater aspirations for education, motivation, and school commitment
- decreased delinquency, crime, and lower arrest rates
- decreased incidence of teenage pregnancy
- increased high school graduation rates
- higher enrollments in post-secondary education
- lower rates of unemployment

The main factor in all this is the opportunity for using discourse that quality early childhood settings offer. In fact, we can tell what schools need to be doing at every level by looking at what good early childhood education offers. What it offers is the widest possible exposure to experience-based language use. Through their interactions with classmates and teachers, young children are introduced to new meanings, and they get constant opportunities to use talk in making those meanings their own. Moreover, this is as true for children using a first or a second language. For young immigrant children, it is much better educationally to be engaged in discourse that supports their first language and uses it as a bridge to learning the dominant language than to be sitting in silence listening to others use a language which is not yet their own.

The First Languages of Immigrant Children

Clearly discourse plays the central role in learning. No matter what the subject area, students make new concepts their own largely through the use of language. In other words, when they listen and talk, read and write about what they are learning, and relate this to what they already know, they are learning. Like early childhood settings, junior and primary schools that provide bilingual education to immigrant students need an environment that encourages students to use language to explore concepts, solve problems, organize information, share discoveries, formulate hypotheses, and explain personal ideas. Students need frequent opportunities to interact in small group discussions that focus on exploring new concepts. They need regular opportunities to work together around shared media, to shape new media creations, and to interpret the creations of others.

All these things happen easily if young children are surrounded by others who speak their own language. But for most of the history of schools in English-speaking countries, immigrant children have not had this valuable start to their education. Almost everywhere in the English-speaking world, the standard practice after enrolling immigrant and refugee students is to ignore their minority languages and give them as much ESL as possible. Often teachers and administrators go beyond ignoring the minority language. Sometimes, they forbid its use in the school environment, arguing that to allow its use in any way would interfere with the learning of English and prevent students from becoming fully involved in the majority culture.

Recently, much more thought has been given to the fairness and the educational effectiveness of this policy. People are more aware of what happens when schools do not build on children's first languages in the early to middle school years. They realize how important the signs and symbols that children experience in learning their first language are for brain development. These signs, especially words and other expressions, shape the early brain development of the young. Although this is not a shaping in any final sense, it is wrong to think that the different encounters with cultural signs that immigrant children have had, are irrelevant to their learning in the new setting. Acting on this false belief is likely to disadvantage children intellectually. It also stops them from making use of the best vehicle available to them for engaging with their new culture: their first language.

There are powerful intellectual and cultural benefits in maintaining young children's first languages in education. By giving immigrant students carefully designed bilingual education, schools give them benefits that go well beyond those offered by ESL education.

The Advantages of Being Bilingual

Until the 1950s, most research on bilingualism saw it as a rather unhelpful human possession, useful mainly for professional interpreters. Bilingualism was seen as a problem for education to remove, mainly through intensive teaching in the majority language and by bringing students quickly into the majority culture. But highly successful programs in the 1960s, especially those provided for anglophones in French immersion programs in Montreal, helped to bring about change. New theories developed that took account of sociocultural factors in the development of bilingualism. They also looked at other things like motivation, language mastery, the status of languages, and matters of demography. This work added weight to the growing body of evidence suggesting that there are real intellectual and sociocultural advantages in having a bilingual education. Although recent research confirms the great benefits of bilingual education, the effects of the earlier distortions continue in some places.

Since the 1960s, evidence has been growing to confirm a point that might seem obvious with the benefit of hindsight: bilingual children have much more exposure to using language, which should translate into improved performances in most of the areas of activity where language and thought converge. Indeed, research in the physical sciences has long supported this claim: Bilinguals are said to mature earlier than monolinguals, both in the development of cerebral lateralization for language use and in acquiring skills for linguistic abstraction (Albert & Obler, 1979). But there are other advantages too. For example, maintaining the minority language is said by many to develop a desirable form of cultural diversity in societies; it promotes ethnic identity; it leads to social adaptability; it adds to the psychological security of the child; and it develops linguistic awareness (Crystal, 1987).

The bilingual research also shows that becoming bilingual has cognitive advantages for the learner (Cummins, 1996). While Colin Baker (1988) warns against overestimating these advantages, especially in relation to everyday mental functioning, there is growing evidence for the following:

- bilinguals are superior to monolinguals on divergent thinking tests
- bilinguals have some advantage in their analytical orientation to language
- bilinguals also show some increased social sensitivity in situations requiring verbal communication
- bilinguals have some advantages in thinking clearly and in analytical functioning

These advantages of bilingualism prompted further questions about the value of offering bilingual education more widely. The main question to address is whether schools for language minorities are better at what they do if they offer bilingual programs. The evidence suggests that they can be.

The Advantages of Bilingual Education for Young Immigrant Children

Quality bilingual education is a recent development which even now is in its early stages of evolution. But these programs are developing rapidly in some places to serve very different national needs: as a step in moving towards recognizing a single or several national languages; as a way of making national contact with a world language; as a way of putting to use the multilingual resources that immigrants bring to a country; and as a way of extending language rights and social justice to linguistic minorities. As mentioned, this kind of bilingual education is still not widely available in English-speaking countries, for reasons that are partly historical and partly ideological.

Cummins and Corson (1997) provide a guide to the research in bilingual education itself. The reviews from many countries overturn some earlier views about bilingualism and education:

- they offer strong evidence that quality bilingual programs have been influential in developing language skills and building academic achievement generally
- they show the common view that immersion programs are only effective with the very young to be mistaken
- they suggest that in some respects older learners have advantages over younger ones
- they report evidence that lower ability children also benefit from immersion programs
- they conclude that a quality bilingual program will support and aid development in the first language

Cummins' Two Hypotheses

Two theories developed by Cummins provide a backdrop to recent research. In 1976, he published his 'threshold hypothesis' (See Cummins, 1996). This has become influential in explaining differences in the achievement of students in second language programs, and its conclusion is widely supported by research studies in many places, notably in Australia, Italy, and India . According to this theory, there may be minimum or threshold levels of competence that bilingual children must attain in their first languages to avoid cognitive disadvantages and to allow the potentially beneficial aspects of becoming bilingual to influence cognitive functioning. This hypothesis helps explain many different things about the educational success and failure of minority language groups. As a basis for educational policy, it suggests that minority language maintenance should be available to all minority children until the years of middle childhood, if their academic achievement and intellectual growth is not to suffer.

A second hypothesis from Cummins (1996) is also relevant here. The 'interdependence hypothesis' looks at the relationship between the learner's first and second languages. There are aspects of language proficiency that are common to both first and second languages: aspects that are interdependent. As a result, less instruction in the second language often results in higher second language proficiency scores for students who are young users of a minority language. But more instruction in their second language results in higher second language proficiency scores for majority language students.

Three key points about minority bilingual education follow from these two theories:

- a high level of proficiency in both languages is likely to be an intellectual advantage to children in all subjects, when compared with their monolingual classmates
- in social situations where there is likely to be serious erosion of the first (minority) language, then that language needs maintaining if academic performance is not to suffer
- high-level second language proficiency depends on well developed first language proficiency (i.e., like the proficiency in their first language that older ESL students already have)

Arguing from these three points, Cummins (1996) concludes that young children from immigrant minority groups profit from bilingual programs if their first language plays the major role, because this lays a language foundation that cannot otherwise be guaranteed. This contrasts with the findings for children from majority language backgrounds, who benefit from bilingual programs in which the second language is used more frequently. In this second case, a firm foundation in the majority first language develops quite naturally, because it is the language of wider communication in the society. Similarly, older immigrant students, whose first languages are already well developed, get the most benefits from English-only programs where their first language is not supported.

Maintenance Bilingual Programs at Work

Increasingly, maintenance bilingual education programs are living up to the research on bilingualism itself. Bilingual programs for minority language children are the subject of extensive study and development in many places (Cummins & Corson, 1997). For example, in the Netherlands a bilingual maintenance approach to the education of minority children is favoured because it proves as effective in promoting majority language learning as other approaches, and even requires less time to be devoted to the teaching and learning of Dutch (Vallen & Stijnen, 1987). Other Dutch programs for the young children of Turkish and Moroccan immigrant workers suggest that minority language teaching for children from these backgrounds has no negative educational or social effects (Appel, 1988). Also in the Netherlands, Verhoeven (1994) finds strong support for Cummins' interdependence hypothesis in two programs where Turkish background children improved their first and their second language literacy, following a heavy stress on instruction in Turkish.

Another overview of developments deals with programs over twenty years in Mexico, the USA, Sweden, and Canada (Moorfield, 1987). In each of these, children began school speaking a minority language and that language was used as the main or only medium of instruction. Later, there was a gradual transition to instruction in both the minority and the majority language. Academic progress achieved in each case was much better than in programs where minority language children were taught entirely in the majority language. Student self-esteem, pride in their cultural background, and group solidarity also increased in each case. In other settings too, where bilingualism and biliteracy are important social advantages, initial and advanced literacy in two languages becomes possible, and full bilingualism becomes a natural acquisition for all children (García & Otheguy, 1987).

In the United States, Wong Fillmore and her associates (1985) conducted research into the effectiveness of different instructional practices in developing the English academic language skills of Hispanic and Chinese minority language students. She reports four major instructional factors as significant:

• high quality teaching, including clear lesson organization, directions and explanations, appropriate aids, attention to higher level skills, and opportunities for oral activities
• high quality instructional language, including clarity, coherence, use of contexts, paraphrasing, responding to student feedback, and discussion of grammar and vocabulary
• effective classroom management with stress on academic rather than on non-academic activities
• provision of equal opportunities for the practice of English

Effective classrooms in these studies displayed a balance of teacher-directed and individualized activities. In bilingual classrooms, students did best when the languages were presented separately without translations. But there were differences in the learning styles for the Chinese and the Hispanic students, which seem consistent with broadly different cultural discourse norms. For example, the Hispanic students gained most from interaction with their peers; the Chinese gained most in structured and fairly quiet classrooms.

A long-term comparison study in the United States examined three approaches to bilingual schooling for Hispanic children (Chamot, 1988):

• immersion strategy, in which content subjects are taught through simplified English

- early-exit or short term transitional bilingual programs of 2-to-3 years
- late-exit or long-term transitional bilingual programs of 5-to-6 years

Researchers report that long-term bilingual programs are most effective in promoting progress in both Spanish and English, and that immersion programs lead to a greater use of English by students in school itself. But comparison studies like these are very difficult to organize, because of the huge variations in bilingual practice that actually exist in schools. Studies by Moll (1992) and García & Otheguy (1987) suggest that the range of possible programs and the complex visions people have for them go well beyond the common stereotypes about what US bilingual schooling really tries to do. Meanwhile other researchers report that many US bilingual classrooms are bilingual in name only, and really are little more than regular classrooms (Wong Fillmore & Valdez, 1986). Many classes make little use of the children's first language, which might help explain the results of a study by Ramirez (1992) that report no significant differences in student achievement between three different 'bilingual' approaches.

Other factors are at work, too. These are captured in Ogbu's (1987) distinction between voluntary and involuntary minorities (see chap. 3). Hornberger (1990a), for example, notes the difference between Puerto Rican and Cambodian students in achieving biliteracy. The bilingual language practices of the Puerto Ricans are sustained by their community's voluntary presence in Philadelphia, which allows its people to maintain long-term contacts with their homeland, helping them preserve their cultural identity. In contrast, the involuntary, refugee Cambodians have few support structures for their language, and this reduces their chances of achieving the same levels of biliteracy that the Spanish-dominant Puerto Ricans enjoy. The relative isolation of the Cambodians means that their learning context is situated squarely in the second language of English and in the mainstream culture of America.

Elsewhere in the United States, Spanish-dominant children benefit academically and in English language acquisition when their mother tongue is used as the language of instruction in the early school years (Campos & Keatinge, 1988; Gándara, 1994). Finally, a synthesis of research covering all of the United States, finds that bilingual education is much more effective than monolingual approaches. It promotes long-term academic gains and also leads to improvements that continue to grow in consistent ways (Collier, 1992).

In Sweden, a policy of active bilingualism has been the goal for immigrant pupils' language learning since 1975; and it has been a legal right since 1977. Every immigrant child there, from any minority group large enough to warrant it, must have the opportunity to attend a mother tongue medium class. Classes for the large Finnish minority in suburban Stockholm are among the longest established. These are segregated into classes using Finnish as the medium of instruction, with Swedish taught as a second language (Hagman & Lahdenperä, 1988).

After nine years of operation, researchers base their conclusions on comparisons with other Finnish children and other immigrant groups who have not had this history of instruction in their mother tongues. By the end of compulsory schooling, the segregated Finnish maintenance children still managed to integrate themselves into their Swedish comprehensive school and had built up their academic self-confidence, identity, and proficiency in Swedish, too. Also, the same students from the Finnish maintenance classes show much higher figures for entry into further education.

In Britain, the MOTET project in Bradford (Fitzpatrick, 1987) reports the effects of bilingual education in a one-year experimental program with infant children whose home language was Panjabi. The class program aimed to preserve a 'parity of esteem' between English and Panjabi by giving equal time and space to each language. The study concluded that there were no negative effects from bilingual education. Instead, there were the positive effects of mother tongue maintenance, as well as a level of progress in English equivalent to a matched control group who had not had a bilingual program.

In anglophone Canada, the more long-standing attention given to the needs of francophone minorities also promoted research and changes in policy and practice for immigrant children. Clearly, subtractive bilingual education is unsuitable for francophone Canadians who live in anglophone areas (see the section on established linguistic minorities later in this chapter). They certainly need English to live in that environment, but the evidence confirms that strong French-maintenance approaches are the best way to insure that they get this. For example, francophone minority children in Ontario schools, who get most of their education in French as the medium of instruction, tend to achieve much better in education and to succeed better in the world of work than those submerged in English or in only nominally bilingual schools (Churchill, Frenette & Quazi, 1986). Although this finding is relevant not just to Canadian-born linguistic minority children but also to immigrant Canadian children, maintenance forms of bilingual education for immigrant Canadians are still rare, as they are, too, for immigrants in the United States.

PROVIDING BILINGUAL EDUCATION

Where programs are available, different responses are made to maintaining and developing immigrant children's first languages. In general, these responses are of two types: firstly 'bilingual immersion education' which aims to maintain children's mother tongue and culture as far as possible; and secondly add-on 'heritage language programs', which try to maintain the minority language to some extent, while still allowing quick transition to the dominant language if necessary through ESL classes. In the next two sub-sections, I look at each of these approaches.

Bilingual Education: Supporting First Languages in School and Classroom

Schools and teachers are addressing many basic questions when they plan bilingual education. The planning involved is complex because it asks teachers to support students' first languages while giving them English at the same time. Here are some of the questions that have to be considered. I elaborate on these elsewhere (Corson, 1999):

1. What needs to be done to staff the first language maintenance and development program?
2. What in-service provisions are being made to develop staff proficiency in first language maintenance?
3. What procedures can be introduced for community consultation, for recruiting bilingual teachers, for providing aids and resources, and for attracting adequate funding?
4. What can the school do to encourage minority parents to maintain and use their languages?
5. How can parents be involved?

Sometimes, schools are frustrated in their efforts because minority families are reluctant to use their language outside the home. Often, this happens because they feel ashamed of their first language, following several generations of minority language intolerance in English-speaking countries. When this happens, children can easily lose their motivation because they see their first language has no place of prestige in the wider community. Clearly the school itself has an important role to play here. Joshua Fishman (1980) suggests 'reward systems' to stimulate the use of the minority language. For example, where bilingualism is supported officially in a country, the school system, government, the law, libraries and other instrumentalities all show by their actions and policies that minority and majority languages have equal status. And inside schools, similar approaches are possible on a smaller scale, even in non-bilingual countries. At the end of this chapter, I provide a list of ways to value first languages that can be used even in schools that do not have bilingual education programs.

The help of minority parents themselves is central to all this (Leman, 1997). Consequently, teachers in bilingual schools are often interested in finding answers to these questions:

- What sort of role can parents have in the school to supplement what teachers can offer?
- Is there a need for community education about the aims of bilingual programs?
- Would parents value an introduction to the bilingual approaches used or even training themselves?
- How can parents mix regularly with students in lesson time?

- How far can the school extend into the home in language matters?

Clearly, this last question is more important for some children than for others. If the minority language is not maintained outside the school to a high level of fluency, then the school needs to make special arrangements. I turn to these matters again in the conclusion to the chapter.

The costs of bilingual education can also be a concern. In dealing with this, partial immersion programs, like those used in the prairie provinces of Canada, are less expensive and they seem more effective than heritage language programs (Gillett, 1987). For this reason, Gillett suggests that an expansion of bilingual immersion education should be the next step in the development of immigrant language education in that country. A further problem apparent in many bilingual education programs is that the minority languages are treated in isolation from the context and culture of students themselves. This treatment of language in isolation from its context was also a characteristic of the early bilingual research.

Cultural Factors and Assessment

In most early studies on bilingualism, cultural factors other than the minority language itself were discounted. Other aspects of cultural capital that minority children bring to school got little attention. Yet, these were often the very things that caused the discontinuities and inequalities in school performance that were measured but never explained by researchers. As recently as the 1980s in the United States, instruction in the minority language for some of the time was the only accommodation that seemed to be made by teachers to the cultural differences of children (Iglesias, 1985). Few of the recommendations, from sociolinguists for example, about matching discourse norms and other signs with those used in the minority culture, were actually put into practice. A key point that comes from research on this matter, especially in classes for the very young, is that the pedagogical signs and organizational structures in schools need to match, as closely as possible, those used in the children's home community (Hornberger, 1990b; Tompkins, 1998). To do this, and perhaps reverse the failure rates of some language minorities could involve policy changes similar in kind to reforms in schools serving aboriginal students that were touched on in chapter 3.

These cultural differences become influential when bilingual children are being assessed. Often, culturally different children come to school knowing very different kinds of things from other children. Even when they use English words and other signs, the rules of use they have for them can be quite different. So, when they meet the assessment methods that teachers use, they sometimes are asked to display knowledge about "x, y" when what they really know about is "y, z." Often, in regular schools, they are never asked to display their knowledge about "y, z." Furthermore they are usually asked to display their knowledge in unfamiliar ways. For example, in Hawaii and elsewhere in the Pacific, many children from Polynesian cultures seem more 'oral and aural' in their interactions with the world, because these senses are highlighted in their cultural practices. But the formal schooling they usually get is mainly 'visual', with a heavy stress on academic literacy and few opportunities for group work.

In some schools, this different cultural orientation is taken into account in the school's planning. Dance, drama, groupwork, and music become more central to the program, because teachers can see how central they are to the cultures represented and to the children's real interests. They also become more central in the school's assessment system and its professional development program, where teachers themselves begin to engage with the children's cultures. All this suggests again that being able to see part of the world from the different culture's point of view is an ability that teachers need to strive for. Again, as far as possible, the culture of the child needs to be in the mind of the teacher.

Here too, Cummins' work (1989) provides a key reference. He draws attention to the over-representation of minority language children in classes for the 'learning disabled'. Other North American writers also confirm that this is a very serious issue which especially affects African Americans and Latino-Americans (Artiles & Trent, 1994). Cummins attributes this over-representation to routine mistakes using psychological tests with linguistic minority children. In particular, he warns against tests that measure only things that count as 'intelligent' within the dominant group, while excluding any culturally-specific ways that minority children have learned as 'intelligent'. He suggests that intelligence tests tell us little about previous learning, because the previous learning experiences of culturally different children are not fully sampled. At the same time, he warns against testing children in their first language, if it has not been recently used or if it is affected by heavy and recent exposure to the dominant language.

Another partial explanation for the over-referral of minority language students to special education services is the pressure that teachers work under, and the very real increase in pressure that minority language students can bring to regular classrooms. A factor in over-referral can be a teacher's sincere belief that he or she is unable to provide adequate instruction for a given child from a diverse background. At the same time, a developing problem in parts of the United States is the *under-representation* of linguistic minority students in special education classes for the learning disabled. This under-use of referral services is thought to be a reaction against the litigation and protests that have accompanied some high-profile cases of over-representation. Researchers are beginning to document the plight of low-achieving minority language students left unwisely but with good intentions in regular clasrooms (Gersten & Woodward, 1994).

Elsewhere, Cummins (1989) discusses bias-free language testing. For fairer assessment, one of the trained people testing minority children's language should be a fluent user of the children's mother tongue. Assessments made in the second language need to be used with care and never as the sole basis for placing the children in special education classes, even for long-term residents of the country. He warns that teachers can be over-optimistic about minority children's language ability. Often, the students understand undemanding English in relaxed conversations, but their ability to use English in the classroom might not meet the demands of academic proficiency.

Assessing and Teaching Exceptional Minority Language Students

For assessing exceptional minority language pupils, Cummins (1984) offers the following main points:

*   For children already diagnosed with language disorders, assessment and instruction should mainly concentrate on helping them to interact either with others or with a written text, rather than on the production of language forms. The task is for teachers to separate the effects of the children's language barrier from the effects of their language disorders, and this can only come from attending to their practical competence in both the first and second languages.
*   For children already diagnosed as hearing-impaired, descriptive assessment in both languages (including, perhaps, a sign language) is of more value than assessment that compares them with others or with norms. The focus is on what children can do rather than on what they lack.
*   For candidates in gifted and talented programs, teacher observation is central. One useful piece of evidence may be the child's rapid progress in learning the majority tongue (assuming that 5-to-7 years is the average time needed to catch up in their language proficiency for doing academic work). A major motivating factor is curricular and extra-curricular activities that encourage that display. Gifted and talented children will be no less represented among the language minority children than among the majority.

Students with few literacy skills in their first language also come under the 'exceptional' heading. To meet the needs of these students, Else Hamayan (1997) summarizes some of the better approaches that do not involve watering down the curriculum. These use the following strategies:

*   meaning-based instruction
*   instruction in the student's stronger language (i.e., usually first language maintenance)
*   literacy instruction that allows literacy to emerge holistically and developmentally

- a curriculum connected to the students' homes and personal experiences
- lessons structured to focus on tasks
- lessons structured to cluster new concepts together
- lessons structured to allow students to learn collaboratively
- lessons structured to allow students to use technology
- lessons structured to allow students to learn by doing

Heritage Language Programs

Heritage programs can work as an appendix to the regular school timetable, or they can be integrated into the school day. Established programs operate in parts of Australia, Canada, and Britain, and advocates are working to establish them in the United States as well. They are taught by fluent speakers of the immigrant language who are sometimes trained teachers, but often not.

These programs can represent significant changes to the structure of schooling. This is because they stress community languages and redefine what counts as legitimate school knowledge and practice. In contrast, ESL programs are often seen more positively by people, because they link immigrant students into the traditional curriculum. Heritage programs also value the linguistic capital of minority groups and this can be threatening to some people. These programs often redefine the qualities that teachers need to have, which also leads to some opposition among regular teachers. Teachers can be frustrated by the complications involved in putting the programs into the school timetable. But there are wider factors to do with racism and cultural privilege that also affect the success of heritage language programs. For example, Reva Joshee and Jeff Bullard (1992) report that a large majority of immigrant community members in Ontario support heritage language maintenance through the school, but the majority culture population opposes this.

The power of the dominant cultural group does decide the language of most school classrooms. It is difficult to break this power, especially where economic control is involved. So, most heritage language programs are offered outside normal school time, often at weekends and outside the school itself. Elsewhere, I discuss the strength and weaknesses of these programs (Corson, 1998). At the core of the problem is the question of making the programs more meaningful, which already exercises the minds of teachers themselves. Grace Feuerverger (1997) interviewed many heritage language teachers and highlights the marginal existence they have. Based on their views, her suggestions underline the need for changes in policy and practice:

- professional development to give teachers a sense of their professional identity and importance
- the forming of partnerships between heritage language teachers and regular teachers

- regular teachers who themselves place value on the heritage languages
- credit status within the school's program for heritage language courses
- more integration of the programs into the regular school day
- more attention to the heritage cultures, as well as to the languages
- supportive administrators who express that support to the students and other teachers

The solution to several of these is to integrate the programs into the regular school day and into its timetable. But even where this happens, the courses are usually aimed only at the languages of established heritage groups, and not at the languages of recent arrivals who may be the very ones who need urgent language maintenance. So, while these programs do serve a purpose, it may not be the purpose that their supporters expect. Also, it is far from certain that they are the best way for improving the education of recent immigrant language minorities who need the more integrating forms of bilingual education described above.

ESTABLISHED LINGUISTIC MINORITIES

Chapters 3 and 4 discussed some of the involuntary minorities who live in English-speaking countries. But there are other involuntary linguistic minorities who have rather different educational needs. Like the immigrant students I have been discussing so far, these established linguistic minorities have strong claims to bilingual education. But unlike immigrants, those claims continue beyond middle childhood. Increasingly in many places, linguistic minorities are getting all of their education in bilingual settings.

The large Hispanic populations in the south-west of the United States, the speakers of Celtic languages in Wales, Ireland, and Scotland, and the francophone minorities in anglophone parts of Canada, are all different in their needs and interests from newly arrived people and from aboriginal peoples. All these established minorities are European in their cultural history. As a result, they seem to share most aspects of the dominant culture with their English-speaking neighbours. But this can be misleading. In fact, the cultures of linguistic minority communities are often very different from the majority culture in ways that are still not widely studied.

Outsiders often miss the extent of these cultural differences. They wrongly conclude that the different educational needs of these minorities can be met just by giving them first language support, in a school setting that remains part of the dominant culture in all other respects. But often the educational needs of linguistic minority communities extend well beyond simple language issues.

Spanish-Speaking and Celtic-Speaking Established Minorities

In the United States, there has been a long history of bilingual education for Spanish-speaking residents. This began in the Cuban immigrant communities in southern Florida and spread to the south-west parts of the country that border on Mexico (Faltis, 1997). Developments across the country have been frequent, although they have also been intermittent because of strong political opposition to the idea of a bilingual and multicultural United States. New developments seem likely, following a shift in the federal guidelines for bilingual funding in the 1990s. Funding is now contingent upon a school's ability to demonstrate that it has a plan for making bilingual education a part of a whole school effort to address the needs of non-English proficient children and adolescents. This means that teachers, administrators, and curriculum specialists in schools that serve large numbers of language-minority students have to retool themselves to meet this challenge (Faltis, 1997), and developing a school language policy is a rational and straightforward way of going about this.

In Britain, the three Celtic languages are at different stages of revival (Baker, 1997). The Welsh language is already a success story, offering a model that other small European languages are following. Scots Celtic is also reviving, although a little less spectacularly than Welsh. In Ireland, there has been a large increase in all-Irish schools, even beyond the Celtic-speaking areas of the country. Like other small languages, it should do better within a united Europe that gives greater recognition to the continent's smaller languages. But in all three cases, the cultural differences between Celtic first language speakers and their neighbours, who speak English as their first language, are not great enough to warrant extensive cultural support in fully separate schools.

Despite the fact that the cultural differences are relatively slight, the need for ancestral cultural reproduction is certainly driving the revival of all the Celtic languages, as Colin Baker (1997) confirms. At the same time, many of the Celtic speakers are affected more by factors of social class or region of living than by differences in ethnic identity and cultural allegiance. The Welsh tend to be Welsh, the Scots tend to be Scots, and the Irish tend to be Irish, whichever language they speak. But this is not so much the case in North America, where linguistic minorities are less ready to believe that they have 'countries' of their own. In North America, linguistic minorities have cultural allegiances that are rather different from their English-speaking neighbours. Moreover, in North America, those neighbours are less proud and sometimes intolerant of the differences.

Some Relevant Research from North America

Two-way bilingual education has generated considerable interest in the United States (Lindholm, 1997). This approach promotes language development for linguistic minority and language majority students who work alongside one another in the same classroom. More than 200 programs are operating across the country and they work very well for both minority and majority language students. Indeed, by grades 6 or 7, the minority first language speakers consistently reach or come close to grade norms in their English academic skills, confirming an inverse relationship between exposure to English and achievement in English when two-way programs are compared with all-English immersion programs. At the same time, native-English speaking students achieve high levels of biliteracy proficiency with no cost to their academic development in English. Rebecca Freeman (1996) reviews an exemplary two-way program operating at Oyster Bilingual School. I describe the research methods that Freeman uses in chapter 7. This Washington, DC program functions as an English-acquisition plan for limited-English students and as a Spanish-acquisition plan for limited-Spanish students. It aims to give all students sufficient proficiency in both languages to participate in content classes taught in Spanish and English. The Spanish component also serves as a Spanish language maintenance plan for the native Spanish speakers, although it is evident from Freeman's study that the two languages are not distributed or valued equally throughout the school. So, despite its evident success, there might still be a problem for minority language communities with this two-way approach.

In Canadian francophone minority settings, this kind of mixed immersion education has been found to gradually erode francophone children's use and command of French. That contrasts with the British situation where native speakers of the Celtic languages in two-way programs often sit alongside students learning these as second languages and still show little sign of erosion. Perhaps the differences between Canada and Britain can be explained by the high general support that the Celtic languages get from the wider community in the their homelands, which contrasts with the very low support for minority French in anglophone Canada. I should add, too, that there is even less support for minority Spanish in the United States; so perhaps language survival among some minority-Spanish communities could be affected negatively by two-way programs.

As Kathryn Lindholm (1997) points out, the knowledge base in the United States for two-way bilingual programs does not begin to compare in scope with the research conducted in Canada. So a brief outline of the educational situation for francophone minorities in Canada, especially in Ontario, will suggest some of the ways that schools in many places are already meeting the different needs of established linguistic minorities. This survey is drawn from work summarized in Corson & Lemay (1996).

Large francophone communities exist outside Québec in majority-anglophone parts of Canada and the United States, too. The large Acadian community in New Brunswick make up a third of that province's population, and its members spill over into all the other Atlantic provinces of the country (Mackey, 1991). Meanwhile, the country's most populous province, Ontario, has about half a million people who use the French language for significant activities in their lives and who describe themselves as Franco-Ontarian. Indeed, like the Acadians, these people also see themselves as culturally different from the largest French population in Canada, who live in Québec. But those cultural differences do not impinge on their lives as strongly as the other pressures to conform, in both culture and language, that come from English-speaking Ontario. These pressures are similar to those felt by established Spanish minorities in California and New Mexico, and the communities themselves have to work hard to create educational systems that will allow them to maintain their cultures and their languages.

According to legislation in Canada, all official-language minority education is maintenance bilingual education, and French and English are both official languages. Often, though, because the population is highly dispersed and most speech outside of school and beyond the family is in English, there is still a high degree of assimilation towards English and towards 'English' culture. Rather than describing themselves as francophones these days, Franco-Ontarians more often see themselves as "les bilingues." Their bilingualism is the chief marker of their identity, and even their vernacular French is heavily filled with anglicisms of a kind that mainstream French deliberately rejects. It is estimated that the number of francophones in Ontario is falling by half every twenty-to-thirty years, although changes to system-wide educational administration are probably slowing the process. Several factors help promote this assimilation:

- inactivity by provincial governments in supporting the minority language
- the tendency of immersion programs to anglicize francophone children
- lack of minority control over education
- francophone parents who are indifferent about supporting their language
- lack of social opportunities to function in French outside schools

All these things can keep students away from native-speaker proficiency. Also, studies confirm that minority language schooling without home language maintenance does not provide native-speaker proficiency. So, linking all this with Cummins' (1996) two hypotheses, it is clear why Franco-Ontarian students (and Spanish-speaking students in the United States) often are held back in their education and why they are at a particular disadvantage in developing the academic literacy needed for school success.

Based on the average educational levels achieved, illiteracy levels among Franco-Ontarians are around twice those of the anglophone population of the province. One out of every three students is at risk of becoming illiterate in French. In an effort to explain this, Wagner (1991) sees an 'illiteracy of oppression' and an 'illiteracy of resistance' at work here. Chapter 4's discussion of 'critical literacy' looks at the implications of Wagner's work and suggests some ways to address the issues he raises.

Another factor at work here is the 'non-standard' nature of Franco-Ontarian varieties of French (see chap. 4). This point is relevant to the non-standard varieties of Spanish used in established communities in the United States. The problem is complicated by the Ontario school system itself. Instead of education in and around these local varieties, old and new learners of French in Ontario's schools sometimes encounter a French variety from Québec, or, more usually, the more dominant variety from metropolitan France. Rarely, if ever, does the local variety get preferred treatment. I return to this point in chapter 7.

Changing Practices

The Minority Language as Vehicle of Instruction.   As suggested already, children from minority groups generally profit from bilingual programs in which their first language plays the major role, because this lays a language foundation that cannot otherwise be guaranteed. The research evidence in Canada supports these conclusions. In programs of different kinds, it is clear that a culturally appropriate course of study that teaches all subjects in the minority language gives better results, and it does so without compromising attainments in the majority language. Again, the best kind of program also values the non-standard variety that children bring with them to school and provides its instruction in a context that is thoroughly congruent with the minority culture. These findings are strongly supported through research with established minorities in a range of countries, including the United States (Cummins & Corson, 1997).

Reducing Assimilationary Pressures.   Rampant assimilation is a problem in many places. Lack of home support is often a factor that promotes this assimilation, because schools can only do so much and cannot replace the family and community in promoting language vitality (Churchill, Frenette & Quazi, 1986). Without a dynamic curriculum that promotes belief in the language's value and increases competence and use of the mother tongue in the home, there is no way to stop this kind of assimilation. Building on the additive/subtractive notion of bilingual education, Landry and Allard (1987) urge minority families and minority schools to act in concert to offset unwanted contact with the majority culture and its language. As Joshua Fishman (1996) notes: "Vernaculars are acquired in infancy, in the family, which means in intimacy. They are handed on that way, in intimacy and in infancy" (p. 192).

Where linguistic minorities are not in control of their own schooling, this counterbalance is likely to be missing. So, Landry and Allard (1987) also argue that complete control of institutions is needed to ensure that a maximum number of contexts is available where mother tongue usage is encouraged. They say that deliberate steps are needed that place high value on the minority language, because lack of prestige for a language often leads to assimilation of its speakers to the dominant language. For example, in most Canadian provinces now, francophone minority communities control their own boards of education and direct the operation of their own schools (Corson & Lemay, 1996).

Linguistic Minority Literacy and Teaching Methods.   Students need much more than a grounding in the technical skills of reading and writing. Minority students are unlikely to succeed in the academic culture of literacy if they have a low sense of their own cultural identity. Accordingly, successful schools are focussing their intervention on cultural and critical literacies that respond to the sociocultural and sociopolitical situation of learners. Talking about text, not just learning how to read it, is central to all this. These things gradually lead to individual and group empowerment, and so counteract the 'illiteracies of oppression and resistance' described in chapter 4.

Where established minority students are successful in schools, the pedagogy in use is culturally liberating. It goes well beyond reproducing dominant aspects of the majority culture. It gives legitimacy to the minority students' culture. Again, it respects their language variety, while exposing them to other varieties and communicating the empowering ways in which those varieties can be used. In shaping the curriculum and designing their teaching methods, teachers in these schools promote a rich dialogic process between the school, the community, and the student. They consult the interests of all those with interests at stake. As a result, teachers in these schools are agents of change and liberation. And already the minority communities are beginning to train them to prepare for this role.

Again, maximum control of schools by linguistic minority communities ensures that there are as many contexts as possible where mother tongue usage is encouraged and valued. Indeed, successful schools are also working to offset the constant contact with the majority culture and language that minority language children receive outside schools. They are trying to build this idea into their formally agreed policies so that it impacts across the school and its provisions. Similarly, the pedagogy in these schools is culturally liberating: It becomes more empowering when it recognizes the minority students' culture and when it shows unqualified respect for their variety of language. And similar changes are also flowing into the education of another prominent language minority, whose cultural and linguistic rights are at last being recognized more widely.

THE EDUCATION OF THE SIGNING DEAF

The natural sign languages of Deaf communities are fully-fledged languages, like any other languages, and these sign languages differ from each other as much as sound-based languages. Also, there are families of sign languages, and they have no necessary relationship to the sound-based languages that surround them. In short, sign languages are unwritten, face-to-face languages (Branson & Miller, 1997b).

More often than not, educational policies have reduced the status of these languages by banning their use altogether or by changing them into signed versions of the dominant spoken language. These restrictions on the use of sign languages in schools allow the hearing establishment to exercise symbolic power over Deaf communities. But recent years have seen changes throughout the English-speaking world. Various Deaf communities, who use their own native sign languages, have begun to challenge more traditional views in this area. These signing Deaf communities now consider themselves distinct linguistic minorities and cultural groups who possess all the solidarity and support structures that go with that sense of identity.

As in other areas of bilingual and bicultural education, Deaf communities are now questioning why education only proceeds through the dominant language. They are asking why the learning styles of hearing people should dominate classroom practices, and why only the cultures that belong to hearing people are valued in schools. In this section, I look at these changes in policy and practice that are returning cultural and educational power to signing Deaf minorities, and also improving the education of Deaf children.

Deaf Sign Languages and Mainstreaming

'Signed English' is a different sign language from the sign languages developed by Deaf communities themselves. Signed versions of national spoken or written languages, like Signed English, are not fully fledged, natural languages. They use 'frozen signs' or single unchanging signs for each word, or word part, in the spoken language. As a result, they lack the dynamism and creativity of natural sign languages. These are changing all the time, like all natural languages (Branson & Miller, 1997a).

Sign languages that develop naturally are community languages, and there are many of these. They include British Sign Language (BSL), for example. This is used by 50,000 people in Britain, making it the fourth most used indigenous language, after English, Welsh and Scottish Gaelic. These signed languages also include the American Sign Language (ASL) used in anglophone parts of North America, and 'La Langue des Signes Québécoise' (LSQ) used in francophone areas. There are natural sign languages in use in every country. In fact, there are non-standard varieties of major sign languages that differ as much from one another as do the non-standard varieties of spoken languages, making them mutually uninterpretable in some cases. Moreover, these sign languages can communicate any of the range of meanings and nuances of other languages:

ASL is capable of expressing the full dimension of human experience including opinions, theory, history and poetry. We now know that ASL is a language that uses handshapes, palm orientation, location, movement and non-manual signals (body and head shifting, body movement and facial markers) with its own content, grammar and formalized rules for use. (Gibson, Small & Mason, 1997, pp. 235–236)

If given the chance, Deaf children learn and use a sign language whether they come from a family background where signing is the custom or not. In Britain, for example, more than 60% of Deaf children have learned to sign by 7 years (Kyle & Woll, 1985). But a sign language is usually learned at school, where other Deaf children and an occasional Deaf adult serve as models. For instance, signing is the favoured form of communication among the Ontario Deaf communities in Canada (Mason, personal communication, 1993), and the two sign languages in use in the province are now acknowledged, along with English and French, as official languages of instruction for schools in the province. Similar statutes, supporting the use of ASL in schools, are in place in Alberta and Manitoba (Gibson, Small & Mason, 1997). Signing also provides the most immediate form of communication available to Deaf children. And in Ontario, the learning of a sign language supports the acquisition of literacy in English or French (Mason, 1994) in ways that many educationists are only beginning to appreciate.

Again the 'interdependence hypothesis' helps explains this process. That hypothesis highlights the supportive relationship that exists between the learner's first language and a new second language. Like ESL students who are new to English, Deaf children's first (signing) language can also support the learning of English literacy if the sign language is maintained to a high enough level of proficiency. This leads to certain conclusions about the education of Deaf signing children. In particular, educational policies that put Deaf signing children into regular classrooms come into question.

The mainstreaming of exceptional children, by placing them in regular classrooms, is seen as a universal good in progressive educational settings. And it is certainly a good practice for most exceptional students. But it is not suitable for most signing Deaf students. In fact, research and authoritative opinion increasingly argues against the mainstreaming of signing Deaf students, because these students are at risk in regular classrooms:

> What is most apparent generally … is that deaf children are unable to interact, do not contribute to class lessons through speech, are subjected to distorted and exaggerated mouthings by teachers and pupils in order to convey specific information (i.e. not natural language interaction) and are unlikely to have secure peer group friendships. (Kyle & Woll, 1985, p. 239).

In fact, if placed in regular English-based classrooms, Deaf signing students can be seriously held back in their education. This is because they do not 'speak' English, and sometimes only a few are fully proficient in signed English. In regular classes, they have no opportunity to communicate in their own favoured language, which is the Deaf signing language of their own community. Instead, they are pressured to acquire oral ways of communicating and this keeps them away from the complex, academic ideas that a Deaf sign language can be used to express. Moreover, all this has a very negative effect on Deaf communities themselves.

As Branson and Miller (1995) observe, in the eyes of the hearing establishment, mainstreaming reinforces the cultural and linguistic incompetence of the Deaf. It helps to marginalize their communities as effectively as ever; and it reinforces their status as 'disabled' people who are in need of 'care'. As one close observer of the operation of mainstreaming notes, "it is the most dangerous move yet against the early development of a Deaf person's character, self-confidence and basic sense of identity" (Ladd, 1991, p. 88). For these and other reasons, mainstreaming seems little more than an "administrative solution with no real base in clinical practice or educational services" (Rodda, Grove & Finch, 1986, p. 153).

School and Classroom Practices for Deaf Signing Students

Because developments in this area are recent and still not widely studied, there is some disagreement about what the best practices might be. The issue is also complicated by the fact that students have varying degrees of deafness that allow some to communicate more readily in non-signed ways than others. This means that the integration of some Deaf signing students is possible for part of the school day and that special classrooms for Deaf signing students, sited in regular schools, are still seen as one way of providing for this language minority.

As a result, some expert opinion favours partial integration of some students for some of the school day, while other students remain highly segregated but still work in the same school setting with hearing students (Mason, personal communication, 1993). Other expert opinion also favours a special class for signing Deaf students in a regular school, using special teachers who are bilingual in English and the sign language of the local community or perhaps who are members of the Deaf community themselves.

Studies of partial integration in Britain, carried out at various ages, have not been encouraging (MacKinnon & Densham, 1989). Instead, fully separate schools for the signing Deaf are seen by many as the most suitable and cost-effective measure (St Louis, personal communication, 1993). In many North American settings, for example, schools of this kind are moving towards using ASL as a medium of classroom instruction (Cummins & Danesi, 1990). Gradually, the favoured alternative to mainstreaming in North America is to offer signing Deaf students a form of bilingual immersion education in their two languages: ASL and English or LSQ and French. This immersion education is presented in separate classes or schools for the Deaf by specialist teachers who are bilingual themselves in the languages and also familiar with the culture of the Deaf signing community.

Judging by the assessments of Deaf community members themselves, these new approaches seem overdue and they are very welcome. Heather Gibson is a Deaf educator whose sister and brother are also Deaf. In fact, ASL was the first language of all three. As children, they dreamed of sharing that language with other Deaf people. Gibson says that, from an early age, using ASL was as important to her as breathing, yet few people then believed that using ASL was the most effective way for Deaf people to communicate. Now, she is the first Deaf woman vice-principal in Ontario. She has been honoured for her work establishing a bilingual and bicultural Deaf program at her school for the Deaf, and she described developments at the school in this way:

> The dream we had has not come to fruition yet, but parts of it are a reality now. We do have more deaf teachers working in the system … In the past that didn't exist. We've also seen more deaf organizations and individuals come in and be part of our deaf education system. It's a critical thing for deaf children to see. These individuals aren't just role models but mentors and advocates for the children. Students have full access to the school curriculum and that's because we're using ASL, our first language. That allows open access to an education. (Black, 1997, p. A5).

This approach is spreading quickly in the English-speaking world as more people begin to recognize that the signing Deaf are minority language users who have a distinct culture of their own to share and transmit. Certain organizational arrangements seem to suit these schools (Israelite, Ewoldt & Hoffmeister, 1992):

- they have teachers who are knowledgeable about the linguistic properties of native sign language
- they have teachers who know about cultural issues in the Deaf and hearing communities
- they see Deaf teachers or teaching assistants as essential to their students' successful development
- their curriculums give wide opportunities to share personal experiences in the signed language
- their assessment teams include at least one Deaf professional more proficient than the student
- they guarantee parent education as part of Deaf education: in signing, culture, and interaction modes

At the same time, like other students in bilingual education, the signing Deaf in these schools follow a curriculum that gives them the best of both worlds. They have their first signing language supported, including exposure to the culture of the Deaf community which gives that language its meaning; and they also receive literacy in English, because they will live and work in an English-dominant society. The Canadian Association of the Deaf (1990), for instance, places a higher priority on the acquisition of literacy in English or French than it does on oral language skills in English or French because of the importance for the Deaf of having literacy for finding work and succeeding in post-secondary education. Accordingly, a core English or French curriculum is still very important for the signing Deaf, because they need to be highly literate and expert in that language. What would a core curriculum look like, if written for signing Deaf students?

An English curriculum taught in a separate school for the Deaf would address the same sets of core competencies and use similar teaching methods to those used in the regular school. But where the core curriculum for other students stresses 'talk', the Deaf core curriculum would stress 'signing' as follows:

- high proficiency in English literacy, using signing as the medium of instruction
- learning about the English language, using signing as the medium of instruction
- instead of 'talking about text', using signing to discuss text
- instead of 'talking about literature', using signing to discuss literature
- instead of 'talking about media', using signing to discuss media

Other ways of organizing instruction are also being tried, especially for younger students. For example, a bilingual immersion arrangement allows hearing students to work alongside the Deaf and become naturally bilingual in the signed language and in their first language. In Canada, a day-care project integrates signing Deaf students in this way with hearing students in a bilingual/bicultural program using English and ASL (Evans & Zimmer, 1993). All the hearing children have some kind of contact with the Deaf community, like a Deaf parent or sibling. In this immersion setting, half the staff are Deaf and the rest are hearing, while the choice of language for classroom interaction is dictated by person and not by activities. In other words, the students themselves choose the language for any interaction.

This program helps all the children develop pride in both cultures. The signing Deaf children also develop a more positive self-identity and better language skills. The studies so far indicate that all the children are learning either ASL or English as a second language, according to their background. Only 20% of the signing Deaf children have some type of language delay after completing the program, compared to 70% who were delayed at the beginning of the program. The most important conclusion drawn from the language assessment data, is that "all children (whether they are hearing, Deaf, of Deaf parents, or hearing parents) have the potential to develop effective bilingual/bicultural skills when exposed to the appropriate environment and language models" (Evans & Zimmer, 1993, p. 69).

Meanwhile, in the United States, several schools for Deaf students are also becoming bilingual/bicultural in their programs. Among the better known are the Learning Center for Deaf Children in Framingham MA, the Indiana School for the Deaf, and the California School for the Deaf in Fremont (Gibson, Small, & Mason, 1997). Experimental bilingual programs in the United States use storytelling to develop young students use of ASL and their use of ASL in learning English. Here, the curriculum focuses on a series of stories that address separate aspects of language. In one program, the teacher is a native Deaf signer who is bilingual in English and experienced in the art of storytelling. This program's early success, with 4-to-7-year-olds, led to its further development. A second program also used role-playing, storytelling by the students, and story writing. Here, the students engaged in lots of code-switching, using English with their teachers and ASL with other students, and their ASL stories became more elaborated and had clearer transitions (Israelite, Ewoldt & Hoffmeister, 1992).

In languages other than English, there are more long-standing developments. Students in France and Switzerland receive bilingual/bicultural primary education where the native sign language is used by all participants, both adults and children, for all non-written communication. In both places, the teaching of French proceeds mainly through written language. Other programs too are developing at more senior levels of education (Israelite, Ewoldt & Hoffmeister, 1992). In Scandinavia, the move towards a full bilingual/bicultural approach is still taking place but, in many respects, it is ahead of North American developments. Research from Sweden and Denmark shows that the reading, writing, and overall academic levels of Deaf students in bilingual programs are on par with hearing children the same age (Gibson, Small, & Mason, 1997).

These few developments suggest a little of the range of reforms. Part of this is the development of effective sign language curricula for the teaching of sign languages in schools and in universities. In fact, it is central to increasing educational opportunities for Deaf signing students (Branson & Miller, 1997b). Most important is the need to end the cycle of low expectations for the signing Deaf. In short, "the participants in the program must subscribe to the belief that Deaf people can be expected to learn as much as hearing children" (Johnson, Liddell, & Erting, 1989, p. 12).

THE ESL EDUCATION OF OLDER IMMIGRANT CHILDREN

By the time immigrant children reach middle childhood, their first languages are usually well enough maintained to support the learning of a second language without first language support. As a result, high schools meet most of the needs of immigrant adolescent students by giving them the widest possible academic and informal exposure to English taught as a second language.

Students needing ESL support range from those with little or no knowledge of English, who have just arrived in the country, to those who are fluent in social communication in English but have difficulty with their academic communication. However, students placed between these two points differ in more than just their experience of English. There is as wide a spread of academic potential among ESL children as among other groups of children. For example, immigrant children with specific learning problems get encouraging results learning English if they are given the same special conditions that they would receive in first language education. These children with exceptional needs learn English as a second language with no hindrance to their first language or to their general development (Bruck,

1984). Accordingly, there is no need to exempt students with disabilities from second language study, as is often done in the United States (Hamayan, 1997).

At the same time, there are many other ESL priorities that schools need to balance against one another. The list below is a summary of responses from principals and ESL specialists in schools who were asked to rank the different groups of immigrant students seeking help in English (Commonwealth Schools Commission, 1984). The students judged most in need come first:

- recent arrivals with hardly any English skills
- students unable to participate in mainstream classes due to lack of English language proficiency
- students whose parents speak no English
- students unable to participate in mainstream classes due to lack of subject content knowledge or skills
- students in transition from elementary to high school and from junior to senior high school
- students in the early years of primary and high school
- gifted and talented ESL students

Nevertheless, even getting to the point where this sort of ranking is possible means completing certain tasks of identification, placement, and assessment, issues which I treat more fully elsewhere (Corson, 1999). Certain arrangements outside the classroom are also necessary. To support, monitor, and evaluate the ESL program, school staff address questions like these:

- How can the school display a positive attitude towards the students' first languages and towards users of that language (see the concluding section to this chapter)?
- What additional staffing levels are desirable and possible?
- Is an ESL coordinator needed for the school?
- Should the school have an across the curriculum language support team?
- How will in-service training in ESL be provided for classroom teachers?
- How will in-service training be provided for ESL teachers?
- How will children with specific learning difficulties and other exceptional pupils be integrated into the program (see Hamayan, 1997)?
- When and how will the ESL program be evaluated?
- What organizational arrangements best suit the needs of the students and the school?

ESL teachers are not the only ones responsible for the learning of ESL students in a high school. In some places, the number of ESL teachers is falling as a few more regular teachers are equipped with ESL training as part of their teacher education (Clegg, 1996; Reid, 1988). Although this change in policy is still in its early days, the responsibility for ESL work in any school is always shared across the curriculum in any case. The work done by specialist ESL teachers is supported and extended by other teachers who come into contact with the students. While ESL teachers are the experts in this area, with special insights into student strengths and weaknesses that can be shared with other staff, the need for cooperative planning is important. And there are many ways to integrate ESL into the school's organizational patterns.

Because of the wide range of ESL needs that students have, schools prefer to choose from a broad range of ESL options. In the larger, language minority communities, schools often provide more than one of the following options, which I also elaborate on elsewhere (Corson, 1999):

- reception units
- integrated and cooperative teaching
- paired teaching
- parallel teaching and programing
- withdrawal teaching
- ESL extension
- correspondence school enrolment
- peer support systems
- enrollment in ESL evening classes
- first language support
- development of study skills
- familiarization programs
- language support across the curriculum
- incidental teaching
- rotation teaching
- special purpose teaching

ESL Teaching Approaches and Provisions for High School Students

Language learning and conceptual understanding develop when students engage in purposeful talk with others. However, even to get to this stage, the task that new ESL students meet in high schools is a daunting one. Moreover, the size of the task they face is affected by life experiences unique to individual children:

- their length of residence in their new country
- the traumatic life experiences that they lived through before arrival
- the length and continuity of their ESL education in elementary school
- the level of proficiency that they have in their first language
- all of the other social class-related factors discussed in earlier chapters
- their access to prior education in their homeland, if any.

Students in the last category, from backgrounds where first language literacy levels are low, have special needs. They are typically three or more years below their age-appropriate grade level, and their acquisition of literacy in English is usually slow and difficult. For these students, Else Hamayan (1997) sees problems in the nature of ESL literacy programs themselves. These programs are usually based on phonetic approaches that assume mastery of an English sound system that most new arrivals just do not have. She suggests that partially literate students would benefit from programs that stress meaning-based literacy experiences that match their oral language use quite closely.

All the things listed above can place severe limitations on ESL students. Most have to catch up academically while learning to use English and also while integrating into a wholly new culture and society. Yet, the usual outcome of high school ESL education is the full integration of students into regular classrooms, so students are managing to do all of this, even in the face of these many obstacles. How do high schools help in this?

Learning to Use the Academic Language of English

For most ESL students, it can take 5-to-7 years to acquire a second language to a level of proficiency adequate to begin to deal with ordinary high school classroom activities. Under ideal conditions, students can do less complex things quite quickly in their second language. But almost all ESL students have some difficulties with most of the curriculum offered in high schools. In fact, just to begin using the signs of academic language, against the background of their complex and precise rules of use, ESL students have to acquire certain competencies. None of these is easy to master in the language of a new culture:

> *Linguistic competence:* to use and interpret the structural elements of English.
> *Sociolinguistic competence:* to use language appropriately for any given situation.
> *Discourse competence:* to detect coherence of separate utterances in meaningful patterns.
> *Social competence:* empathy and the ability to handle social situations using language.
> *Sociocultural competence:* familiarity with the real-world context where English is used.
> *Strategic competence:* to use verbal and non-verbal strategies to make up for any gaps in English knowledge.

Studies of second language learning suggest that the following factors are important in extending communicative competence generally:

- learning efficiency improves as motivation increases (examination success, job prospects etc.)
- motivation increases when pupils can decide for themselves when they are ready to produce second language utterances
- pupil understanding of educational objectives and sharing in the task of setting objectives increases motivation markedly
- learners need input in the target language at a level that can be understood
- learning efficiency improves along with the strength of affiliative motivation (joining a respected group)
- a low level of anxiety is needed in the learning setting and anxiety reduces in a supportive learning environment with non-authoritarian teaching
- learners need a high level of self-confidence and a low level of self-consciousness in the learning task
- input needs to be just ahead of the learners' stage of rule development for it to support or disconfirm interlanguage rules that they already possess
- group work is superior to teacher-led activities in increasing coverage of content, amount of interaction or production, and accuracy of production
- teacher-led activities is superior in providing input that is extensive and needs a high level of accuracy
- communicative games and information gap tasks can extend interactive behaviours in the second language significantly, which helps learning
- learner proficiency correlates positively with the amount of language production in classrooms
- brief repetition and rephrasing of a message by teachers in the second language assists immediate learning
- many learners benefit when teachers draw attention to the learners' progress by interpreting the learners' English production and relating it explicitly to knowledge of the rules of the language
- peers used as models of language-in-use improve learning
- learning at more advanced levels is improved by wide interaction with adults and by a range of social contacts.

But going beyond these basic things, a great deal of research has gone into finding the 'best' approach for teaching a second language in a formal setting. Until quite recently, the 'communicative method' was the dominant approach because it laid stress on the learner's ability to function in a truly communicative setting, where the different competencies listed above could develop. But this method was still based on studying words, structures, functions, topics, or situations where the signs of English were set against rules of use rather divorced from all their real-world complexities. So these units of learning had little real significance from the learner's point of view. In other words, they were not 'meaningful acquisition units'. More recently, a 'task-based approach' is more favoured and has begun to supplement or replace earlier approaches. Tasks are items of class work that involve students in learning the new language while they concentrate mainly on meaning (i.e., use), rather than form (Long & Crookes, 1992; Skehan, 1996).

Much discussion has gone into defining more precisely what 'tasks' really are, in an ESL setting. In general, a task is some activity set in the real world of the student that leads to some outcome that gives the task, and the language it involves, a meaning or significance in the world of the learner. At the same time, a 'task-based' approach does not eliminate the need to teach language forms, like syntax and vocabulary knowledge. In fact, second language acquisition research clearly supports the idea of combining task-based language teaching with close attention to teaching about form (Allwright, 1997; Crandall, 1997). In other words, instruction focused on the relevant forms to be used is often necessary before the task, and instruction focused on the use of the forms in performance of the task is often valuable afterwards. I say more about the elements of a task-based syllabus in a later section.

As part of mastering the many different and difficult tasks of the high school curriculum, adolescent ESL students always have to 'get inside' the academic concepts that are the very stuff of that curriculum. These academic concepts are the meanings of specialist words, expressions, and other abstract signs whose use allows communication in complex areas.

Learning Academic Concepts in English as a Second Language

Interest in the role of words in learning English as a second language is now at the heart of ESL practice. But with only an occasional exception, the early work in linguistic studies gave scant attention to vocabulary, or neglected it entirely (Meara, 1982). So the upsurge of interest in vocabulary in the 1980s and 1990s, among ESL and other second language researchers, is a notable shift.

Many immigrant ESL students have special difficulties using English for academic purposes. The Graeco-Latin vocabulary of English creates special difficulties for children from some sociocultural backgrounds. This academic vocabulary is different in important ways from the basic vocabulary of English. Apart from conceptual difficulty, academic words tend to be much longer; they tend to be different in shape; they are drawn almost entirely from Latin and Greek, rather than from Anglo-Saxon sources; and they appear very rarely or not at all in everyday language use. Academic Graeco-Latin words are mainly literary in their rules of use. Most native speakers begin to encounter these words in quantity in their upper primary school reading and in the formal secondary school setting. So their introduction in literature or textbooks, rather than in conversation, restricts people's access to them. Printed texts provide much more exposure to these words than oral ones. For example, even children's books contain 50% more rare words than either adult prime-time television or the conversations of university graduates, while popular magazines have three times as many rare words as television and informal conversation.

Students coming from some backgrounds, especially from non-European backgrounds, can have serious problems with this kind of academic vocabulary and the related academic concepts. Elsewhere, I discuss approaches to teaching and learning these words (Corson, 1995b). The major part of the problem is knowing when and how to use the words effectively, so a good language learning environment in high schools is one that develops ESL students' critical language awareness as well. This always includes a study of the special place and function that academic words can have in English. Unfortunately, this sort of information is not usually passed on in regular ESL classes.

For example, it is important for second language learners to know that sometimes these English words, borrowed from Latin and Greek, are used in rather distancing ways to show unnecessary formality or exercise power. Giving students this critical kind of language awareness helps take some of the unwanted rules of use away from these words: rules of use that exclude some people from interaction, rather than others; rules of use that give the word user a different status from the one that is needed in the context; and rules of use that suggest a level of language evaluation that is not needed by the subject matter.

All these negative attributes of academic words are things that teachers of English and other high school subjects are beginning to give more thought to. In formal teaching situations, it is too easy to insist on the use of these academic words, even when they are not really needed in the context. It is easy to place too much value on the academic vocabularies of the school and, in so doing, devalue the vocabularies of students. At the same time, everyone needs to know that, when an academic word suits the meaning of the moment, its use really does help communication within one of the academic meaning systems of English.

Because academic words appear in certain precise and limited areas of discourse, their learnability really depends on ESL learners having rich contacts with the specialist areas in which they appear, as well as frequent contacts with the words themselves. Their meanings become clearer by trying them out in talk, linking them to the students' own intentions and purposes, and hearing them used in reply. In this way, the conceptual difficulty gradually falls away. This happens more easily when learners can negotiate their own meanings with more experienced users. Indeed, it suggests a clear conclusion for any form of education: We improve our grasp of academic concepts through conversations about the subject matter that uses the signs that give a name to those concepts.

Talking About Text in ESL and Regular Classrooms

Research does suggest an important role for reading experience in promoting vocabulary development, especially for younger children and young adults. But adolescents close to the end of their compulsory schooling have real problems learning and using academic concepts if they only meet them in their reading. This is because high school students meet academic demands that are unlike the more moderate demands placed on younger children. They are also unlike the demands placed on young adult university students, who are well inside specialist meaning systems to a much greater extent. While mastering the background knowledge of a number of complex fields, adolescents are asked to master the rules of use for huge numbers of new words, and these meanings are novel, unusual, and often change in different contexts and across meaning systems. To do this, students need far more than just coming across words in print. They need wide opportunities to engage in motivated talk about the texts that they read, or view, or that they hear read to them.

The increased integration of school-age ESL students into regular classrooms in many places is beginning to give them these wider opportunities to interact in natural language settings with native speakers. In mainstream classes, the motivation to use language with proficient classmates is higher; and social contacts and models of proficient usage are more numerous. These natural language conversations with native English speakers, linked to instructional exchanges, seem the best way to stimulate the learning and use of the kind of English needed to succeed in senior education (Crandall, 1997; Singleton, 1997)

It is clear that second language learners have many more opportunities to use the target language in groupwork than in teacher-led activities. But it is also clear that the changes that occur in student/student interactions give more meaning to the input received from the teacher, and the student talk itself is changed by conversational features, like requests from others in the group for clarification. One good way to provide this learning environment is in regular classrooms supported by regular teachers who are ESL specialists themselves. In this setting, students interact with their English-speaking classmates and a subject teacher skilled in working with ESL students. In this respect, two of the six syllabus models suggested by Krahnke (1987) for the foreign language classroom seem relevant. In both these models, ESL students get good opportunities to interact with their English-speaking classmates under the guidance of a subject teacher skilled in working with ESL students.

First, a 'content-based model' gives priority to the learning of some curriculum content or other as the aim of the syllabus. Although this content-based model is designed for foreign language teaching, it could be readily adapted to regular classrooms that integrate ESL students, because in these settings the usual curriculum content that all students need to master, will always have some priority over language learning (to the extent that those two things can ever be separated).

Second, a 'task-based model' also seems relevant. As suggested already, this offers a syllabus made up of "a series of complex and purposeful tasks that the students want or need to perform with the language" (Krahnke, 1987, p. 11). Here again, the syllabus has a purpose other than language learning, as happens in any regular classroom that addresses the academic content of technical and other specialist subjects. In these regular settings, students are confronted with tasks that provide logical steps or stages in the overall curriculum. And ESL students are no different. They also need to master these tasks to succeed in education. Within such a syllabus, for example, computer technology now offers opportunities for motivating interactions that can put ESL students in touch with a variety of task-based text types that reach well beyond the capability of traditional classrooms (Cummins & Sayers, 1995). This task-based model offers many other opportunities to senior students, asking them to engage critically with their own communities, to compare various experiences that are mentioned in ESL texts with events in their own lives, and to discuss the validity of different views of the world and the interests promoted by those views (see Morgan, 1998).

But at present, few regular high school teachers are trained in ESL teaching, and many are uncertain about integrating ESL students into their classes. Viv Edwards and Angela Redfern (1992) have researched this issue and they do advocate much more integration of students into regular classrooms. However they cannot see it working with the teachers who presently staff most schools. Even ESL teachers, convinced of the benefits of a move to the mainstream, tend to resist full integration. Nor is there much professional development of practising teachers in this area. Indeed in English-speaking countries there is little or no provision in present teacher education courses to give newly graduated teachers this proficiency. As Jim Cummins observes:

> So with minimal training being provided at preservice level, minimal professional development funds at school level, the reality is that the vast majority of regular teachers are quite unprepared to teach ESL students, unprepared often in both senses of the term (personal communication).

Consequently, for the foreseeable future at least, the bulk of ESL work will continue to fall on ESL specialists. Fortunately there is already a lot of 'talking about text' in good ESL programs, but students begin to miss out on this kind of academic talk when they enter regular classes, where subject specialists make less use of interactive teaching approaches. So, perhaps ESL teachers have a special modelling role here, as I suggest in the next section.

Studying Romance Languages

Another learning experience helpful for academic vocabulary development is studying second languages other than English. For example, there were once quite pronounced English vocabulary advantages in studying Latin and Ancient Greek, and these advantages are still relevant to learning and using academic words. But today these advantages are more widely available elsewhere, through the study of

Romance languages. Moreover the things outlined below are not just of value to ESL students.

Students used to get wide exposure to the history of English words when translating into and out of Latin and Greek. This was always seen as an interesting if minor bonus that went with the teaching of these subjects; but this process of looking at the roots, affixes, and other parts of words seems very important. It helps give students information that is useful for word learning and use. The words and their meanings become more transparent for a language user if their concrete roots in another language are known. Without this, English academic words often remain 'hard' words whose form and meaning seem strange to those coming to them for the first time.

Because this kind of learning is quite rare in natural language settings, courses of second or third language study can give rich benefits for ESL development. With Latin and Greek less often taught now, the Romance languages seem more useful (French, Italian, Spanish, Portuguese, Romanian, etc.). Romance language students seem well placed in learning academic English because of the similarity that many English academic words already have for them. The evidence that students transfer knowledge from one language to another is now strong, especially where the two languages are similar (see Corson, 1995b, 1998).

But ESL adolescents, who are studying one of the major Romance languages as a third language, are often successful students already, probably without having any Romance language study. In addition, Romance language students are only a small minority of students in school systems in English-speaking countries. So, if all ESL students are going to get the lexical advantages that come from studying Romance languages, other approaches are needed.

ESL Language Awareness and Critical Language Awareness

Studies in language awareness are very helpful, not only for learning about academic words and not only for ESL students. There are many other things that language learners need to know about language, so many in fact that they cannot be listed here in any detail (see van Lier & Corson, 1997). But if all the many kinds of language awareness could always be found in the natural language experiences of people, then courses of language awareness would not be needed in formal education. Unfortunately, ESL learners rarely get these experiences in natural language settings, so schools need to provide them instead.

A good language learning environment in schools also develops ESL students' *critical* language awareness (see chap. 4). They can learn about things like 'labelling', 'sexist language', 'discursive bias', 'prejudice in language', 'rhetorical language', and 'discourse and discrimination'. At the same time, ESL students need to know about the use and functions of academic words, because this sort of information is not usually passed on in regular ESL classes. Again, it is important for second language learners to know that sometimes English words, borrowed from Latin and Greek, are used in rather negative ways, to show unnecessary formality, or to exercise power.

School Policies for Collaboration and Support from ESL Specialists

Because they are skilled in using interactive teaching methods, ESL specialists are a resource in a school that other teachers often draw on. But too often, ESL teachers fill marginal roles in the staff of schools, and their work is not given the same respect as teachers of mainstream students. Nina Bascia (1996) sees critical connections between how minority teachers interact with and advocate for minority students, and how the same teachers are treated by colleagues and school administrators. Often, the advocacy work that these teachers do, helping culturally or linguistically different students get respect in schools, is not formally recognized in any way. Instead, the teachers' role is only to solve other teachers' 'problems'. As a result, the problems cease to be the problems of those other teachers. They get hidden away in the school's structures and have to be solved over and over again.

ESL teachers often have little influence over their colleagues in practical and normative ways. Because of their lack of influence in changing formal school practices, their schools go on to re-create the same problems with every new generation of students. Bascia sees a need for changes in administrative conditions to give more weight to the expertise and insights of these teachers who are presently on the fringes of schools. A school language policy can help build effective collaboration between regular subject teachers and ESL teachers. Various ways of organizing this collaboration are tried with success in many places: Examples include 'integrated and cooperative teaching', 'paired teaching', 'parallel teaching and programming', and 'rotation teaching'. Perhaps again, as a very long-term goal, all regular classroom teachers will eventually learn to be ESL teachers themselves, so that a school's teaching body becomes a highly proficient ESL teaching force.

Yet, even under these conditions, ESL specialists would still be needed. Certain ESL students always need a program that gives intensive and partial support outside regular classrooms. This is because some ESL students are highly traumatized when they arrive in a new country, and they need the close contact they can establish with ESL teachers who are sympathetic to their needs and really know what they are doing. Also, at higher grade levels, the language demands placed on newly arrived students are so great that an ESL support program of some kind is often necessary. Furthermore, specialist provisions for gifted and other exceptional ESL students are essential, because there are just as many exceptional ESL students as there are exceptional mainstream students.

To deal with these complex matters of curriculum, learning, and teaching, high schools in many places find it useful to draw up a 'school ESL language policy'. This kind of action plan ensures a number of things: that all teachers know their role in the ESL students' education; that they are willing to work within that role; or that they can get the support or training they need if they currently lack the expertise. These policies also cover ESL assessment.

ESL Assessment, Evaluation, Guidance and Resources

Listed below are some brief and readable guides to the selection, use, and limitations of tests of various kinds that address the major second language learning competencies:

* testing of reading in a second langage (Weir, 1997)
* testing of writing in a second langage (Cumming, 1997)
* testing of listening in a second langage (Buck, 1997)
* testing of speaking in a second langage (Crandall, 1997)
* assessment of speech and language disorders (Baker & Chenery, 1997)
* accountability in language assessment (Norton, 1997)
* ethics in language testing (Hamp-Lyons, 1997)

Usually, a staff member in each school is responsible for tracking each student's ESL development and even for passing information about individual proficiency levels to a system record that can be referred to by any school that an ESL student attends within the system. Under these arrangements, assessment and evaluation of ESL language proficiency get rigorous monitoring. Also, appropriate guidance and counselling is normally available in the students' first languages, especially where their learning is affected by some disability or by some emotional problem that has its roots in traumatic experiences elsewhere.

One area that schools are giving more attention to is communicating directly and regularly with parents in their own first languages. There is much that parents can do to support ESL students in their learning. There is also a lot of information about ESL outcomes, stages of acquisition, and the format of report cards to give to parents. So, appropriate translation and interpreting services are an integral part of the regular provisions for ESL.

At the same time, ESL students still have to cope with the regular English curriculum as they get more proficiency. Sometimes, there are special ESL English courses for academic credit that parallel regular English courses, but ESL students will usually spend most of their time in English working alongside regular students. Media studies is a core curriculum area introducing secondary students to the media in their country, including ways of using it critically and coping with its seductive and varied messages. This sort of course seems very relevant to the needs of ESL students.

Media Studies and Media Literacy

The list below includes the four activities that everyone sees as part of the core curriculum in English language instruction. However, the last four activities have really come into their own only in recent decades.

- listening: attending to the oral language of others and giving meaning to it
- speaking: expressing meaning to others in oral language
- reading: attending to the written language of others and giving meaning to it
- writing: expressing meaning to others in written language
- moving: using facial expression, gesturing, and movement to express meaning
- watching: attending and giving meaning to the movements of others
- representing: using visual effects to express meaning to others
- viewing: attending and giving meaning to visual effects created by others

For many young people, and in most present-day jobs, these last four activities now assume an importance that gives them a core place in curriculum planning. These are the basic competencies of media literacy.

Media education is education about technology, but it does not stop at the 'how it works' and 'how to operate it' stage. It asks students to think critically about technology and its cultural and sociological significance, as well as its place in business and science. Media education asks students to look critically at information, regardless of its source or medium. It asks them to see the media as industries whose owners have agendas of their own. It helps students to distinguish between commercial messages, casual communication, and the messages of propagandists. Above all, it suggests that students recognize that our commonsense judgments are usually filled with prejudice and error, which colours everything that we come into contact with. Clearly media education has close links with critical language awareness.

To meet its aims, media education looks at all the language activities, especially 'watching', 'viewing', 'representing', 'writing', and 'moving'. But there is an even more pressing need in using computer technology that is almost upon us. This is fully consistent with the idea that 'talking about text' is the practical curriculum foundation of high school education:

> Talking and listening must form a major focus of interest for the future. It is unlikely that the use of computers in the classroom will ever be the same again once teachers and students become used to the ability to control a computer with speech, to dictate and see their words appear on the screen and to ask the computer to speak their words. (Abbott, 1997, p. 186)

This innovation will produce different kinds of speech control, that will impact on traditional spelling and punctuation. Already we see the 'cyberspeak' of the Internet developing its own ways of mimicking stress or intonation. Also the nature of the collaborative writing process will change when instant transcriptions of discussion become an everyday matter. Teachers of English and ESL teachers will have a more challenging role as these developments spread as students take more advantage of the success of the Internet as a site for publishing: "Already, it is being used by senior pupils in isolated schools in rural Scotland to 'discuss' their literature projects with distant peers, to exchange notes and ideas on texts in supportive networks" (McGonigal, 1997, p. 255).

The value of the Internet for getting ESL students to work with one another across cultural and linguistic boundaries, to pursue joint projects, and to resolve common problems is already well understood by some. Cummins and Sayers (1995) give portraits of culturally diverse students using the Internet in this way:

- between a refugee camp in Croatia, New York, and Catalan schools in Spain
- a partnership between classes in Maine and Quebec City
- students dealing with ethnic prejudice in New York and San Francisco schools
- parent/school collaborative desktop publishing in San Diego
- folklore investigations in California and Connecticut
- community action between students in the United States and Nicaragua
- computer networking between Palestinian and Israeli teachers and students
- a holocaust project linking Israel, Argentina, Australia, Russia and Poland

Clearly, activities like these promote higher-order thinking and literacy skills, perhaps to a greater extent than many of the traditional activities that secondary schools give curriculum space to. As Cummins and Sayers (1995) observe:

> The information superhighway offers unprecedented opportunities for educators to create collaborative learning environments that will stimulate critical thinking skills and academic excellence among *all* students ...In short, computer-mediated learning networks can act as a catalyst for collaborative critical inquiry that is fundamental in preparing students to participate actively in a democratic society. (pp. 15, 172)

At the same time, there are problems in all this that need the checks and balances of formal guidelines, set out in a school language plan: "Desktop publishing makes it more possible than ever before to see children becoming authors of their own literature, but computer spelling and grammar checkers seem to undermine traditional aspects of authority and craft" (McGonigal, 1997, p. 255). Teachers meet a real dilemma on this point. Can we justify the time and space needed in school for spelling, punctuation, and grammar when the new technology itself teaches many students that complete mastery of those skills is becoming redundant for much of the time? At the same time, most teachers have few doubts about the importance of these basic things.

CONCLUSION: VALUING FIRST LANGUAGES

In line with the view of social justice presented in Chapter 2, most decisions about minority languages in pluralist societies would be made and implemented at the level of the single school. Every school, even every classroom, is a new setting for working out fair arrangements. To make sure that educational professionals have the information they need, local minority language communities in many places are indeed helping to decide the direction of their children's schools (see chap. 7). They are having a say in which languages get valued in their own children's schools and how the schools themselves organize their language programs.

This does not mean that minority languages are appearing on every school's curriculum, because many minority parents and communities prefer schools to put their efforts into teaching English. As suggested in chapter 2, sometimes community education is needed to convince parents of the value of supporting the first languages of younger children. But at a minimum, majority culture schools need to value the languages of minority students. Yet, how can the many different minority languages that are spoken now, in most English-speaking countries, be valued by schools in more than token ways?

In this chapter, I have suggested that the ideal way to do this for young children's first languages is to provide bilingual immersion programs. However, in practice, this sort of provision is beyond the reach of most schools and school systems where many different languages are in use. In these settings, schools are trying to value minority languages in other ways. Below are some suggestions for supporting first language development, even when the school only teaches in English (for sources, see Corson, 1998):

Staff and Visitors

- recruit people who can tutor minority language students fluently using their first languages
- hire as many staff members as possible who share the children's language and culture
- invite guests from the minority language cultures and show them respect
- employ professionals who understand the influence of home language and culture on children's development
- provide leaders, mentors, and models of culturally sensitive practices
- make wide use of the languages and skills of community members in the school

Curriculum and Teaching

- adopt an anti-bias curriculum
- support teaching with images that represent the different cultures
- provide books in the minority languages in the school library and include bilingual books
- have books and recorded collections in the minority languages in classrooms
- learn basic words in the community languages
- provide classroom opportunities for children to communicate with others in their first language (in cooperative learning groups, etc.)
- create units of work that incorporate other languages
- encourage students to write in their first language for school newspapers and magazines

Parents and Communities

- involve parents in daily activities and collaborate with families
- ask families for culturally relevant information
- find translators for parent meetings and interviews
- respect family cultural beliefs and practices
- have programs that mediate the cultural discontinuities between the children's homes and the school
- present English courses to parents at the same time as their children are studying their first languages
- involve children and parents together in family literacy programs

Professional Development

- pursue additional research on which to base culturally sensitive practices
- begin by finding out about the languages and varieties used by pupils in the school
- arrange professional development that shares information in all these areas
- give leadership in professional development to ESL and minority teachers
- draw up a school language policy as a year-long exercise in professional development

School Organization

- base management on clear principles that promote culturally sensitive practices
- provide signs that welcome people in the different languages
- have bilingual or multilingual signs wherever signs are needed
- use the minority languages in newsletters and other official school communication

- display pictures and objects from the various cultures around the school
- invite ESL students to use their first language at assemblies, prizegivings, and other official functions
- involve the minority language communities in the school's management
- commit school resources to immigrant language maintenance in the community
- deliberately value minority languages in the administrative discourse of the school
- speak about other languages with respect
- above all, ask teachers to allow the minority languages to be used freely whenever possible

DISCUSSION STARTERS

1. Consider the sociological differences between minority languages and non-standard varieties that are suggested on page 101. Do the users of different languages and varieties in your part of the world conform to these sociological differences? If there are exceptions, what historical factors caused them?
2. Think about school systems you have experienced. Where do those school systems or schools sit on Churchill's ascending ladder of six levels? How could you nudge them towards higher levels of fair treatment?
3. Explain Cummins' two hypotheses in your own words. Why is the maintenance of a young immigrant child's first language important for later language development? Using the hypotheses as a starting point, what areas of minority language education would you reform if you could? If you were or are a teacher, how would you change your own teaching practices?
4. How does bilingual education differ from ESL education? Review the various approaches to organizing ESL education mentioned in this chapter. Which ones are already used by schools in your area? Which of the others could easily be adopted for your local high school's students? How would schools in your system need to be changed to make use of these different approaches?
5. Do the experiences of Franco-Ontarian schools offer leads that could be re-applied to linguistic minority students elsewhere (for example, with the more established Spanish language minorities in the United States)? How could schools and teachers apply those ideas? What obstacles outside schools stand in the way?
6. Why has the mainstreaming of signing Deaf students lost much of its support among signing Deaf communities themselves? Are there other ways of organizing the education of Deaf children that work well in your area? What are these? Do other social groups have a similar case for separate schooling?
7. Many teachers work in schools where there is great student diversity, and many different immigrant languages are in use. In these settings, what can

teachers reasonably do to give value to immigrant students' first languages? Which of these things would schools in your area be willing to insert into their planning and practices? How could you put more of these ideas to work in schools?

6

Gender and Discourse Norms

The skit is based loosely on a format known from television contests. The student council president, Marcel, acts as master of ceremonies. He announces that the school will now pick the school "stud" … Four boys from the senior grades are called up to sit in a row on the stage. Marcel passes from one boy to the next, asking each one a question … To the third, Ali, he poses the following question: "What is the role of women in society?" Ali is visibly uneasy, and fails to answer. Luc says that he will answer the question, and eventually Marcel gives him the microphone. Luc answers: "To serve and please men." The audience responds loudly, with many boys cheering and some girls booing.

—*Heller (1999, p. 193)*

Schools are rarely genteel, sensitive places. Most senior schools persist as sites where archaic male values get reproduced by successive intakes of students. Meanwhile, girls and boys looking for fair treatment in these institutions often differ markedly in their discourse norms. These differences are known to have consequences for educational success, especially for girls coming from immigrant or other marginal backgrounds. This means that many culturally different girls are doubly disadvantaged in schools, and their group interests go unrecognized.

This chapter begins by considering the different discourse norms that research suggests are more typical of one sex than the other. By laying out this evidence, I am not implying that these different norms are much more than trends that are a little more characteristic of one sex than the other. But they are trends that get reproduced rather uncritically, from one generation to another; and they do seem to carry weighty implications for the life chances of males and females.

A key factor at work in this area is the imbalance in power that exists between men and women in most settings. Although power is not the only factor influencing gendered relations, it influences other important contextual and interpersonal factors, like intimacy and desire, in powerful ways. Accordingly, an aim of recent research into language and gender is to understand the differences that appear in discourse between men and women within particular contexts, especially in set-

152

tings where unequal power relations traditionally prevail. This chapter discusses these settings of inequality. It then links them with the imbalances in power in schools, in classrooms, and in the wider world, that tend to favour some discourse norms over others, sometimes with terrible consequences.

Education plays the chief role in reinforcing all this, because of its place in the secondary socialization of children. At different stages, it rewards boys and girls in different ways for modelling their own gendered norms of interaction and behaviour. Also the evidence suggests that education, especially at senior levels, places an unequal value on competitive discourse practices, often at the expense of cooperative ones. This means that the more 'cooperative' signs and rules of use that girls tend to acquire in their early lives attract less and less value as children progress through schools.

The chapter also collates insights into the special problems first-generation immigrant girls can have. And finally, it argues towards more worthwhile policies and fairer school practices.

GENDERED LIFE CHANCES: OPTIONS AND LIGATURES

Education usually gives people two types of life chances: additional 'options' in their lives, which give a greater range of choices in their future as a result of their education; and stronger 'ligatures,' which are the bonds between individuals and groups that develop as a result of their experiences in education. Clearly, there are gender and cultural differences in access to options and ligatures (Dahrendorf, 1978), and these differences relate directly to gendered practices and norms that the institution of education helps to reproduce and reinforce.

The 'Harvard Project on Human Potential' underlines the gendered dimension in the distribution of options and ligatures (LeVine & White, 1986). It offers the example of women in developing countries, who seem poor in options but richer in ligatures. But because ligatures provide some of the most important benefits in life, like support, structure, motivation, and a sense of respect and continuity, it is likely that women with few options in their lives, in some developing country settings, still experience their lives as highly satisfying. For example, Benedicta Egbo (2000) reports that non-literate rural women in Nigeria are often very poor in options, because of their lowly rated job and functional skills, but many are rich in ligatures because of their strong friendship and support groups. Western observers, weighing up the absence of options in the lives of these women, might think that their life chances as a whole were highly unattractive. Certainly, Egbo's study does show the value of literacy for rural women in Sub-Saharan Africa, especially its role in raising economic independence and giving them control over their own bodies through greater use of contraception and a readiness to refuse genital mutilation.

People living among capitalist social relations, in market economies, can easily see the role that 'options' have in offering increased life chances to those who have them. However, many have more difficulty seeing the place 'ligatures' have as life chances. This might be because the value of ligatures has become hidden for many people in the rush to develop and extend capitalist economic options. Yet in many societies, and among most cultural groups, ligatures are positive ends in themselves, to be pursued as a goal in life. They are not just a means to other ends, like the ligatures that people in market economies sometimes value more highly. I am thinking here, for instance, of the range of aboriginal peoples discussed in chapter 3. Even in the midst of the rich options that their countries offer to citizens, it is often the ligatures that mean much more to indigenous peoples, even when that valuing of ligatures leads to a reduction in their options. Sometimes, these ligatures, developed between ancestral people, are so binding as human interests that they become almost physical needs whose loss creates great levels of sadness, or even morbidity.

In capitalist countries, most education systems are good at providing students with options, but very weak at providing ligatures. Nevertheless, in English-speaking countries many recent immigrants come from ethnic communities where ligatures are prized. For some, such as the millions of refugees from Indo-China, Africa, or the Balkans, ligatures of one kind or another may be all that remain to them of their former lives. For others, like the ancestral peoples mentioned above, cultural interests support their ligatures; and often these interests reach well beyond the understanding of people from outside those cultures. Specifically, when these cultural interests are those of women, they are often disguised by power relationships that make the interests of dominant males seem the universal norm.

In this chapter, I am looking at differences in the life chances that male and female students get from their schooling, especially life chances affected by the highly specialized and artificial discourse practices that schools value. I suggest that girls derive much more in the way of ligatures from the more informal discourse practices of their education than boys do. Boys seem to get more options for themselves, partly because of their greater readiness to monopolize the formal discourses of senior schooling, and to capitalize on the competitive bias inherent in those discourses. Moreover, boys from dominant family backgrounds manage to develop a more limited set of ligatures through their education, deriving from their contacts with other similarly privileged males (the 'old school tie' and the 'old boys network'). They are able to convert these ligatures of reciprocity into life chances that become powerful options for later use.

FEMALE DISCOURSE NORMS AND MALE POWER

Across societies, power is the variable that separates men and women. Female exclusion from public spheres of action also tends to exclude them from the language games where dominant ideologies are created, and from the sign systems used to express those ideas. For example, all the many societies and cultures studied in Philips, Steele and Tanz (1987) have key public-speaking roles and speech activities in which women participate rarely, or not at all. But in the same societies, men are not notably excluded from the key activities and language games of women; and men are also able to define the activities that attract status. In short, men in these societies have greater command of the discourses of power than women.

From her ethnographic studies in Papua New Guinea, Bambi Schieffelin (1987) suggests that it is the activities engaged in by women compared with the activities engaged in by men, rather than gender itself, that associate with the linguistic choices that are made: Men engaging in women's activities tend to use language in much the same way as the women would. Again, the key variable in this is differential access to power. For instance, when men place themselves in relatively powerless situations, identified by the activities they are engaged in, their language tends to be indistinguishable from that of women in the same activities. If women themselves are under-valued in that society, then the activities that they engage in, and the language used by them, will be under-valued. The social solidarity of people doing these same activities, regardless of their sex, is expressed through the language they use.

As research into language and gender becomes more searching, the power implicit in wider social structures is becoming a more important issue (Wodak, 1997). Early research, such as that by Lakoff (1975), was based on explicit and straightforward linguistic features discovered in the speech of women compared with men. Gradually, it became clearer that differences in interaction styles between women and men are affected by sociocultural practices and values rather removed from any obvious connection with language. And other studies of gendered discourse outside the dominant Western pattern of usage have questioned other more enduring conclusions reached in earlier research. At the same time, some differences do appear with regularity across cultures and social groups.

For example, it does seem that women as a group use a wider range of pitch frequencies and more intonation in their speech than men do as a group (McConnell-Ginet, Borker & Furman, 1980; Philips, 1980); and it also seems that women as a group talk less than men, at least in mixed-sex interactions. However, a classic sociolinguistic 'pattern' portraying women and girls as choosing standard or 'correct' forms more often than males (Pauwels, 1991; Romaine, 1978), seems in other research to be an overgeneralization (Coates & Cameron, 1988). Perhaps its identification as a pattern was due to an inadequate sociological conception of the specific conditions of women's lives, and from the over-readiness of researchers to attribute particular psychological dispositions, such as conservativism and status seeking, to women as a group (Cameron & Coates, 1985). As it happens, women from some cultural minority groups, influenced by local conditions and contexts, seem to be even more colloquial than their male peers.

The quote below neatly captures the errant generalizations that often affect this area of inquiry and commentary:

> Women's language has been said to reflect their conservatism, prestige conscious-
> ness, upward mobility, insecurity, deference, nurturance, emotional expressivity,
> connectedness, sensitivity to others, solidarity. And men's language is heard as evinc-
> ing their toughness, lack of affect, competitiveness, independence, competence, hier-
> archy, control. (Eckert & McConnell-Ginet, 1992a, p. 90)

All these contradictions suggest that the preferred place to site an analysis is really the unique community of practice that different discourses create for different groups of people, as they continually renegotiate their subject positions and their identities within multiple and competing discourses. What it means for a given person to be 'prestige conscious', 'nurturant', or 'competitive' actually changes across different communities of practice and sociocultural groups. So the broad generalizations implied by these descriptors are more likely to mislead than guide our inquiries or interpretations. For example, Eckert (1990) observes that although middle class women in the United States are more likely than men to discuss personal topics, this is not necessarily true of working class women. And of course, even within local sociocultural groups, individuals always behave in ways that confound any stereotype.

In general, however, women and men usually belong to the language games of different subcultures that have quite different ways of empowering people. This is apparent in cultural groups where differences in male and female roles and activities are highly ordered, as in many Islamic cultures, in Orthodox Jewry, or in fundamentalist Christian communities. For example, Israeli Orthodox women observe *Tsniut* (modesty) as a central value in their own subculture (Oryan, 1997). This value dictates many performances and rituals that are manifested in a variety of discourse norms, such as word and topic choice, timing or length of spoken contributions, and a special use of prosody. And these norms differ strikingly from the men's norms. The Orthodox men and women learn different norms for interaction within and between the sexes; and each set of norms is modelled and prescribed by influential others. In their turn, the men and women live out those norms, taking them for granted as the way their own culture is and should be. But there are more than subcultural differences at work here.

Powerful structures, reflecting the out-dated values of dominant male social groups who lived generations ago, still affect the discourses of today's men and women. This happens even though the people concerned are far removed in time from those out-dated values, which were tied originally to the traditional roles men occupied in the economic market or workforce, and that women occupied in domestic settings. And in their turn, the people of several centuries ago who actually lived out those values, were influenced by highly respected discourses of power, like the surviving literary texts of Greece and Rome which rigidly stratified men and women; and which then, as esteemed texts, legitimized that stratification for many centuries. Influenced as they are by these influential values from the past, women as a group still get relatively few chances to reform practices that go much beyond surface forms of discourse. In other words, women still have relatively little influence over discourses that really count in people's lives. And history shows that control over discourse is the most important power to seize, if people want to escape the unwanted power of others. In place of this important linguistic capital, women of generations ago accumulated only the kind of symbolic capital that would add to the prestige and economic capital of their menfolk. Among the many things that contributed to a woman's symbolic capital then, were her unsullied reputation outside the home, her religious devoutness, her approved and approving circle of women friends, and, above all, her public devotion to husband and family.

This kind of explanation for differences in discourse practices, based on the effects of sociocultural and historical dominance, is a necessary balance to add to a simple cultural explanation of difference, if only because subcultures of women are themselves clearly susceptible to wider power forces within cultures. At the same time of course, women usually have their own discourse norms that are not necessarily defined in reference to dominant male norms, or clearly determined by historically dominant male values. For example, in societies with a high level of formal education, the models of language regarded as prestigious by many women are drawn from the class of educated women élites, whose own preferred norms can vary considerably from their male peers. So, the context or setting of discourse, including the class, gender, and cultural interests of all the participants, heavily influences discourse practice.

COOPERATIVE AND COMPETITIVE
DISCOURSE PRACTICES AMONG ADULTS

A developing aim of research into language and gender is to understand the differences that appear in discourse between men and women within particular contexts, especially in capitalist societies where unequal power relations traditionally prevail. A key example is the setting of the home, where women have to work harder than men to maintain conversations, asking more questions and supporting and encouraging male responses (Fishman, 1983). In their turn, men in the home tend to respond less frequently to women's attempts at interaction. Pamela Fishman concludes that men control the content and rhythm of conversation in this way. They establish their right to define what the interaction should be about and they determine when and where interaction should occur. In an extension of Fishman's study, DeFrancisco (1991) recorded heterosexual married couples, interviewing her participants after the events. Her research confirms that women do more of the conversational work in marital relations, but are more often silenced by the men's behaviour, especially by what they describe as men's 'patronizing', 'put-down', or 'teachy' behaviour.

Also in Fishman's research, the number of statements made by men is very close to the number of questions asked by women. While men make twice as many statements, women ask more than twice as many questions to which the men often decline to respond, although the women almost always respond to male statements. So, what is going on here? Does the exercise of latent or explicit power explain this pattern of differences? I believe that it does largely explain it, although an adequate explanation of any single interaction would always include more than a simple, one-sided quest for dominance by the male participants. In any interaction, participants are constantly adapting themselves in their search for meaning and value. For men, that search could have aims well removed from any simple quest for dominance through the interaction. Yet, as often as not, their discourse will still manifest longstanding norms that are more characteristic of men's traditional activities than of women's. As part of their socialization into gendered discursive ideologies, men more often deploy verbal and non-verbal signs that help them keep control of discourse. Meanwhile, the signs deployed by women often suggest quite different purposes and values that are to do with creating ligatures with other interactants. Since the sexes develop these interactive trends through socialisation and enculturation, it is possible to explain the observed differences by reference to power relations that are long established or legitimated as norms for interaction. These reside within the power structures, the archaic values, the socialization practices, and the discourse arrangements of societies.

The influence of unequal power relationships is evident, too, in the patterns of interruptions and silences recorded in male-female conversations. This second set of patterns suggests that men from market-oriented, capitalist backgrounds tend to exercise rigorous topic control in their conversations (Fasold, 1990), especially in the workplace (Kendall & Tannen, 1997). On the one hand, they often interrupt in such a way as to flout conventions about when to speak and when to remain silent; on the other, they decline to support the topics that women are developing. This marked tendency is consistent with other findings. For instance, women are the ones who initiate conversational topics, while men control topic development by their minimally responsive behaviour (Klann-Delius, 1987). Also, women give and receive more compliments and apologies than men, although men do apologize more often to powerful people, and they do engage in polite talk when it suits them: to begin a romantic relationship, for example (Holmes, 1995).

Of course, there are vast cultural and social differences in norms for politeness. While Nigerian men seem to exercise firm control over conversations, using interruptions and other control devices rather like their counterparts in many other places (Nwoye, 1998), the language of courtesy in Japanese reveals quite different norms. Courteous speech is used by all within the speech community to a large extent, although even here there are marked differences when women are making assertions or requests (Takahara, 1991) or when they are adopting new social roles in the male world of work that place different demands on their discourse (Smith, 1992). And among the Mayan peoples in Mexico, even when women are not being polite with one another, they still use norms of politeness to add a sharp edge of irony to their noncooperativeness (Brown, 1993).

Again, all these different patterns of interaction are much more than mere linguistic trends. Rather, they reflect conventional levels of respect that dominant members of societies have historically shown for the different thoughts, interests, views, activities, and rights of men and women. Paula Treichler and Cheris Kramarae (1983) summarize several other characteristically male practices that contrast with female practices: Males more often seem to interpret questions as requests for information; they often ignore the comments of previous speakers; they make declarations of fact and opinion more frequently; and they talk more often, at greater length. Men also use taboo expressions in their speech much more commonly (Smith, 1985) in an exercise of power that disadvantages them as often as it empowers. For example, research studies from Sweden, Brazil, and the United States report women using far less profanity and obscenity than men, a pattern found in girls' and boys' speech, as well. At the same time, when women are 'backstage' in the company of close friends, they seem more willing to subvert and challenge these norms of politeness (Coates, 1998) although, by finding this private outlet for their more 'frontstage' frustrations, they are helping to sustain male dominance and to legitimate certain patterns as a male-only preserve.

Other research also emphasizes the cooperative versus competitive dimension that appears in men's and women's interaction styles in Western capitalist settings. While many men shift topics rapidly, apparently hearing other people's problems as requests for solutions and their questions as requests for information, women tend to use questions more to maintain conversations. Women also tend to acknowledge any previous contributions that are made to the discussion. They interpret signs of verbal aggression as personal, negative, and disruptive. For many women, this male competitive style of interacting prevents conversations from being used for positive ends: to show care and responsibility; to negotiate or express a relationship; to support and cooperate; and to establish a sharing, engaging, and communal exchange (Maltz & Borker, 1983). At the same time, men may still feel that they are doing all this through their interactions, albeit in their own way, using signs that are more identified with themselves.

But interpreting this evidence in a different way, Deborah Cameron (1985) questions whether women really are more cooperative in their talk than men. She wonders if their observed willingness to adopt a cooperative style might not be an artifact of feminist gatherings, where participants are urged not to interrupt, or raise their voices, or show deviance from solidarity. Less attractive interactive functions can be served in this way, such as binding conversational partners to a specific attitude for political purposes while constraining genuine criticism. This interpretation is probably more relevant to certain communities of practice than to others. Penelope Eckert (1990) studies groups of adolescent girls in the United States who are constantly engaged in negotiating consensus in their interactions. Not one topic is left behind without reaching an expression of consensus that sometimes has to be forced onto the unwilling. Crucially, too, Diane Reay (1991) observes another consensual pattern among British girls as young as 7 years of age, who also avoid strategies of questioning and challenging one anothers' ideas when working in a single sex group. Reay suggests that acting consensually in this way is not the same as being democratic, since democratic interaction always allows the possibility of conflict, which is something the young girls in her study try to avoid in much the same way as Eckert's (1990) adolescents and Cameron's (1985) adult women do. This strategic use of so-called 'cooperative' discourse by women, then, seems far removed from an ideal kind of speech situation; but it is certainly no more distant from it than the more obviously competitive discourse practices often adopted by men.

On the evidence, there is not much to admire in the informal competitive talk of Western males, in many contexts of interaction at least. Men's talk resembles a form of display, involving joke telling, boasting, ribbing, and verbal aggression. Even here, though, there are differences from culture to culture. Present-day discourse norms in Australia, for example, are much affected by the generations of males from working class backgrounds who hugely outnumbered females in that country from the late eighteenth to the mid-nineteenth century. Even in the late twentieth century, Australia's culture remained essentially male-working class in many of its aspects; and its discourses show the effects of that masculinized history. Recognizing the disabling nature of this for females, many Australian women have made some of the male discourse norms their own, especially the good-natured ribbing and banter so characteristic of everyday, informal interactions in that country. With deliberate intent, many women adopted and learned how to use these signs in different communities of practice: to reduce somewhat the imbalances in power that have historically favoured men in their country; and to claim a measure of control for themselves in mixed-sex interactions. In more precise settings elsewhere too, like the highly masculinized work activity that female police officers have to perform (McElhinny, 1995), women are resisting the pressures to conform to existing gendered ideologies. They are creating different social identities for themselves in the process .

For men in single-sex and in mixed-sex groups, conversation often seems a matter of getting control of the interaction and then keeping it. Men tend to take longer turns at talk and have a greater rate of controlling pauses filled with vocalizations like 'um' and 'ah'. In contrast, women smile more often and direct their gaze longer at their conversational partners. Although women give many nods and responses such as 'yes' and 'mmm' to signal they are listening attentively, men often give barely minimal responses to the talk of others, or give none at all (Maltz & Borker, 1983). Indeed, the different signs used by the sexes can suggest to observers that while women are relating to one another through their language, men are reporting (Wodak, 1981).

All these contrasting trends in male-female discourse leave room for misunderstandings to arise in mixed-sex conversations. This occurs especially when women, apparently at least, are trying to manage affiliative goals, but have to do so within domains of interaction that are controlled by men whose attention, apparently at least, is on the outcome of the interaction, not on its processes. And this discursive quandary has a major impact in capitalist societies, where the process of winning access to positions of institutional power often depends on possessing the kind of verbal skills needed to function successfully in roles created to meet the historical values and discourse norms of dominant males.

When women take on gendered administrative or professional roles, and conform temporarily to discourse norms that are not their own, they risk being misperceived as pseudo-male, because to succeed they have to adopt signs whose rules of use are more associated with males. At the same time, during their occupancy of these gendered roles, they often lose the personal satisfaction that comes from achieving their own affiliative goals in interaction through a use of their own preferred discourse norms. On the other hand, women commonly enjoy institutional and career success. Through a use of normed signs that bring a more relational and egalitarian definition to the work situation, they manage to modify their professional interactions by minimizing status differences and by downplaying their own authority (Kendall & Tannen, 1997). So when women hold administrative posts, under conditions that allow them to shape the roles and norms of the posts according to their own acquired preferences, they often succeed very well in exercising leadership (Shakeshaft & Perry, 1995; Wodak, 1995), even in areas like school administration where masculinity has historically been the powerful defining force (Blount, 1999).

This increasing success of women in leadership roles might be because the cooperative set of conversational signs that women tend to deploy (Troemel-Ploetz, 1994) allows them to marshall a greater range of effective leadership strategies: like sharing power with others rather than struggling over it; or constructing equality rather than conversational asymmetry; or protecting face, rather than winning empty victories. All this is not to say, though, that the many preferred styles of women can be characterized as 'women's language'; or that there are 'two cultures' interacting when mixed-sex groups converse. Again, any differences that research uncovers are always limited in their range of reference to the precise sociocultural group from which they were drawn, and to the social context in which the differences were observed. Lack of concern for the context of situation, including the cultural identities of the interactants, seems a frequent weakness in the early research on sex and language.

I have already mentioned Lakoff's seminal exploration of 'women's language'. This was critically extended by O'Barr & Atkins (1980), who also based their research on the observed frequency of different features of language. After examining more than 150 hours of courtroom testimony by women and men, they suggest that a better name for the language used more often by women would be 'powerless language'. They argue that the tendency of women to use 'powerless language' more often than men is due to the greater tendency of women to occupy relatively powerless positions in many social contexts. Men are likely to use this language (provided always that they are proficient in deploying its signs) when they are placed in positions of disempowerment, or in situations where they lack the expertise necessary to control the interaction. In other words, social status and/or expertise in specific contexts is reflected in the discourse norms adopted by those doing the interacting.

But other research modifies even this conclusion somewhat. In situations where women possess the de facto power that comes from having genuine expertise, their power is not always enough to outweigh structural and historical differences in power that are linked to sex. These structural differences include symbolic constructs to do with sex that tend to constitute women's perceived identity, of which a particular set of discourse norms more commonly used by women (sometimes called 'women's language') is one. Indeed, the literature offers many examples that underline this tendency: When female experts are in discussion with male non-experts (Smith, 1985), the expert females are perceived as less dominant and less in control even than the non-expert males. Valerie Walkerdine (1987) reports a study where two 4-year- old boys refuse to assume the role of powerless objects in their teacher's discourse, and with her consent recast her as the powerless 'woman as sex object' of their own discourse. Elsewhere, speakers of either sex are more polite with male ticket-sellers than they are with female ticket-sellers in a railway station (Brouwer, 1982); and in professional-client interaction in a legal-aid setting, the level of authoritarian or participatory interaction varies according to the sex of the client and the professional (Bogoch, 1994).

Others find women using more 'women's style' in a range of contexts: in laboratory conversations, in interactions with police in a police station, and in requesting information (Crosby & Nyquist, 1977). But pointedly, women and men are both much more hesitant and indirect than the male police officials at work in their own police station setting. Similarly, in the railway station study, "all of the kinds of utterances that women are characteristically supposed to use more often than men—utterances indicating insecurity and politeness—were used more often by both women and men when speaking to the male ticket seller" (Brouwer, Gerritson, & de Haan, 1979, p. 47). Again, too, the reluctance to be direct and plain-spoken, so often portrayed as a female norm, does not seem a common characteristic of African American women in general; and it even seems quite the opposite of the prevailing norm for women in the Malagasy Republic, where women and men learn discourse norms that reverse those more commonly reported elsewhere (Eckert & McConnell-Ginet, 1992b; Keenan, 1974; Tannen, 1982).

It seems that where sex differences in discourse norms do emerge, they are strongly influenced by the particular context, including the sex, gendered identity, and perceived power of the addressee. Different inequalities that exist in power, dominance, expertise, and status intersect with gender, class, and cultural differences; and they receive expression in different forms of discourse in different discourse settings. But it is important to stress that these apparently coercive expressions of power are rarely overwhelming influences. Free agents will always try to find ways to counter structural forms of determination. Indeed, efforts to resist dominant discourse structures are often observed; and they go on all around us (Hall & Bucholtz, 1995).

Yet, the effects of widespread, prevailing ideologies of gendered interaction, made possible through enculturation and socialization into the discourses of different language games, are so great and so pervasive that they are taken-for-granted for much of the time by most people. As Foucault (1980) argues, the development of particular forms of language meets the needs of the powerful, but often without much deliberate exercise of influence by the powerful. The symbolic violence, of which Bourdieu (1981) speaks, happens because the conflicts that take place over and around discourse are so one-sided. The balance of power consistently favours some rather than others; and these hegemonic, one-sided patterns get reproduced from generation to generation. In response to the more competitive male patterns of interaction, women seem to collaborate in their own discursive oppression, usually accepting the hegemonic relationship in a naturalizing rather than a critical way. Instead of modifying or even adopting the male discursive practices that are often so unlike their own, females adopt more cooperative practices that tend to reinforce males in the belief that their own signs are acceptably normal.

These different norms, some appearing more competitive and some more cooperative, become ideological impositions that females accept in taken-for-granted ways. And so do males. Parents model and pass these discursive patterns on to boys and girls in early childhood. As I suggest below, the same patterns are already established in the discourse norms of school age children, well before they enter their first school. The norms become sex-specific cultural interests that males and females feel disposed to defend; and these normed tendencies persevere, distinguishing male from female discourse practices. So, from early childhood onwards, most males and females seem to manifest and develop a broadly different understanding of the form and the purpose of conversational interactions.

In short, while girls and women from many cultures tend to see conversation more as a cooperative activity, men and boys tend to see it more often as a competitive exchange. In doing so, members of the two sexes make their own interpretations of the gendered rules of use that attach to each other's signs. Then, in complex ways, these interpretations reinforce and subtly reshape the meanings that the signs have for present-day males and females; and so on for future generations. For example, when a patriarch two centuries ago felt free to abruptly interrupt a female member of his family, without any fear of resistance, that act plainly signalled the generalized and formal power most fathers had to command unquestioned obedience from all members of their households. The interruption itself was a sign resonant with cultural meanings based on the peremptory ways in which that sign could be used by fathers.

Today, if a male uses the 'same' sign, and gets away with his interruption, the sign's rules of use are much modified. If the interruption passes unresisted by others, it is more likely conveying the slightly elevated prestige and informal privilege that dominant males still retain. Yet this much more vague and informal position of privilege that males can now have, is still quite influential in household settings, as we have seen. But that presumption of privilege also transfers to more public settings, where one-sided interruptions are often tolerated still: in many workplaces, especially in the military or the police; or wherever sports coaching takes place. Although it might seem much the same sign, used two centuries apart, its present-day rules of use signal a gradual transformation in the overt power of dominant males. At the same time, some of the sign's more archaic rules of use, even now suggesting unquestioned obedience, continue in the setting of the school which persists as a masculinized environment. And these meanings today extend to teachers of both sexes, who often interact with students rather like the patriarchs of old, assuming unquestioned interactive rights and using the signs that go with them.

Moreover, when children continually witness a model of communication in which the male competitive approach consistently prevails, they tend to regard that dominance as naturalistically necessary: not just as the way things are, but as the way they should be. This in turn reinforces the positions of dominance that males occupy in social systems, since their competitive norms are reinforced even by those who have neither the wish nor the disposition to adopt those norms themselves. So while research largely confirms the popular view that women and girls are good at interpersonal skills, such as sympathetic listening, careful questioning, and sustaining flagging conversations (Cheshire & Jenkins, 1991), these skills probably derive from imbalances of power in the social world that force women and girls to make a cooperative virtue out of an asymmetrical necessity.

More specifically, education plays one of the key roles in all this, because of the dominant place it has in the secondary socialization of children. At different stages, it rewards boys and girls in subtle or blatant ways for modelling their own gendered norms of interaction and behaviour. Also, especially at its senior levels, education places unequal value on competitive discursive practices usually at the expense of cooperative practices and the ligatures they create. This means that the cooperative and consensual signs which girls rather than boys acquire in their early lives, attract less and less value as children progress through school. Meanwhile, boys grow up in schools still modelled on discourse practices whose historical roots lie in the competitive values of dominant males who lived more than a century ago. So, almost inevitably, conventional schooling gives more value to the gendered discourse practices of boys; and many boys get more options from their education as a result.

COOPERATIVE AND COMPETITIVE
DISCOURSE PRACTICES AMONG CHILDREN

Compared with studies of adult sex differences, studies of boys' and girls' language that are not based on assumed, inherited differences between the sexes are still few, and most can be summarized briefly. Firstly, those early studies that examine cooperation and competition in conversations between boys and girls have found the same patterns of male dominance, even among children aged 3-to-4 years, as exist among adults (Esposito, 1979; Klann-Delius, 1987). For example, in conversations between boy-girl pairs, the boys interrupt twice as often as the girls (Esposito, 1979). Yet, this pattern of dominance through interruptions does not appear when boys have conversations with older people. In these settings with adult interlocutors, boys tend to give even more listener responses than girls (Dittman, 1977). Again, symbolic structures of dominance seem influential in this pattern: The need to recognize and conform to power relationships, in this instance dominance based on age, seems to influence the discourse of boys who, in turn, reflect the pattern by reversing it in their discourse with girls. Moreover, these patterns of dominance seem to correlate with the behaviour of parents and teachers when they interact with girls and boys (Klann-Delius, 1987). These highly significant adults make more listener responses and fewer interruptions when boys are talking than when girls are.

As in the cross-cultural research on adult male and female norms, the community of practice that positions boys and girls seems to affect their discourse norms in marked ways. In other words, the setting, the activity in which the children are engaged, and the social identities of the children themselves combine in influence. For example, Penny Eckert (1989) was not looking for much sexual differentiation in language when she studied two groups of high school students, the one group buying into the school's norms for success and the other resisting them. Yet, she found marked levels of gendered differentiation across settings and social identities. I illustrate her work a little later. Similarly, in her studies of African-American, elementary school girls and boys, Marjorie Goodwin (1980; 1990) reports that in some play activities the sexes are alike in the social identities they try to construct for themselves, while in others they are quite different. Moreover, illustrating the role of diversity within this diversity, she says that "the same individuals articulate talk and gender differently as they move from one activity to another" (1990, p. 9). Significant sex differences also appear among older children in the specific community of practice created by oral English examinations in England and Wales, where mixed groups of adolescent boys and girls are asked to show their oral proficiency in collaborative discussion (Cheshire & Jenkins, 1991; Jenkins & Cheshire, 1990). While boys and girls in these formal conversational activities offer a similar number of minimal responses to other interactants, such as 'yeah' or 'mmm', these signs have quite different rules of use for the girls than they do for the boys. For girls, the responses usually signal conversational support; but boys tend to use them to gain a foothold in the conversation. Also, in this formal oral setting, boys seem to make more inappropriate remarks that close down discussions. In respect to both these findings, it is hard to escape the conclusion that it is exposure to the language games of single-sex male or female groups that influences the conversational behaviour of both boys and girls in this examination setting. Indeed, there seems to be strong support for this inference in other studies looking at single-sex group interaction.

Girls in US high schools, for example, spend a great deal of time engaging in 'girl talk'. This is a "typically female speech event involving long and detailed personal discussions about people, norms and beliefs" (Eckert, 1990, p. 91). Their 'girl talk' teaches young women about the roles of adult women and the discourse norms that go with those roles. But its use specifically in senior levels of education also gives adolescent girls valuable opportunities to develop the kind of 'symbolic capital' so esteemed in the competitive world of high schools. In school settings, individuals are expected to accumulate marks of social success by being seen to influence important school and social activities. But girls are at a special disadvantage because the stress on competitive status that exists in high schools conflicts with tendencies in their own discourse norms. In chapter 7, I look more closely at the research methods Eckert used in her study.

Also, when immersed in play activities, even younger girls and boys have very different modes and methods of interaction in their single-sex groups (Thorne, 1986). Indeed, these norms are reinforced by careful segregation of the sexes in many social settings. In their recreational activities, girls tend to be less public than boys. They engage with one another in small groups or in friendship pairs, in locations where confidences can be exchanged in strict privacy. Other symbol systems reinforce this tendency, especially the contrasting sets of signs found in the forms of recreation that the sexes enjoy. For example, girls' play tends to be more cooperative, with a focus on collaborative rather than competitive pastimes. Their choice of games sends a powerful message to younger girls and boys. And the turn-taking that features in girls' play also shows up in their conversations with friends around the games. As a result, scrupulous attention to the rules of turn-taking is often treated more seriously by girls than by boys. When disagreements occur in girls' groups, speakers tend to express these disagreements indirectly by using fewer direct imperatives and more phrases that solicit engagement or promote a sense of groupness.

Although these verbal differences between the sexes seem to diminish somewhat in the more egalitarian and 'fraternal' contexts that young, mixed-sex siblings create during unstructured play activities (Sheldon, 1997), the gender-reinforcing power of non-verbal sign systems comes into its own when toddlers communicate without words in mixed-sex groups. Susan Grieshaber and Susan Danby (1999) powerfully demonstrate this point using videotaped observations of 2- and 3-year-olds in an Australian childcare setting. In what the researchers describe as a preamble to the gendered play of older preschool children (Danby & Baker, 1998), the children at play—around a water trough in this childcare setting—use a sophisticated form of non-verbal communication to tell each other when to move, where to go, and which storylines to take up. Clearly, there is much more than mere parallel play going on here. Although the children hardly use spoken language at all, they all appear to be very sensitive to the signs that each one uses. And the chief message communicated in the signs they use, is the dominance of the boys in all the little games that they play.

Through their participation in single-sex language games, boys and girls acquire different rules for creating and interpreting discourse; and these rules of use seem to be modelled on male or female adult roles that infants begin to acquire from their earliest moments, as they begin to position themselves as gendered individuals. These differences even show up in more private acts of communication, like expressive writing, where young boys position themselves as 'doers' who take risks. These are the kinds of risk-taking skills, too, that the language games of computers and the Internet tend to reward (Alloway & Gilbert, 1997) and which present-day education increasingly favours to the distinct advantage of boys. In contrast, young girls are more likely to write longer and more complex texts that win academic approval but which bring them fewer options in the wider world (Kanaris, 1999). Meanwhile, in their public interactions, children re-apply their gendered norms in mixed contexts, often doing so in dysfunctional ways, as they continue to do as adults. The cycle of communication and frequent miscommunication continues when the norms are reproduced in mixed- and single-sex adult interactions, producing the gendered types of practice summarized in the previous section.

Research also suggests that these informal but influential norms carry over into adulthood and inform the kinds of communication that single-sex adult groups develop (Maltz & Borker, 1983). These differences, preserved in the discourse conventions of the two sexes, often produce that significant degree of miscommunication between women and men in general that I have already noted. Typically, in their turn, very young boys and girls reproduce the differences, acquiring the rules of use along with the sign systems of adult males and females, who were once small boys and girls themselves. Indeed, the ideologies associated with these conventional rules become habitual dispositions when adults encourage young children to be acquiescent and uncritical of the world around them. Accordingly, the young readily become socialized into reproducing these discursive patterns themselves on most occasions, always allowing, however, that most girls are quite proficient at resisting the norms when they feel the need to assert themselves (Goodwin, 1988), just as males are often proficient in modelling cooperative speech when the occasion suits them (Cameron, 1997).

So it is important to stress again that there are always attempts to resist all this reproduction of norms, as children negotiate their locations within the flux and flow of multiple discourses. Yet, much of this process of reproduction has an automatic character to it, since the ideologies are far from explicit and they go unrecognized at the time of their transfer. For most of the time, they are transferred unconsciously in the models offered by innocent adults who themselves take the signs and their rules of use for granted. So, it would be wrong to say that schools are manipulating the behaviour of boys and girls, or that children are intentionally indoctrinated into acquiring male or female discourse conventions. While this is not the purpose of schools, it is often their function.

GENDERED PRACTICES REINFORCED IN SCHOOLS

Much has been written describing conventional schools as competitive agencies of social control. And I find it hard to mount much of an argument against this view. In almost everything schools do, they are comparing and sorting children, evaluating their
performances against one another, or against some arbitrary norm that disadvantages
some children while it advantages others. Moreover, there is only a modicum of fairness and social justice in the way schools go about doing all of this. These same institutions are also powerful agencies of social control in other respects (Corson, 1995a)
because of the discursive power they exercise and because of their place in an established hierarchy of social formations which can always be oppressive, even in the most
benign of political climates. I want to concentrate in this section on the ways classroom practices, in particular, reinforce and reward the competitive discourse tendencies of children, while marginalizing cooperative tendencies. Classrooms do this in
ways that give certain important options to the many boys who spend much of their
lives learning to use and practise competitive forms of interaction.

In all the countries studied in Alison Kelly's review of sex differences in
teacher-pupil interaction (1988), there are strong indications that female and
male teachers tend to pay less attention to girls than to boys at all ages, in various socio-economic and ethnic groupings, and in all subjects. Her review
looked at 81 quantitative studies of primary and secondary schools, across all
ages, school levels, subjects, and socio-economic and ethnic groupings. Furthermore, girls apparently get less behavioural criticism, fewer instructional
contacts, fewer high-level questions and academic criticism, and slightly less
praise than boys. While girls volunteer to answer questions just as often as
boys, they are less likely to call answers out. Kelly's analysis also indicated that
male teachers give slightly more attention to boys than to girls. Similar patterns
of unequal interactive support continue to appear in more recent studies when
both sexes are at work in the same classroom (Bjerrum Nielsen & Davies, 1997)
and the same patterns persevere at all levels, from pre-school to university
(AAUW, 1995; Mael, 1998).

So it seems that teachers are reading and responding to student behaviour and
student identities quite differently. For instance, according to Scandinavian studies cited by Harriet Bjerrum Nielsen and Bronwyn Davies (1997), a rather typical
discourse unit in an elementary school classroom goes as follows:

1. teacher asks a question
2. a girl raises her hand and is appointed to answer
3. the girl does so briefly and her answer is usually correct
4. a boy interrupts with an interesting comment on the topic
5. the teacher leaves the girl and engages in an exchange with the boy
6. other boys then join the discussion
7. the girls silently await the next question or whisper together

These studies also indicate that teachers tend to respond to the *form* of girls' contributions, but to the *content* of boys' contributions. Another study reported by Bjerrum Nielsen and Davies (1997) found that the student's own level of academic achievement, which often corresponds to socio-economic and ethnic background, affects boys more than girls. Slow achieving boys get more behavioural criticism, but high achieving boys 'receive the best of everything'. At the same time, low achieving girls get the least teacher attention in classroom talk, although other studies have found this to be the case for high achieving girls (Kelly, 1988).

These patterns from Scandinavia also appear in other non-English speaking contexts. In Québec, Claudine Baudoux and Antoine Noircent (1993) look at interactional differences between francophone girls, boys, and teachers during the last year of high school. Here, the girls seem to keep themselves back from whole class interactions. They quite deliberately give themselves a subordinate role, both physically and intellectually, in the classroom; but they still adopt strategies that compensate for these differences in power, strategies that allow them to meet their own personal goals in school and resist the worst effects of the disabling treatment they receive.

Remarkably perhaps, it is well known that all these differences in interaction occur despite teachers' assertions that they do not treat nor wish to treat girls and boys differently (Sadker & Sadker, 1985). Furthermore, teachers are often unaware of their differential treatment of girls and boys. For example, respected teachers in one US study routinely gave boys more opportunities to use science instruments and equipment than girls. Another US study reports cultural bias in teachers' treatment of immigrant students in science classes, with immigrant girls at the bottom in both the respect they receive and in their actual treatment (Corson, 1998). So, in rather straightforward ways, the ideologies teachers hold, as part of their core professional practices, continually reward the competitive norms of many majority culture boys. These same sets of signs that dominant boys tend to use are intricately associated with their male identities. In fact, the rules of use that relate to the signs have been historically overlaid by that maleness. So, the meanings they convey help reinforce the greater influence boys have, but often without much deliberate exercise of power by the boys themselves. Again, this communication of adult practical ideologies has an automatic character to it. Many studies confirm that teachers even disbelieve the evidence when confronted with it. Indeed, it is common for both male and female teachers to defend their actual practices with the sincere disclaimer that 'we treat them all the same, here' (Biggs & Edwards, 1991; Fennema & Peterson, 1985; Morse & Handley, 1985).

Other research on finer aspects of teacher-pupil discourse has also appeared, looking for example at variations in the type of questions asked by teachers, and at the allocation of turns in interaction. There are reports that teachers direct more open-ended questions at boys in the early years of schooling, and more yes/no questions at girls (Fichtelius, Johansson & Nordin, 1980). Consistent with the Scandinavian findings, there is also evidence in Michelle Stanworth's study (1983), that male and female British pupils in late adolescence experience the classroom as a place where boys are the focus of teacher-pupil interactions, while girls are on the margins. Even teachers describe themselves as more interested in the boys, and they are seen by their pupils as more concerned with the boys. They are also more aware of the identities of boys, and they are more willing to allow the boys to upstage the girls in interaction. Indeed, in the same study, many of the girls who are not admired by their female classmates, manifest interactional norms that are more characteristic of boys, even though these are the very norms that the same girls admire in the boys. And this is an example of Gramsci's (1948) idea of hegemony at work. In their perceptions of one another, the girls pillory the use of discourse practices that could allow them to compete with the boys. By so doing they help in their own oppression.

In extra-curricular work, and in other social exchanges outside the classroom, different but consistent patterns of male dominance emerge. In Monica Heller's (1999) long-term study of a francophone school in Ontario, most of the public discourse heard in school council meetings, at celebrations, and dances, is produced by the males; and much of it is directed towards reproducing gender stereotypes that allow the males to continue to dominate public interactions. Often they do this through a use of highly gendered sign systems that girls everywhere seem much less disposed to use, like clowning, poking fun, or telling jokes. As in Eckert's study (1990), when interacting in their single-sex groups, the girls engage in consensus-building and relational girl talk; but when they are in the boys' company, they do little more than position themselves with respect to these dominant male discourses. Of course, these discourses vary depending on the ethnolinguistic background of the male in-group: The Québécois males portray themselves as the tough, rugged, authentic Canadian francophones. Others who are fully bilingual in French and English signal that they are plugged into the full range of North American popular culture, displaying this in their music, dress, and sporting tastes. And the francophone males of African extraction position themselves as anti-colonialist, anti-racist, street-wise guardians of the European French standard. But in all these male language games, there is little room for authentic female interests, and even less for female discourse norms. And this cycle of unequal discursive reproduction does its work from generation to generation of students, as they come up through the school.

Bjerrum Nielsen & Davies (1997) provide a comprehensive summary of the effects of years of similar, differential treatment on adolescent girls. Although girls are often praised in the elementary years, during which they usually perform better and are more satisfied with school, that satisfaction and the satisfaction of teachers with them drops away in secondary school. As part of the serious decline in self-esteem that girls often show around puberty, just the act of speaking up in class becomes a time of great anxiety. Some girls manage to adopt the more 'masculine' signs they see valued in school, but in doing so they put their friendship with other girls at serious risk. Others respond to boys' more competitive displays by becoming silent or oppositional. Although they get better marks than boys, girls' class-room participation seems to change for the worse in adolescence. While they still tend to meet all the explicit school demands for obedient behaviour, they still lose out. They become less compliant to the benign will of teachers, less self confident, and less interested in taking part in classroom discussions.

Meanwhile, the more inventive and individualistic behaviour of the boys matches the implicit and real norms for academic success in competitive institutions. No doubt, as they mature, more boys are able to capitalize on the greater leeway for clowning, ribbing, and boasting that is allowed them in classrooms and which positions them more at centre stage. These systems of signs are part of the linguistic capital that attracts high status when it is linked with males. Gradually, as more opportunities arrive for adolescent boys to interact in these ways with their teachers and with each other, the girls tend to be left out and get treated more and more as rather uninteresting students.

In Summary

The growing number of studies to date outlining sex differences in school settings now offer more than preliminary indications of patterns of interaction that probably exist more generally. When coupled with other evidence about adult discursive practices and about the norms for interaction that children in single-sex groups adopt, there are grounds here to suggest two developmental trends in discourse norms as girls and boys reach towards maturity.

Firstly, in mixed group and whole class contexts, throughout their school careers, girls as a group continue to use the cooperative, consensual interactional patterns that they are accustomed to using in their own groups and which are valued in junior schools. Boys as a group tend to shed these patterns, adopting instead the more competitive discourse norms met and acquired in their single-sex interactions, which are ultimately modelled on adult single-sex norms and increasingly influenced by them as boys mature. The boys become better placed to appropriate the senior school's linguistic resources because its norms of interaction match the dominant norms boys bring from their own homes and communities; and they coincide with the disposition to use those norms that boys acquire and which the language games of the social world continue to attribute to males.

Secondly, as a result of their own participation in the language games of single-sex groups, whose interaction is modelled on the adult female pattern, girls as a group continue to develop competence and interest in a more conversational and cooperative approach to their classwork; while boys as a group thrive more on a competitive and individualist approach to the curriculum because they increasingly participate in language games compatible with that approach, and also because schooling itself, at its more senior levels, still does little to reward and reinforce the use of cooperative interactional patterns that would be more consistent with girls' acquired cultural interests and likely preferences.

INFLUENCES BEYOND THE SCHOOL

Probably, then, many girls are excluded from genuine participation in the kinds of intellectually developing activities that are more appropriate to their acquired discursive interests, because of the interactional styles and the classroom techniques that traditional schools use and which many teachers adopt, often against their will. Yet, there is an observed willingness among girls to work cooperatively at senior school level in interactive activities. I summarize the evidence for this claim later. It licenses a greater use of oral language work in the senior school. It also suggests that after consulting their preferences, girls, and boys too, should be allowed to approach the curriculum in this way, if that is their expressed interest.

Indeed, if schools everywhere placed greater emphasis on cooperative work, especially at senior levels, then more prestige would attach to these ligature-building discourse norms more generally in societies. This is because the senior levels of education remain the most prestigious in many people's minds, so the practices they endorse tend to acquire the same prestige. In short, they become high-status sociocultural practices outside schools because of the institutional privileging that schools give them, just as the practice of giving public lectures once held great prestige, by analogy with its now slightly diminished place in higher education.

Girls get options from their schooling, too, of course. And in a few places, girls now enjoy higher success rates in senior school education than boys, notably in England and Wales, Australia, and Ontario (Alloway & Gilbert, 1997; Baxter, 1999; Corson & Lemay, 1996), although perhaps not in the US (AAUW, 1995). This change is happening even in those areas of the curriculum where boys were once dominant, like the sciences and mathematics. In those different school systems, educationists are giving more attention to the use of 'ligature-building' interactive pedagogies in high school education, especially group work and team approaches to assessment. The latter are gradually replacing the external, solitary, and norm-referenced forms of teaching and assessment that encourage competition and individual performance, discouraging cooperative learning and interaction with peers.

Perhaps as a result of this change already affecting schools in some places, the many ligatures people already create with one another are slowly becoming more valued socially, which is more in line with their real importance. Their formal status in social life is gradually increasing, as males and females come to see them as the highly desirable acquisitions they are. But girls and women in some cultures are already immensely advantaged by the ligatures they develop with one another, inside and outside schools. And these ligatures are now turning into career options, as girls more often than boys put their interactive skills to work, developing and maintaining bonds in all the many life and work situations where these skills are valued and necessary (Waite, 1997; Wodak, 1995).

All this suggests that some of the changes within schools are influencing the discourse norms of wider societies in positive ways. But at the same time, malignant language games still at work in those wider societies are influencing the norms of boys and girls themselves; and they are doing so with much more negative results. As boys, in particular, search for meaning and value in their encounters with the world, some are acquiring rules of use that have terrible consequences for themselves, their schools, and others working in schools. Writing after a series of violent episodes involving firearms in US schools in the late 1990s, Beverley MacPhail (1999) warns that we are reaping what we sow in the way we rear boys.

MacPhail says that the cause of most violent episodes, like the many school tragedies that involve firearms, is clear to those feminists who have made careers out of studying male violence. Like my own analysis in this chapter, hers centres on gender and power. For her, all these horrific acts of violence seem to have a chilling commonality: They are all perpetrated by white males who felt isolated, powerless, ridiculed, and rejected. In explanation, she says that, while feminism has successfully expanded the range of gender-role stereotypes for girls and women to live out, society has been less willing to encourage more flexible sex roles for males. The language games surrounding boys still teach them to be dominant, competitive, detached from others, and dissociated from their feelings; and all these attributes create an impossible role for them to adopt. It harms the boys who adopt it, and also the ones who resist it. The ones who adopt it learn to ridicule and belittle women, or other men perceived as weak. Meanwhile, boys not projecting these male sex-role attributes, are called girls, sissies, or wimps; or they get other undesirable tags that fuel their resentment and increase their anger. Finally, gendered ways of expressing these emotions turn into tragically different results for boys and girls.

On the one hand, women are socialized into turning their feelings of powerlessness and anger inward. Usually, they find ways to take comfort in the ligatures shared with other women. As MacPhail says, women walk away from the job, talk to friends, or take the matter to the courts. In contrast, many of the language games that males live out teach them to direct their feelings outward. Worse still, in the most popular language games from the United States—wherever that country's power reaches—men are taught to defend their masculinity by striking out. Picking up a gun gives them the symbol of power and control society repeatedly tells them they are entitled to. By reading the symbol systems of movies and video games, where violence is transformed into heroic and exciting events, boys get a strong message that violent acts are acceptable. These acts are signs whose rules of use 'make sense'. Boys learn these rules when they are given play-guns at age 2 years and real guns at 12 years of age. And when every other movie advertisement they see, projects a hero with a gun in his hand. Guns themselves, of course, are the most potent signs of all. Their rules of use are shaped by the language games in which they appear; and they are usually violent language games. With more than 200 million of them in private hands in the United States, that genie is forever out of the bottle. It might not be returned, for generations to come.

So, when males strike out at women, or at more dominant males, or at powerful male-ordered systems that have caused them pain, they are behaving in ways that seem quite normal to them, because the rules implicit in the system of signs that surrounds them supports and glorifies exactly this kind of violent response. Eventually, it produces adult males who take violence for granted as a way of solving human problems, and then as an instrument of public policy.

Meanwhile, girls get quite different messages. These are most starkly evidenced in the strictly segregated aisles of toy-shops, where bright pink aisles filled with toys that invite girls to interact positively with the world stand next to camouflage-coloured aisles that look like miniature arsenals. Females must be 'nice' and avoid jeopardizing interpersonal harmony (Sheldon, 1997), otherwise they risk censure from their peers or adults. So, little girls learn to say things with a smile; they learn to avoid any hint of conflict-talk, at least in formal settings. Elsewhere of course, other arrangements obtain, especially in mixed sex-groups, as described above. For example, girls and boys from some sociocultural backgrounds seem much more alike in their verbal norms, even though their non-verbal signs usually leave little doubt about where the real influence lies. Also, many girls from upper-middle class backgrounds learn to "mask their exercise of power during conflicts, with polite language" (Sheldon, 1997, p. 229). Like many upper-middle class boys, and most culturally different boys reared in stratified communities where formal ligatures are highly valued, the girls manage to be 'nice' and to be powerful at the same time.

Children with backgrounds in diverse cultural meaning systems tend to respond to the world differently; and as chapter 3 argues, their discourse norms tend to reflect their own community's values and cultural practices. When culturally different boys and girls join a new society and enter its culture, they bring memories of all their former embodied sign systems. Sometimes, these other systems advantage them, and at other times, they are disabling. For instance, when encountering the real and imagined violence constantly found in the media in North America, immigrant and refugee children sometimes recollect painful memories of actual episodes experienced in their lives elsewhere. The influence of many vivid sign systems can make children of diversity react differently to their school experience. Pointedly, the two sexes often differ in their reactions, as well.

THE DIFFERENT NORMS OF IMMIGRANT GIRLS

Perhaps the least visible groups in pluralist societies are girls who come from certain immigrant and refugee cultures. They are doubly marginalized: first as members of different cultures; and then as females within those cultures. More than this, their invisibility in education is also increased by their marginal place in research and practice. This happens because the study and practice of multicultural education still tends to treat members of any single culture as a homogeneous group, with little regard for sex. At the same time, early feminist theory and practice tended to minimize the cultural differences between women, because of the need to treat broad issues of gender discrimination that affect all women. Although serious and multiple disadvantages do affect girls from immigrant cultures, this double effect gets scant attention in the literature to date. In this section, I collate some of the little that we know about this area at present. I try to highlight the unequal power arrangements in schools that affect the discourse norms of many immigrant girls.

Let me stress, at the outset, that individuals and groups of immigrant girls are very different from one another in their cultural values, their life histories, and their hopes about education. In assembling some of the sparse evidence here, I am not making any claims that can be generalized to all immigrant girls, and especially not to all individuals within the groups described in the literature. Dealing with diversity means always treating every person with the expectation that he or she is uniquely different and lives a life independent of any stereotype.

Immigrant Girls

Some groups of girls are now more subject to risk of educational failure than others. In the United States, for example, research that looks at sex, race, and ethnicity "reveals critical vulnerabilities among various groups of girls" (AAUW, 1995, p. 34), yet little recent research has been done in that country linking sex, class, and culture with low achievement. It is certain that many non-immigrant girls who come from low-income, but majority culture, backgrounds are still in positions of unusual risk when compared with their male peers. They still participate in language games, inside and outside schools, that close off whole avenues of life for them: avenues that include employment and life-style options that girls from more privileged backgrounds often take for granted these days. Despite this, the groups that seem most at risk are the girls from certain immigrant cultural backgrounds.

Schools often misperceive the preferences and abilities of immigrant girls because of stereotypes that circulate in societies, and among some teachers. No doubt some individual immigrant girls do hear life stories, in their own communities, about their future opportunities that make them feel inferior to their male relatives. Although this is hardly the case for all girls from a given immigrant background, sometimes schools build on stereotypes of that kind. The false belief that immigrant girls are subjected to male power in every sphere of their home lives, can create an image for these girls quite unlike the actual one they experience outside school. And of course, it is also a very different image from the one that they would prefer for themselves.

In other words, while teachers may see many immigrant girls as passive victims of cultural forces, the reality of their cultural experiences can be life-affirming. It might be a positive lived reality in many ways. But unfortunately, as Tsolidis (1990) warns, "rarely is the thought entertained that the source of ethnic minority girls' problems may be other than their cultures" (p. 58). These stereotypes, held by teachers and others about immigrant girls, can be disabling for them if teachers are unaware of what lies behind the discourse norms that girls exhibit. The following quote comes from an experienced secondary science teacher who talks about the many students in her London girls' school. She makes some generalizations that probably most teachers would agree with:

> Girls, particularly working class and immigrant girls, lack confidence in themselves and their abilities, especially in unfamiliar areas. Having spent a lot of time watching them, I have noticed that girls exert pressures on each other which reinforce this lack of confidence. There is pressure not to brag, 'show yourself up' or make a fuss; otherwise you may be labelled 'big-headed'. Discretion and modesty are valued, while outspokeness and self-assertion are suspect, if not 'punished' by the group (unless they express anti-authoritarianism).

> Imagine a girl attempting to formulate a question in a science lesson under such pressures. She is likely to expose her vulnerability in two ways. First, she risks the censure of the whole group. Second, she almost certainly risks being dismissed and thus unintentionally ridiculed by the teacher for failing to pose the question in a sufficiently abstract frame of reference to be recognized by that teacher. In such a context, girls may readily reject scientific knowledge wholesale as being at odds with their own experiences. (Baran, 1987, p. 91)

Structural arrangements in schools and classrooms often affect children from different cultural backgrounds very differently. Some girls and boys do appear at home in the setting of the school. They are supported by the mutually understood conceptual frameworks that they share with teachers and classmates from similar backgrounds. These children are empowered in the setting of the school by the orientation to the world that they bring from the home. Accordingly, they are ready to convert the already valuable and similar conceptual frameworks entered in the home, into the high status academic language games that the school offers.

Other children are not empowered in this way; and their confidence in classrooms is affected. Many immigrant students are acutely aware of their family's lack of high status cultural capital and the power that attends it. They come from family circumstances where unemployment is common. Many others have parents who fill low-status and intermittent jobs, often spent with others from similar immigrant backgrounds. Many have a family history set in a rural culture, which is the main life experience that the family draws upon. Many have experienced war, or had first-hand contact with violence before or after entering their new culture. Taken together, these experiences are filled with powerful symbols whose rules of use become memories that can impact on immigrant childrens' perceptions of self.

They are positioned in life by these sign systems, and the stories they tell themselves about their place in the world often tend to reflect all of this.

At the same time, these views of self and circumstance can be very different from the views that teachers believe immigrant girls hold about themselves. For example, teachers in an Australian study (Tsolidis, 1990) believed that "ethnic minority communities expected these girls to marry young and become young mothers, and this was the expectation they taught to." The teachers, however, did not check with the girls to see if these views of theirs were misperceptions or not. So, there is good reason to wonder "how responsible are teachers for the creation of self-fulfilling prophecies?" (p. 65). Indeed, the evidence in the same study confirms that the immigrant girls were seeking greatly enhanced future prospects for themselves; and these things were foremost in their minds. As important, their families also went well beyond simply agreeing with them on this. One girl's comment shows the very high expectations that immigrant families often have of education, and the pressure for success that it can place on their offspring:

> I honestly believe that my parents want to give me what they were deprived of when they were young. They often say that they wish that they were educated so they wouldn't be treated like "dirt" by the boss. I can always see tears forming in their eyes when we discuss the matter. This makes me feel a bit depressed because you can see that being uneducated really has its hardships. (Tsolidis, 1990, p. 64)

Students coming from backgrounds like this often want things from schools that some teachers feel are inappropriate for them. So their family priorities and their own wishes often focus on a future quite unlike that forecast by their teachers. And their teachers, working from good intentions but bad stereotypes, can become an obstacle to those hopes.

As discussion in chapter 5 suggests, first-generation immigrant students often bring conceptual frameworks and discourse norms that are inconsistent with what teachers ask from them. In particular, clear and strong patterns of misunderstanding and mismatches in interaction between teachers and immigrant female students appear in Canadian, New Zealand, British, and US research.

For example in Canada, Goli Rezai-Rashti (1994) looks at immigrant female students in schools where racism and sexism are seen as 'systemic'. In other words, the discrimination in these schools was due not so much to the deliberately biased actions of people, as it was to biases in the structures of the schools themselves: in their rules, their taken-for-granted practices, their organizational values. Here the relationships between the students and teachers are framed in what Rezai-Rashti calls 'colonial discourse'. In this discourse, the pressure on them to assimilate often leads the girls to reject their first language and culture. Instead they are urged to replace these things with the trappings of a capitalist consumer culture that the girls adopt only reluctantly, just to fit in with dominant North American norms. However, the educators themselves apparently miss the point of all this. Wrongly, she says, the teachers are likely to see students as rebelling against the perceived repressive culture of their own communities. Seldom are students' problems seen within the context of the systemic racism present in the actual relationship created between educators and students. Furthermore, this readiness of the educators to find fault with the home cultures of the students allows the teachers to overlook the sexism prevalent in their own English-speaking culture, while still blaming the sexism found in the immigrant cultures.

In a New Zealand girls' high school, working class girls from immigrant Pacific Island families get only rare moments of teacher interaction, while middle class majority culture girls get most of the teachers' attention (Jones, 1987). The immigrant girls explain their reluctance to engage in the verbal competition of class interactions as due to their fear of being singled out. They mention the cultural value of *ma* (modesty and shame) and their fear of being the centre of attention. In response, the teachers react to this by being more sensitive to the discomfort their questioning causes the immigrant girls. They reduce the public demands that they make on the girls, but they do not substitute alternative pedagogies. As a result, in a complex way, teachers reward European cultural norms and reproduce discourse patterns in those students who have the disposition to receive them. But they discourage the patterns of the Pacific Island girls while reproducing in the girls the same patterns that they discourage. Accordingly, the immigrant girls do not get equal opportunities to learn, and they become more passive receivers of knowledge. In this way, they fit the image and the identity that their teachers create for them.

Some other evidence from New Zealand suggests that there is psychological reluctance and inability on the part of teachers to promote extended interactions with culturally different girls, even when they have much more extended interactions with other children (Cazden, 1990). Elsewhere, there are indications, too, that it is the teachers' failure to create suitable conditions that cause these inequalities. For example, a study of Panjabi new entrant children in Britain finds no differences in the patterns of interaction initiated by the children themselves with their teachers. However, there are significant differences in the patterns of interaction initiated by teachers (Biggs & Edwards, 1991). The Panjabi children seek the teachers' advice and help, in much the same way as other children. In response, the teachers spend less time interacting with the immigrant children. It would seem that, because different amounts of time and different kinds of teacher interaction are associated with different groups of children, the reluctance lies with the teachers.

These studies are interesting and important. But because some are impressionistic only, while others are small-scale and rather limited in scope, they leave many questions unanswered about the wider lives of immigrant girls when compared with their formal lives in English-speaking schools. More thorough and finely tuned research is only just beginning to appear, especially research that looks at the educational and the life experiences unique to single cultural groups. One ethnographic study looked at schools and girls in a medium-sized mid-Western city in the United States (Goldstein, 1988). It follows the education and integration of Hmong refugee girls from rural Indo-China. In it, Goldstein points out that "the educational practices and messages of school often conflict with those in the minority-culture home and community," but she warns that, to understand all this, "it is essential to consider how gender mediates the point at which ethnic and dominant cultures intersect" (pp. 1-2).

In the Hmong culture, authority passes along the male line. Also, the culture's view of personhood is that the group is more important than the individual, a view that is similar to many of the aboriginal cultures discussed in chapter 3. Moreover, in this respect at least, the Hmong culture is not unlike the majority of the world's cultures. But this emphasis on the group is very different from middle class North American cultural norms; and it affects discourse norms differently, too, and in important ways. Another key difference is that, unlike North Americans, the Hmong do not recognize adolescence as a special developmental period. This means that teenagers are considered as young adults. They have the same adult responsibilities as older people, but these responsibilities in turn are determined by their sex. For instance, male adults are more involved in the discourses of public roles, and females in private roles. In fact, in their home setting in Laos, females seldom leave their village neighbourhood.

Apparently the girls' teachers misunderstood or were unaware of much of this background. And they sent messages to these students that blocked the girls' integration into school, rather than encouraging it. In one high school, the Hmong girls were put in a bilingual program specially targeted on the Hmong as a group, which isolated them from their American peers and labelled them explicitly as 'different', but implicitly as 'inferior' to those from the dominant culture. Gender differences were not considered in this bilingual program's organization of classroom interactions, or in the curriculum knowledge that was presented, even though the differently gendered Hmong norms of interaction required it. At the same time, gender biases were clear in the teachers' presentations, and in the selection of curriculum material.

In another high school, the Hmong girls were placed in low-level, transitional, special education classes, where the academic content took second place to other disciplinary concerns. Again, because of their consistently good behaviour, they were separated from other students and encouraged to work together, so that they could help each other and not trouble the teachers too much. This made their problems worse, because routine interactions with the American children, who might help them in their learning, were difficult to promote. Further problems came from the lack of knowledge that the American students had about the Hmong and their practices. For the American students, the gendered separation of social activities by the Hmong was hard to accept, and this created further social distancing. One Hmong student, who was regarded as an adult in her own community, reported that she "invariably ended up feeling like a child in their company" (Goldstein, 1988, p. 17).

A second ethnographic study from the United States looks at the lives of Cambodian women and girls in Philadelphia (Sylvester, 1996). It discusses two different stereotypes of Cambodians in the United States, one positive and one negative, that affect their lives as students. Clearly, stereotypes of any kind are best avoided because, as Sylvester's study suggests, their effects can never be controlled or even predicted. First, there is the 'model minority' stereotype that many people wrongly attach to the identities of all Asian immigrants. Students from some Asian backgrounds find it difficult to live up to the 'myth of the model minority' that comes from the academic success that a few Asian students achieve in difficult areas. In Canada, Maclear (1994) describes the problems that journalists and editorial writers create for Asian children by over-emphasizing academic success stories that suggest children of Asian backgrounds are different in their natural talents and skills from other groups of children. Yet, success in education comes no more easily to most of them than it does to any others. Secondly, Sylvester mentions the more negative stereotype of Cambodian immigrants as poor, illiterate farmers who are unable to organize their lives for themselves in the United States or succeed easily in its schools. She finds that neither stereotype matches the reality of the students' lives, yet both affect the education they receive. She also reports that, unlike the practices recommended in chapter 5, the schools treat the linguistic capital of these students as a problem to be removed, rather than as a resource to be built upon.

Summary

Although there are few studies that put gender and cultural differences in student norms together, those to date more than hint at the special problems first-generation immigrant girls can have. In pulling this together, I have done a lot of guesswork based only on sparse evidence. So, it needs to be stressed that many groups of immigrant girls and many individuals within those groups would not fit the summary below. As Kaye Haw (1998) found in her study of the attitudes toward academic success held by Muslim girls, the effects of different discourses pertaining to school context, parental background, past and present experiences of migration, strength of cultural allegiance, and different sociological conditions affecting the wider community all positioned different immigrant girls differently, even those attending Haw's two single-sex schools in the one British city. So there is reason for caution when interpreting what follows. In fact, the summary is bulleted to highlight how speculative and limited it all is. We can expect that future research will throw more light on the many different ways that education can affect girls from different cultures:

- In the language games of their own communities, some groups of immigrant girls seem to get fewer opportunities than other children to show communicative dominance or exercise their independence. At the same time, in schools, immigrant girls meet even worse imbalances in communication.

Their teachers tend to leave them to their own devices, except when working with the whole class. In turn, the girls also find the academic expectations schools have for them are different and they are affected by stereotypes that paint many immigrant girls as passive, compliant, lacking in ambition, or even naturally gifted. In response, teachers tend to leave them alone, sometimes feeling sorry for them or preferring not to trouble them by insisting on standards they have for others. Although many do less well in school than they or their parents would like, the families tend to accept this as their own fault.

- Treated in this way, immigrant girls can come to perceive school discourse in their new country as moving along a single one-way channel. Knowledge passes only from the teacher to the students, with little return interaction from girls like them. Although they see other children asserting themselves by interacting in lively ways, especially the boys, they see themselves mainly as spectators in all this because they are not disposed to present their own cultural capital in school-acceptable ways, nor do they have enough of the capital given high status in the school to increase their own in more than passive ways.

- The immigrant girls also find that the kind of ligatures they share with other girls from similar backgrounds are missing from the public symbols and practices of schools. In their place, there are few opportunities to build close ties with non-immigrant girls and boys who sometimes regard them as strange and a little intimidating. Because there are few signs and symbols in schools to reveal alternative roles in life to them, they often accept roles for themselves that are far more restrictive than they would like them to be. They come to accept a place in life that is very much like the place described for them in the stereotypes of dominant people in their community and in their school. The narratives and stories they hear throughout their childhood give them few alternatives they can easily identify with.

SOFTENING GENDERED SCHOOL DISCOURSES

One priority seems to lie in modifying interactional practices during the early childhood years: in kindergartens, childcare centres, and nurseries. This is where the gendered norms, that children acquire in the wider community, are reinforced institutionally for the first time. It is where children begin to accept that discourse norms of different types apply to boys and girls; that this is the way their world is ordered for them; and, worst of all, that this is the way it should be ordered. These caring institutions can loom large in the small child's world, so the normed practices that they sanction always resonate with the influence of semi-official authority. Gradually, early childhood educators are becoming more alert to the need to support gender equity. They are arranging classrooms that encourage cooperative cross-sex play, without the use of gender stereotyping. They are introducing games and toys that minimize competition, which means minimizing the losing that goes with it. And they are adopting a host of imaginative activities that develop respect for boys and for girls (Schlank & Metzger, 1997). Gradually, then, the different signs and symbols that early childhood educators are inserting into their work are presenting children with different narratives and stories that they can see themselves living inside, if they choose to do so.

The senior school is also an important site for reform. As chapter 3 indicates, oral language activities are still underused in schools for older children. Yet they are central to mastering the curriculum at all levels of education, and for intellectual development itself. Moreover, they are important for building the ligatures that many senior schools seem to be bypassing at present. But even with more stress on oral language work, adolescent girls will still need the kind of classroom context that motivates their own participation. In their teachers and others, they need to witness signs and symbols that are not overlaid by strong hints of male privilege. And they need opportunities that encourage open involvement, despite the signs of pressure they place on one another not to copy the boys' ways of interacting. Just by varying the context of interaction, including the classroom participants, worthwhile change can come about.

For example, there are some indications in senior level classrooms that changes in the topic and the nature of the class activity can produce marked differences in pupil-initiated contacts with teachers. Studies of girls and boys, working in mixed-sex and mixed-ability chemistry laboratories in New Zealand schools, suggest that different interaction patterns can develop with teachers in this type of setting (Burns & Bird, 1987; Burns, Clift, & Duncan, 1991). In these contexts, more girls seek out their teacher's help with learning problems, and it is mainly the boys who admit they are afraid of revealing their incompetence. Pupil laboratory sessions of this type seem to promote different interactive patterns. The more formally gendered signs that prevail in more conventional teaching settings are replaced by signs whose less rigid rules of use seem more inviting to the girls. In turn, the large sex differences found in activities that are tightly controlled by teachers seem to disappear in these informal, practical sessions.

Broadly consistent with the above, there is evidence from England that girls in early adolescence engaged in craft, design, and technology practical sessions have more and longer contacts with their teachers than boys do. The girls interrupt more, and they also make more unsuccessful attempts at initiating contact. So, they compete more in influencing the interactions that take place. Indeed, the usual ratio of teacher-to-pupil contacts found in formal classes actually reverses itself here (Randall, 1987). But other emancipatory signs helped shape the same school setting, sending powerful messages to all participants: The teacher, the head teacher, and the local authority were all strongly committed to providing equal opportunities for girls, and they communicated that fact. So projects of equal interest to the sexes were available and discussed; and there was minimal gender stereotyping in the way that lessons were handled. In this context of female empowerment, the girls received a more just distribution of interactive opportunities, and more control over the discourse, which is something they seized with evident willingness.

Suggestions at the end of chapter 3 about teacher interaction styles also seem relevant here. The tendency of boys to use competitive signs and symbols more readily does make that behaviour seem the more typical male response. But perhaps it is not. A look at cultures removed from the European suggests that competitive signs are not at all a male prerogative, and might not be typical, even of males with a European cultural heritage. Probably, they are less widely used by the majority of males than we think, appearing only dominantly normal because of the dominance they express. In other words, these signs are norms that most people, including most boys, might not prefer if they were given the choice at some early stage in their lives. So, perhaps the real interests of boys would be served too by changing classroom norms, especially the more persistent pedagogical signs that reflect outdated values from a past where dominant males called the tune on almost everything that mattered. For example, teachers could reduce their use of disabling, masculinized practices like the following, which always create blatant imbalances in interactional fairness:

The unrestrained use of the imperative (by the teacher).
The use of the (absolute) right to speak last.
The use of the (absolute) right to contradict.
The use of the (absolute) right to define the world for others.
The use of the (absolute) right to interrupt or to censure.
The use of the (absolute) right to praise or blame in public.

The strong tendency to insert these powerfully negative signs into their professional relations with children is deeply ingrained in many teachers. Yet, the one-sidedness of the rules of use associated, for example, with the teachers' absolute right to contradict, sends a powerful message to children about how the world is ordered and what their place is in it. And it leaves them with fewer reasons for loving an institution that sends such messages. Moreover, the sign is re-acquired by generations of young students who later become teachers and reapply it themselves, thinking that the sign and its attendant rules of use are part of the very stuff of teaching. I believe that none of these teacher ideologies would withstand critical inspection and challenge if they were freely debated in staffrooms. They are areas for gradual change that entire schools could easily subscribe to.

What I am suggesting here involves changing whole-school discourse norms by changing a school's negotiated language policies (Corson, 1999). Indeed, for reform to occur in education, these things need to begin with schools themselves, because, in general, wider school systems and social formations are uninterested in such matters. Gradually, schools themselves are beginning to find out much more about their local communities, about the strengths, weaknesses and attitudes of their teaching staff as a whole, and about their students' preferences. Sometimes teachers are so affected by their own lack of success with boys and girls from certain backgrounds that they see those backgrounds in a prejudiced way and also misinterpret the students' own hopes for themselves. Replacing these stereotypes with information closer to reality means studying the context in some depth, before taking action. There are a range of ways to do this, and in the next chapter I go into some of these methods in more detail. A good starting point, following the approach to deciding social justice discussed in chapter 2, might be to find out more about the actual preferences that girls and boys have concerning school and classroom discourse norms.

For instance, there is considerable support in the literature for extending the use of single-sex classrooms in senior schools, especially in subjects like mathematics where boys are historically over-represented among the more successful. But boys are much more over-represented among the least successful in this subject too (Willms & Jacobsen, 1990). Furthermore, the desperate situation for the hugely disproportionate number of boys who are weak in literacy proficiency, suggests policy actions of a different kind to make the language games of academic literacy more relevant to the interests of boys in particular. More socially critical approaches to literacy, aimed at linking academic literacy with the greater social empowerment of the learner, would obviously be good for boys and girls too. The 'critical literacy' discussed in chapter 4 might attract the interests of many of those boys who are presently distracted by the more enticing and sometimes pernicious language games that surround them.

Single-sex schools at various age levels are also supported in the literature (Mael, 1998). But these are hardly a panacea in every setting, because a harmful level of sexism is still evident across all school types (Lee, Marks & Byrd, 1994); and racist practices, directed at newcomers to a country or at the socially marginalized, are just as possible in single-sex environments as elsewhere. More valuable, perhaps, might be classroom practices that 'teach girls to speak out' (Baxter, 1999), especially young women from other cultures who get little encouragement outside schools to be assertive in the norms they adopt. Immigrant girls are often among the most vulnerable human beings alive. They are exploited, ignored, and denigrated in many social settings; but the school should not be one of those settings. Obviously, changing the discourse norms of schooling in ways that give immigrant girls a sense of their own empowerment is important. In doing this, the example set by professional staff, especially male teachers and administrators, seems vital: "Men teachers have a particular responsibility and opportunity here, because what they say and do influences what kind of masculinity is hegemonic in the school" (Kessler, Ashenden, Connell, & Dowsett, 1985, p. 47). To help the process of change, the following suggestions for teachers and administrators could make schools and classrooms fairer places for everyone: for boys and girls of every background, and for men and women too. They do seem important courtesies for schools to extend to everyone, as part of their classroom and administrative discourse norms:

- reducing the use of impersonal or bureaucratic language in official and informal communication
- softening formal messages with more humour, less pomposity, less condescension, and a use of vivid metaphors linked to the real world of the school
- sending messages to students that use signs personalizing the recipient
- using the first person as subject and only the occasional passive verb in oral and written communication with students and staff
- introducing a language of school and classroom symbols that expresses collaboration, rather than competition and cooperation for shared rewards, rather than winning for personal glory
- taking positive policy action to end the denigration of girls by boys in the school and the classroom
- speaking openly about issues of race and gender discrimination
- taking positive policy action to challenge the pervasiveness of verbal sexual abuse
- fostering a classroom environment where laughter is common, where frequent greetings are given using people's names, where real achievements are recognized through public expressions of congratulation
- creating a classroom environment filled with displays of students' work and where people are relaxed about giving and taking criticism without fear or offence
- giving higher priority to reshaping the gender distribution of interaction in classrooms
- creating school and classroom contexts that encourage girls to assert their right to speak out effectively and persuasively
- singling immigrant girls out for more recognition and remembering their names and using them
- creating a comfortable and non-threatening environment for interaction
- withdrawing from a centre-stage pedagogical role more often, as a deliberate pedagogy, and re-arranging the structures of classroom interaction in ways that favour the language rights of girls
- giving more attention to the purposeful and regular use of oral language by students as a key pedagogy in all areas of learning across the curriculum.

DISCUSSION STARTERS

1. Do you find the distinction between 'options' and 'ligatures' a helpful way of looking at the life chances that people get from their education? Why or why

not? Are there important ligatures, or just options, that conventional schools pass on to their students? What are those ligatures? How could classrooms be re-arranged to build more ligatures? What do these two ideas have to do with signs and their rules of use?

2. "Powerful structures, reflecting the out-dated values of dominant male social groups who lived generations ago, still affect the discourses of today's men and women." How does this happen in practice? In other words, how do signs and their rules of use create this connection between the social world of the past and of the present? Can you give some examples? Is there any hope of re-moving the present-day influence of unjust structures intruding from the past? How might it be done?

3. To reduce power imbalances in specific contexts of interaction between men and women, is it enough for the male and female participants to adopt one an-other's signs? Why or why not?

4. Review the studies that confirm that boys and men appear more competitive in their interactions, while girls and women appear more cooperative. Does this match your own experience in mixed-sex interactions? Can the gendered signs used by men and women disguise their real intentions? How often does this happen? Can you give examples of experiences that illustrate your points?

5. What exactly is it about the gendered signs and symbols that students use, that encourages their teachers to treat boys and girls differently? Give some examples. What could possibly make teachers "disbelieve the evidence when confronted with it"? Is there any way around this dilemma?

6. "The girls pillory the use of discourse practices that could allow them to com-pete with the boys. By so doing, they help in their own oppression." To what extent are girls doing this voluntarily to one another? Is there anything in the masculinized signs themselves that prevents females from borrowing them? If so, what is it?

7. Consider the "two developmental trends in discourse norms as girls and boys reach towards maturity," set out in the paragraphs on pages 171-172. Does the evidence in this chapter support the conclusions that I have reached in these paragraphs? What other conclusions would you reach, using this evidence plus the evidence of your own experience? How might schools be changed to provide fairer treatment for boys and girls?

8. In the section entitled, "Influences Beyond the School," I have kept my dis-cussion to the urgent issue of firearm use, and of violence more generally. What other pressing social and political issues might be interpreted, and per-haps even explained, using ideas like 'discourses', 'language games', 'signs', and 'rules of use'? Begin by trying to account for the way people living in consumer societies accept, and then take-for-granted, the horrible carnage that traffic accidents produce everywhere.

9. "Again, because of their consistently good behaviour, they were separated from other students and encouraged to work together, so that they could help

each other and not trouble the teachers too much." What signs are being interpreted differently here, by the teachers and by the Hmong girls? Speculate about the different rules of use for the signs you have identified, depending on the cultural background of those trying to interpret them. How could the different groups of participants 'get inside' each other's rules of use, and participate in a roughly similar classroom language game?

10. Consider the list of 'disabling teacher practices' on page 183. In the text of the chapter, I suggest that archaic male values lie behind these practices. But what other rules of use are represented by these sets of signs? Can the use of these signs be justified?

7

Research Methods
for Language Diversity
and Education

It is only if social phenomena are genuinely emergent that realist explanations in the human sciences are justified; and it is only if these conditions are satisfied that there is any possibility of human self-emancipation worthy of the name. But, conversely, emergent phenomena require realist explanations and realist explanations possess emancipatory implications. Emancipation depends upon explanation depends on emergence.

—*Bhaskar (1986, pp. 103–104)*

Most of the literature discussed in chapters 3 to 6 was written by people working in applied linguistics or sociolinguistics despite the fact that many researchers in both those disciplines have real reservations about the limitations of their fields of inquiry for doing present-day studies of language diversity in education. The reasons for this ambivalence are evident in the short histories of both these disciplines, when those histories are set alongside the review of social science theory presented in chapter 1. In spite of their quite recent introduction, neither applied linguistics nor sociolinguistics has been much affected by contemporary developments in the philosophy of social research, especially by the critical realism that lies behind the above quote from Roy Bhaskar.

This omission is partly because there was enough for researchers to do while these new language disciplines were establishing themselves, just setting out aims and scope and building an introductory resource of studies. Also, a certain kind of resistance to developments in mainstream social research theory is common in all disciplines in the human sciences, because adherents to any language game, like a discipline, tend to resist pressures to change their game if the impetus for change comes from outside their known conceptual framework. This seems to be the case with the discipline of psycholinguistics, for example, at least those versions of it that touch upon education. Again, not influenced very much by developments surveyed in chapter 1, researchers in psycholinguistics seem to have boxed their discipline into a language game of their own design that resists much concern for social and cultural diversity, while embracing a starkly positivist conception of theory and evidence. In contrast, researchers in the social psychology of language are gradually adjusting their methods in line with new insights, like those now offered by discursive psychology.

In this chapter, I begin with a brief discussion of some changes in orientation currently impacting on 'language diversity and education' research practices. I then mention some of the research methods those changes seem to license. Finally, I present four examples of methods at work, each drawn from discussion in one of the four central chapters in this book.

APPLIED LINGUISTICS, SOCIOLINGUISTICS, AND THE REAL WORLD OF HUMAN INTERACTION

Applied linguistics began to flourish well before any hermeneutic, critical, or postmodern epistemology had become influential in setting the course of inquiry in the human sciences (Pennycook, 1990). Although sociolinguistics has had a slightly shorter disciplinary history, most of its theory and research directions, including its conceptual boundaries, were set in place well before the 'interpretative alternative' began to intrude on the more positivist past. Indeed, sociolinguistics blossomed well before its emancipatory potential was even properly recognized, prompting the editors of one authoritative handbook to observe that "the original euphoria about the possibilities of sociolinguistics has largely subsided; inflated hopes have become more realistic—in some cases, unjustifiably and overhastily abandoned altogether" (Ammon, Dittmar, & Mattheier, 1987, pp. x-xi). The same editors also remarked on the great hopes people in education had placed in sociolinguistics, only to have them dashed.

Gradually, sociolinguistics filled up the narrow space allotted to it within the shifting disciplinary boundaries of the human sciences. To many people, especially those most influenced by disciplinary politics, it became no more, and no less, than a mirror image of the sociology of language, albeit one that overlaps constantly with the latter. Both these disciplines examine the relationship between language and society; but sociolinguistics was categorized as re-applying its findings to language questions and to linguistics; while the sociology of language was categorized as re-applying its findings to cultural questions and to society, which, of course, includes education.

If those categorizations were accurate, most of the preceding chapters in this book could be described more readily under a sociology of language classification, rather than under a sociolinguistics one. However, as Allen Grimshaw (1987) notes, the differences between the two can easily be exaggerated. And since I resist labels applied to my own work, I am not much troubled by any uncertainty that exists here. For me, the whole is a sprawling system of language games, overlapping and loosely connected in some portions but disconnected nowhere. So I agree with Quine's (1966) view: We need to highlight this notion of a single, sprawling system well ahead of the disciplinary boundaries that are "only useful for deans and librarians" (p. 56).

Even the term 'sociology of language' is becoming a little dated now, because people 'inside' this area are extending their interests not just to language, but to all the sign systems that make up discursive practices. The name seems a little inadequate now as a label for what sociolinguists or sociologists of language often do. The sociology of language tries to bring together the language disciplines of psychology, philosophy, linguistics, and anthropology, as well as all the language concerns of education itself. And although it is described by Joshua Fishman (1978) as "an integrated, interdisciplinary, multi-method, and multi-level approach to the study of natural, sequenced and socially situated language behaviour" (p. 811), it rarely manages to do all these things without a good deal of diffidence. For me, a thoroughgoing sociology of language would focus on things to do with the dominant narratives through which the distribution of power, wealth, position, and privilege are accounted for and justified. So, as well as discourse studies, broadly conceived, this means being interested in things like language loyalty, language as a source and symbol of group solidarity and identity, and language as a tool of social stratification and discrimination. More specifically, my focus is on the social, political, and educational aspects of the relationship between discourse and society (Edwards, 1976). And if sociolinguistics is also concerned with all these things, then I am a sociolinguist, too.

Many applied linguists are deeply involved in issues of human emancipation. And sociolinguists have been too, since the earliest days of their discipline. Yet, these interests are still rather muted in the literature, and they have had relatively little abiding impact on the two disciplines more generally. This is especially true of applied linguistics, with its concentration on language teaching. As one authority observed in a transcribed interview, "the training and development of language teaching experts has been very insensitive to economic, social, and political implications of what happens" (Brumfit, as cited in Phillipson, 1992, p. 254). Indeed, applied linguists involved in the delivery of second language programs to culturally different peoples rarely consult the interests, needs, and values of the program recipients in a critically real way, and this is a cause of cautious concern at least, for some inside the field:

> Where I think things have not been really effective has been in the mediation, the way in which these ideas have been integrated into local, social, political and educational conditions ... I don't think we have brought into the operation an awareness of local conditions nor an effective involvement of local people.... so that one can see these

[practices] as in some sense, even though enlightened and benevolent, well-meaning, but nevertheless to some degree impositional (Widdowson, as cited in Phillipson, 1992, p. 254)

Perhaps, then, it is just this perception that language teaching is the central interest of applied linguistics that distorts the function of applied linguistics and diminishes its real potential. Perhaps this same perception links applied linguistics too closely with the concerns of mainstream linguistics and not enough with the concerns of the other human sciences.

A Constraining Theory of Knowledge

Robert Phillipson (1992) notes that it was linguistics, to the exclusion of the social science disciplines, that dominated theory-building in the first phase of applied linguistics expansion on both sides of the Atlantic and that this was even at the expense of education itself. As he looks back on these beginnings, he sees two rather incompatible theories of knowledge that now underpin work in applied linguistics:

> In one, applied linguistics takes over theories and methods from other areas of scientific study, which then have the status of feeder disciplines; in the other it is an autonomous scientific activity requiring the elaboration of its own theoretical base in relation to its intended applications. When all these ambiguities in the term exist, it is not surprising that there is uncertainty about what 'applied linguistics' stands for. (p. 176)

These two theories of knowledge hardly exhaust the range of epistemologies available to applied linguists, and also to sociolinguists. But these two very different points of entry do suggest a sharp ideological cleavage among adherents of the two disciplines. Clearly, on logical grounds, the first of these theories of knowledge, which borrows its ideas and methods from other areas of scientific study, is much more relevant and appropriate to the study of language teaching, and to the study of language in society too of course. This seems to be so because both disciplines draw on topics and issues treated very seriously in psychology, political science, sociology, anthropology, and especially in education itself.

Yet, for many applied linguists, and for many sociolinguists too, it is the second epistemology that governs their work. For much of the time, work goes on independent of the other disciplinary influences. At best, most references to those influences involve the facile borrowing of technical signs, like 'ideology' and 'structure', without much borrowing of the theoretical baggage that gives those signs their precise rules of use. And this epistemological uncertainty creates tensions for many linguists, trained in the one approach to their work, but very aware of the logic of the other. In the first place, they are able to see the unreasonably narrow scope of their actual activities; but at the same time, they can see 'the things that really exist' in the world relevant to their research: things that their work ignores. Above all, applied linguists and sociolinguists are able to see the social 'things' whose existence is paramount for everyone who inhabits the social world: namely, the discursive products of human interaction.

Obviously, applied linguists and sociolinguists go well beyond the ideal concerns of linguistics itself. They step resolutely into the ontological minefield that is the real world of human social interaction. As applied theorists, their concerns go beyond theories of knowledge and theories of meaning. They reach into questions of being itself. As mentioned in chapter 2, a theory of being about the social world (an ontology), asks 'what things really exist in that world?'; and 'how basic are they?'. Clearly, ontological and epistemological questions are closely related to one another, because claims about what exists in the world almost inevitably involve questions about how what exists can actually be known. And by answering these questions, we become a little clearer about where a disciplinary language game intersects with the real world of social interaction.

For critical realists, that point of contact is where a human science discipline encounters the reasons and accounts that real people offer as their own interpretations of the world. In line with other forms of 'scientific realism', Bhaskar's realism (1986) asserts that people's reasons and accounts are 'real' in the sense that their existence and activity as objects of scientific enquiry are absolutely or relatively independent of the enquiry of which they are the objects. In other words, returning to the quote that opened this chapter, they are *emergent* phenomena requiring realist explanations, and those explanations in turn possess emancipatory implications. Both these cardinal points emerging from the current philosophy of social research seem to be relevant to my theme here in two ways: namely, they urge us to embrace other theories and disciplines and to consult the participants in communities of practice.

Embracing Other Theories and Disciplines.   By consulting the reasons and accounts of relevant actors in other theories and disciplines, researchers learn about the values, beliefs, interests, ideologies, and structures that give rules of use to key signs within those disciplinary language games, and which then position their users in certain ways. As Foucault (1972) argues, this locating of integrated frameworks provides 'a field of possible options': a changing space of interweaving discourses from which certain possibilities for emancipatory action can emerge. We need to search out these spaces between disciplines and theories, and at the same time reduce our emphasis on the tightly constrained questions and themes that emerge from singular language games, and which tend to obscure or ignore the spaces.

In practice, this means much more than engaging in collaborative ventures with people from other disciplines, helpful though those might be, especially when linguists manage to build the world views of those others into their own. More specifically, however, it means expanding the language games of applied linguistics and sociolinguistics by inviting into those games others who can bring a very different worldview. This means, in particular, people from other cultures and social positions who can help linguists confront and examine their biases, their commitments to monodisciplinary dogmas and constraining conceptions of their work, and their over-rigid views about what counts as academic standards, especially the kind of standards that produce a flow of new entrants to the field who are almost always 'people like us'. The result of all this might be programs of work better adapted to the postmodern condition, as it plays itself out in increasingly diverse global settings.

In short, I believe the future for research into language diversity generally lies in interdisciplinary approaches to 'discourse studies', broadly conceived, politically aware, and socially situated; and much less in 1970's conceptions of discovery that were largely tied to natural language on its own studied in 'defined' contexts.

Consulting the Participants in Communities of Practice.   The above paragraphs set out no more than the early steps in this critically real process of research. A second priority is to seek out the views and interests of those whose lives and social arrangements provide the focus of any study undertaken. This means that those conducting a study will consult the full range of participants, in that community of practice, about the aims, scope, and direction of the planned research. Deciding the membership of that community of practice, and who their genuine representatives are, is a research activity itself. Once it is completed, researchers need to know what those people are thinking, and take that into account as evidence in reaching conclusions, or in deciding policy and future practice. But this does not mean uncritically going along with their wishes or preferences.

Rather, it means knowing the things they value, the things that oppress them, and having their interests in mind, even if they appear not to know their best interests.

In other words, if justified by the study's findings, it might be necessary to try to change what many participants think. This becomes a part of the action that follows the research itself. For example, a study of minority language speakers might discover that the people want only English in their elementary schools. If on the evidence this seems to be contrary to their best interests, it might be necessary to change that preference, perhaps through some form of community education (see chap. 2).

Ideally, then, an academic researcher or a teacher-researcher really needs to be 'a local' to some extent; or at least have the approval, the mentoring, the trust, and the advice of those who genuinely represent the local people. From my work with indigenous people, I see clear relevance in the ideas below from Graeme Hingangaroa Smith (1990). He sets out four *models for doing culturally appropriate research,* each one responsive to the interests of participants in a community of practice:

1. *The Mentor Model,* in which authoritative people from the community of practice itself guide and mediate the research.
2. *The Adoption Model,* in which researchers are "adopted" by the cultural community and entrusted to do the research with care and responsibility.
3. *The Power-Sharing Model,* in which researchers seek the help of the community and work together towards the research aims.
4. *The Empowering Outcomes Model,* where the research has emancipatory outcomes for the cultural community as its first objective.

Probably, these ideas are relevant to any kind of field research, not just to research with indigenous people. Researchers approaching any cultural group, including the members of single organizations or the staff of institutions like schools, could benefit from adopting one of these four models. Model 4 seems the most complete approach. It asks researchers to build the community's hopes and aims into their research. In a later section, I mention some of these models again, relating them to actual research studies.

Finally, and as an essential conclusion to all this, a research study in progress needs to consult the reasons and accounts of the participants in such a way as to interpret and understand the different language games that position those people. In language diversity and education research, some current methods and researchers already seem closer to doing all this than others.

REALIST ETHNOGRAPHIES
OF EDUCATIONAL COMMUNICATION

As outlined in chapter 2, Pierre Bourdieu tries to produce a genuine sociological framework for his linguistic discussions by bypassing formal linguistic theories that leave no place for the agent's language performance. He also tries to avoid a narrow focus on the details of social interaction, as occurs in those studies that abstract away from the wider structural features that human interactions reproduce. Despite its lack of formal linguistic rigour, his marketplace analogy allows him to steer a difficult middle course. For him, individual and group language codes are not isolated from the social and the historical conditions and discourses in which they are embedded, or from the embodied dispositions and cultural backgrounds that individuals and groups possess. From linguistics, Bourdieu borrows the idea of 'difference,' but he reapplies it with sociocultural instead of mere linguistic force: Words and other symbols have their real-world semantic power not just because of the relations they contract with one another, but also because of their stylistic significance and their pragmatic value in a complex, stratified, social system.

Indeed, Bourdieu's (1966, 1981, 1984) own field research explores the different types of relations to the world that different sociocultural groups possess. The relations he describes are embedded in different sets of dispositions that different people have towards the material world and towards other people. And all these many relations go well beyond 'what can be said' in natural language. Although Bourdieu's central point is widely misunderstood, it is really an anthropological one: All sociocultural groups possess esteemed cultural capital, but it is not always the same form of capital that is recognized and valued in education, or esteemed in other formal sites. By moving from one cultural 'field' or setting to another, power and significance relationships change, and different types of cultural capital become more or less valued. As we have seen repeatedly throughout this book, schools are one of these cultural fields. Often, in opposition to their emancipatory aims, the function of schools is to value certain privileged language games and discourse practices, while excluding others.

Accordingly, as Bourdieu (1981) acknowledges, there are many possible sets of ethnic, gender, and class interests that are very different from one another and that do require different and perhaps incompatible types of treatment in research and policy. For me, an early step in a critically real approach is to discover these interests by consulting those who have them. A later step is to show these interests to be 'real' and explain their operation. Then, the mandatory, final step is to act on those findings through changes to policy or practice that follow from that newly interpreted and explained evidence. In contrast to this, activities of theory-building, research, and policy-making that ignore the voices of sectional interests can do a great deal of harm. Their distance from the reality of different world views, and from the many sign systems that grow out of different sociocultural conditions and interests, places a severely disabling constraint on what those activities can reveal or achieve. Their findings are inevitably distorted, which jeopardizes hopes for emancipatory reform.

The Ethnography of Communication: Interpreting and Explaining

Beginning his work at about the same time as Bourdieu, the US linguistic anthropologist Dell Hymes (1964) fashioned an approach to the study of language diversity that seems quite consistent with Bourdieu's ideas and Bhaskar's (1986) critical realism. Hymes is concerned with every type of human communication, both verbal and non-verbal, so his ideas seem quite consistent, too, with discursive psychology's interest in sign systems of all kinds (see chap. 1). Finally, the research questions he advances can be stretched to cover the three succinct questions Foucault (1982) asks about language and power: where is discourse; how does it operate; and what does it do? Accordingly, an approach that is something like Hymes' ethnography of communication seems highly relevant to researching the full range of issues covered in this book.

Iffat Farah (1997) and Nancy Hornberger (1995) both survey the development of Hymes' ideas, beginning with his call in 1962 for linguistics to greatly broaden its scope of interests. Dating from that time, he urged linguists to include the study of interaction in identified contexts of situation, where communicative form and function are seen as integrally related to one another. In this approach, language diversity researchers would take a community of practice as their situated context. They would investigate that community's communicative habits as part of a whole, "so that any given use of channel and code takes its place as but part of the resources upon which the members of the community draw" (Hymes, 1964, p. 3). To guide investigations, Hymes (1974) offered an array of components that for him are all involved in the study of communicative events (pp. 53–62).

This array covers elements commonly found in linguistic descriptions everywhere, like the setting or the scene, including close attention to matters of place, time, and physical circumstances. It also covers the genres deployed by interactants, the channels they use as vehicles of communication, its tone and manner, and the language varieties put to work. For the most part, these are things that researchers can discover for themselves without necessarily consulting people or going much beyond their own data and their observations.

Hymes (1971), however, wanted to go much further than this. He insisted that researchers also pay close attention to elements like the cultural definition of the occasion, the norms of community that govern interaction and interpretation, and the characteristics of participants, including their different role-relationships. Now, if researchers are to learn about these additional things, they need a much richer engagement with the reasons and accounts of participants. They need to explore what the participants take for granted in their interactions and what they consider unusual in their situated acts of communication.

Finally, Hymes (1971) directed researchers' attention to identifying the expected outcomes and latent goals of participants, which asks for much more than mere interpretation. This task invites researchers to examine the fundamental values in a community; it asks them to interrogate structural forms of oppression that position a community of practice within wider social and political formations, so that a good explanation of the operation of those structures becomes possible. To do this adequately, the researchers must be steeped in a broad range of theories and disciplines. And their presence in that research community must be welcomed and highly valued.

Since that early intervention by Hymes, and by many others following a similar course, the history of research in language diversity and education has turned slowly but gradually in the direction of an ethnography of educational communication. In fact, most of the more relevant studies cited as evidence throughout this book fall firmly within the scope of an ethnography of communication. Many researchers describe their work in exactly that way, and their outputs are listed in comprehensive surveys of the field (Saville-Troike, 1987, 1989). This evidence of a paradigm shift in language diversity and education research is apparent, too, in the methods that are now influential in the area. For example, most of the 20 or more approaches that attract priority in a survey of research methods (Hornberger & Corson, 1997) explore what Jerome Bruner (1996) calls the 'situatedness' of education in society at large. Pointedly, this shift in direction is consistent with the debate on social research and language ideology that is proceeding more generally (see Silverstein & Urban, 1996) and which increasingly spills into the purview of linguistic anthropology (Duranti, 1997). Indeed, in some places, notably in the United States, most of the more insightful 'sociolinguistics' is currently done by linguistic anthropologists who are offering new conceptions of older, positivist methods. For example, Charles Briggs (1986) critically examines his own use of interviews, enlarging the point and purpose of that method in the process.

Accordingly, many of the more current methods now in use approach the study of human sign systems as an activity positioned in the widest possible con-

text, where form and function are not separated from one another, and where issues of social justice and power are regularly considered. At the same time,
researchers applying these methods are hardly attempting an interpretation of
the universe and all it artifacts. Rather, they set the usual limits on themselves
that the real-world of doing research imposes. In other words, they explore only a
single piece of a complex web of relations, networks, and discourses. But it can
never be a bounded context.

   To bring about these changes in method and substance, all kinds of disciplinary
frameworks are entering the research process. Key ideas are now borrowed from anthropology, psychology, sociology, critical and ideology theory, political science,
and from different approaches to curriculum and policy studies in education itself.
As important, the application of these integrated ideas is becoming more completely
theorized than it once was, in the sense that the borrowed rules of use for words and
other signs are closer to the rules of use that apply in those disciplines.

   These more ethnographic approaches see the self-same world that Bhaskar
(1986) sees. It is a world best approached by seeking out the reasons and accounts
people offer to describe the things they value and the things that oppress them. Expressed in their many different systems of signs, these reasons and accounts offer a
necessary starting point for a study. Researchers then try to show the reality of
those structural influences, explaining their operation. And, in general, this approach seems to work well when the different methodological tools used in participant observation are applied. This includes too those participant observation
methods that had their origins when positivism still held sway, and which often
need some form of rehabilitation when put to work for more interpretative purposes. For example, positivist methods like structured interviews and observations, or questionnaires, all have weaknesses when used in an interpretative
research program. But each can be improved in different ways, partly at least by
teaming it with other methods.

   At the same time, many currently used research methods have emerged from
the same post-positivist critique that produced Bhaskar's theorizing. A fuller list
might begin with the following: critical discourse analysis and the other approaches to discourse and content analysis that are now in use; historical analysis
and historical critique; conversational analysis; ideology critique; critical ethnography; and the critical triangulation of different sets of methods. In some limited
way, each of these methods tries to uncover the reality of the accounts and reasons
that suggest the influence of social structures in research theories. When they are
used as multiple approaches in the study of the same phenomenon, these methods
can provide compelling evidence to help uncover and even explain that reality. So,
they provide us with some of the deepest possible means for doing emancipatory
social research (Thompson, 1990). They offer a form of 'depth hermeneutics' that
both interprets and explains human phenomena.

   Now, if all this seems abstracted from the actual world of language diversity and
education, it is easy to bring it back into sharp focus by looking at schools and

classrooms. Those who have used ethnography of communication to study children's language in natural contexts, say that teachers can understand their students' language and learning much better if they know more about children's daily lives in their own community settings. Indeed, a few schools and teachers in some parts of the world are making radical changes to their pedagogy, assessment, and curriculum procedures after doing ethnography of communication research in their local communities. Good ethnography of educational communication seems to have the following basic criteria:

- it involves prolonged and repetitive observation within the actual context
- it disturbs the process of interaction as little as possible
- many of its instruments are developed in the field
- many of the important questions emerge as the study proceeds
- it consults the reasons and accounts of people in the community under study
- it interprets the full range of sign systems used by humans
- it pays close attention to issues of power and discrimination
- it tries to identify values, norms, and structures impacting on the situation
- it tries to understand the sociocultural knowledge participants bring to the context and generate within it and the sign systems they use in those processes

Ethnography of communication comes in several guises (Farah, 1997). These include classroom ethnography (Watson-Gegeo, 1997), micro-ethnography (Garcez, 1997), critical ethnography (May, 1997), and interactional sociolinguistics (Hornberger, 1995; Rampton, 1995). This last is a close cousin of Hymes' (1974) approach. It received its most characteristic and earliest expression in the work of John Gumperz (1976, 1982). All these versions are being used extensively now in the study of bilingual and multicultural classrooms (Martin-Jones, 1997). Although they are increasingly deployed as classroom research methods by teacher researchers themselves (McCarty, 1997), my direction here now turns to exemplary academic uses of methods of this type. Each of the four case studies that follows contributed to the literature that informed one or more of the four central chapters in this book.

FOUR EXAMPLES OF METHODS AT WORK

1. A Bilingual Education Research Study

The sub-title of Rebecca Freeman's (1996) study of dual-language planning at Oyster Bilingual School really captures one of the key points in this chapter and this book as a whole. As one of her respondents explained in interview: "It's much more than language" (p. 557). Using detailed discourse analyses, Freeman shows how the many micro-interactions between educators and students in that school combine with one another to resist many of the oppressive discourses that trouble users of minority languages in the wider society and in other, more conventional, school sites. The discourses circulating throughout Oyster school promote linguistic and cultural diversity as "a resource to be developed by all students, and not a problem that minority students must overcome in order to participate and achieve in schools" (Freeman 1998, p. 233). In this sense, Oyster's 'language-as-resource' orientation (Ruíz, 1984) resists the 'language-as-problem' orientation that still characterizes most bilingual and ESL programs in the United States. Moreover, Freeman's (1996) study itself illustrates the value of using ethnographic and discourse analytic methods of data collection and analysis for studying language diversity and education. Furthermore, the feedback she gave to the staff and the interactions she had with people in the school—before, during, and after her research—make this study fit the *Empowering Outcomes Model* mentioned in an earlier section.

Interviews and Discourse Analyses. Freeman's research assumes that schools, like all social institutions, are constructed realities made by people through discourses around their actions, beliefs, values, and interests. These, in turn, reflect and shape the abstract, over-riding discourses that constitute the institution, while also reflecting and shaping the discourses of wider social formations. In other words, the signs and symbols used in the many language games shared by a school's adherents shape the organization in certain ways rather than in others, giving a school its unique character and values. In her efforts to understand the effects of this ever-dynamic, ideological process on a school's language policies and practices, Freeman designed her research activities to engage all the levels of authority in the institution and all the power relations among those levels. Accordingly, she analyzed the texts of open-ended interviews conducted with people from various levels of authority. These analyses told her about the political interests of policymakers, and the tacit or the overt goals of the school's policy for its various target populations. Then, by triangulating these analyses with other searches of official policy statements, she untangled some of the ways in which the sociopolitical concerns of the school's leaders affected the interpretation and implementation of its language policy.

More specifically, to get this insider's understanding of how the Oyster program functioned, she held ongoing, open-ended interviews and conversations with policymakers, administrators, teachers, parents, and students over a 2-year period. Most of these exchanges were taped and transcribed to provide data she could work with. Using *frame analysis* (following Tannen, 1993), she looked closely at each transcript, trying to interpret people's accounts of what the problems were and for whom; what their goals were for the various target populations; and their sense of whether Oyster had been successful or not. This allowed her to look across texts within similar levels of authority, such as the teachers' level or the administrators'; and to identify recurring themes. For example, she found there was much agreement about the nature of the problems that language minority students face in mainstream US schools; and much agreement about how Oyster managed to soften the effects of those problems. Furthermore, when she compared the different levels of authority with one another, and then too with the policies and other written texts circulating in the school, she was able to see coherence in different people's accounts of the things that made Oyster's bilingual program a successful one. In other words, the intertextual analysis that she did provided an account of the school's ideal language plan as it lay tacitly in the discourse of key participants.

Classroom Observation Studies.   Because her aim was to identify the real principles underlying the language policy at work, Freeman set her analysis of the leaders' discourse alongside her own observations of classrooms at work. At this further level of triangulation, she used a more conventional approach to doing ethnography of communication. Her aim was to find the speech situations and activities that really constituted the school community. The research questions used in her analysis emerged from the discourses she witnessed. In particular, using the ideal plan as a useful backdrop, she evaluated the distribution and valuing of languages in the school; and the valuing of different speakers relative to one another. This revealed discrepancies between the ideal and the actual, which could often be put down to conflicts between discourses at the institutional and the intrusive societal levels of context.

To see how the ideal language plan worked in classrooms, Freeman spent a year with the school's sixth grade; and another year with one of the kindergarten classes. Working as a participant-observer with students and teachers, she made extensive field notes, taping and transcribing interactions as she went, and collecting samples of students' work. She drew on as many sign systems as possible in her attempt to get an insider's understanding of the situation. While doing so, she continually sought comments about her interpretations from the teachers, in this way confirming or disconfirming her own conclusions, and helping herself find new directions and new insights. In spot-checks, she also compared her results from these two grades with activities in other grades in the school. Then, when her analysis was written up, she sought feedback on it from the school's administrators, who explained how they were trying to address discrepancies between the ideal vision they had in mind, and its implementation. Again, a key to interpreting those discrepancies was the unique location of the Oyster program itself. Like programs in any school, this school's curriculum was still positioned by the intrusive discourses of wider social formations, which still helped reproduce oppressive conditions for all the language minority students at Oyster. But despite the irresistible weight of these external factors, schools can sometimes challenge and soften them, in this way better meeting the interests of their students. Sometimes, they transform the wider discourses in the process. Indeed, this became a goal of those behind the dual-language policy at Oyster Bilingual School. Freeman's (1996) study explains how successful they were in meeting this goal.

Interpretation and Explanation.   Originally, the school's bilingual plan was a
mandatory response to the US Bilingual Education Act. However, the school's staff
gradually came to see it as a clear alternative to the existing discourses about language
use and minority group participation in schooling. As mentioned, they came to see
the 'language-as-problem' orientation of mainstream educational and societal discourse as discriminatory; and they rejected it in favor of one that saw 'lan-
guage-as-a-resource'. To make this different orientation work, the Oyster school had
to take itself very seriously as a single community with common interests and common goals, rather than a set of distinct communities of different ethnocultural groups
often in conflict with each other. In fact, the way the school represents itself symboli-
cally, articulates this notion. For example, the parent organization is known as the
'community council'; and all the students wear shirts identifying them as members of
'Oyster Community Bilingual School.' Moreover, these signs seem to permeate the
more mundane and practical discourses of the place. As one parent explained, "You
know, the great thing about this school is it's like a community that crosses language,
cultural, and class lines" (Freeman, 1996, p. 568).

From Freeman's own reading of policy documents and interviews, it seems that
Oyster's bilingual program began as a grass-roots effort coordinated by an active
Hispanic community struggling to meet the needs of a growing Latino population in
Washington, D.C. They convinced the school administrators to move to a 'two-way'
bilingual program (see chapter 5) by recruiting 20 experienced native-Span-
ish-speaking teachers from different South American countries. This two-way program served as an English acquisition plan for the language minority students, and
as a Spanish acquisition plan for students with only limited Spanish proficiency. Its
aim was for all students to develop academic competence sufficient to succeed in
content classes taught in Spanish and in English. Clearly, then, this goal challenged
dominant US discourses about minority language education that emphasize bilingual education that leads to monolingualism in English. Instead, the school promoted first-language maintenance, giving value to a form of additive bilingualism.
In this school, both languages were seen as resources to be valued.

Oyster's struggle against mainstream educational and societal discourses was
also reflected in other aspects of its program and practices. For instance, the teaching staff represented a wide range of cultures and language backgrounds. As confirmed in Freeman's interviews, these teachers helped students promote, value,
and maintain their identities; and they asked students to look critically at the ways
different groups were represented in curriculum content. Moreover, the interaction
in the classrooms she observed was structured to allow students with different discourse norms to negotiate meaning with each other. And all of this was evaluated
using dynamic performance-based assessments, in both languages.

Nevertheless, while Oyster's discourses managed to resist wider discourses about
language use and intergroup relations, there was still some inconsistency between the
ideal plan and its implementation. Most of the discrepancies seemed to come from
structural factors to do with the way schools are organized, the way teachers are

trained and recruited, and the demographic practicalities of the setting in which schools are located. For example, the school's monolingual teachers at first resisted the idea of a two-way bilingual program. Unimpressed by arguments about the social justice of such a program, or much aware of its educational importance, they were initially brought around mainly by arguments about the economic and security benefits the local community would derive as a result of the new initiative. For the staff, wider understanding came later, through a summer institute where different groups of professionals and community members studied and debated these matters. Clearly, then, Oyster's bilingual policy was not handed down from above, as one for the administrators and teachers to implement uncritically. It came up from the community itself. It reflected and responded to people's expressed interests and values.

Other discrepancies were also apparent at the time of Freeman's study. For instance, at that time, there were no Salvadoran teachers in the school, even though the largest Latino student population in Oyster and in the city generally was from El Salvador. The school was aware of this anomaly, however, and the principal already had alternative plans in mind for rectifying it. In addition, all the school's Spanish-dominant teachers could speak English, but not all the English-dominant teachers could speak Spanish. So this imbalance in professional background seemed to send a subtle message to students about the unequal prestige of these two languages, certainly in educational contexts. Furthermore, the policy that English-dominant teachers should speak and be spoken to only in English, and Spanish-dominant teachers should use only Spanish, was often subverted in practice. While Freeman saw hardly any codeswitching to Spanish by English-dominant teachers, there was much shifting to English by the Spanish-dominant teachers. Despite the targeted recruitment of staff, it seems that, in an English-dominant US, there are still limits to what a school like Oyster can do to make Spanish count equally. Nevertheless, through internal measures like common evaluation policies and balanced promotion criteria, the school does seem to be making Spanish count more than it formerly did, in the Oyster community. For example, both the native Spanish-speaking and the native English-speaking students were required to take a basic skills test in Spanish.

There seemed fewer inconsistencies in putting the school's key policy of cultural pluralism to work. Freeman often observed students developing good intercultural communication skills, and working well in diverse groupings in classrooms. They were also heard talking about discrimination, and solving problems of bias inside and outside school. For example, the children responded positively when teachers treated individuals or diverse groups of students fairly; they responded negatively when the contributions of women were omitted from the curriculum, or when the media or local police treated racial groups in stereotyping ways. And they were able to deploy diverse discourses in doing these things: the students might speak out to the teacher in class, or circulate petitions and protest letters, or write stories setting out some alternative and fairer construction of reality. But despite this critical engagement with diversity issues, Freeman still found divisions in students' social interaction inside the school; and these replicated the racial, ethnic, or class divisions in society at large. Indeed, this is something that concerned the teachers and the administrators. Again, Freeman concludes that the interaction between the Oyster educational discourse and mainstream US societal discourses accounted for this inconsistency between ideal policy and actual practices. Societal norms of interaction in Washington, DC, as reinforced by the mass media, rarely show sociocultural groups interacting in integrated ways. Indeed, it is not uncommon for integrated interactions to be negatively stereotyped in these wider and highly influential discourses.

2. A Study of Cultural Discourse Norms

Although this study by Alice Eriks-Brophy and Martha Crago (1994) is much more modest in scope than the Freeman study, it still fits most of the criteria I am arguing for in this chapter, with the exception perhaps of much explicit treatment of power issues in the wider society that position and shape the research context. Nevertheless, their study of three kindergartens and three first-grade classrooms in Northern Quebec, all taught by Inuit teachers, clearly reaches into structural issues of power and discrimination in mainstream schools and classrooms, issues reviewed more fully in chapter 3. Their research examines two key aspects of the organization of classroom discourse: teacher routines of Initiation-Response-Evaluation (IRE) and turn-allocation formats. The two researchers look at transformations that occur in Inuit interactions when cultural values and congruous communicative exchanges are introduced by Inuit teachers who are fully inside the sign systems and language games of the aboriginal culture itself. The two researchers document how Inuit discourse norms appear naturally in classroom interactions between Inuit teachers and Inuit students, and they suggest the ways Western educational modes of discourse might be transformed by accommodating non-mainstream cultural discourse norms.

In one key respect, this study contrasts with the majority of those discussed in chapter 3. The latter often focus on aspects of classroom interaction that seem problematic, which the researchers then try to rectify by making adaptations to the communicative process. In contrast, Eriks-Brophy and Crago examine aspects of classroom interaction that were proceeding smoothly for both teachers and students. They document how participants were co-constructing the classroom interactions and how they all interrelated during these semi-formal conversations. At the same time, these transformations in the discursive setting were bidirectional. Because the culture of the Inuit students was influential in these classrooms, the local culture's values and norms affected interactions. But because the classrooms were also sited within a non-aboriginal educational system, the discourses of the local culture were constantly affected by the intruding norms and practices of the mainstream. Many of the transformations observed were brought about deliberately by the Inuit teachers, who were naturally motivated to promote learning in more culturally congruous ways. Consequently, the researchers argue that the transformational perspective they adopted was quite different from the one taken in other research on discourse norms that identifies and examines *discontinuities* in educational exchanges.

Ethnographically Informed Conversational Analyses.   The focus of Eriks-Brophy and Crago's (1994) study was the teacher-led lesson. They documented discourse patterns and elicitation interactions used between Inuit teachers and Inuit students; they then compared these with the more mainstream classroom interactions described by Mehan (1980). In this way, the researchers hoped to show the natural ways that the patterns of classroom discourse used by mainstream teachers were being transformed by their Inuit teachers so as to achieve a more culturally congruent style of classroom interaction. Their data set was collected over a period of 2 years; it was taken from a variety of sources to provide the multi-layered, multi-modal base essential for ethnographic research. All six classes videotaped in the study were taught in Inuktitut by Inuit teachers who varied in age, educational level, second language background, and teaching experience.

An important feature of this research was the value it placed on the advice and support of two local cultural experts whose participation represented the reasons and accounts of the local community. In this respect, then, Eriks-Brophy and Crago's study fits within the *Mentor Model* mentioned in an earlier section. These cultural experts were both very experienced Inuit teachers who acted as informants and who brought a deep knowledge of their own Inuktitut language and the Inuit culture. They were chosen by 'informed subject selection', a process in which experts who are especially knowledgeable in the field of inquiry are identified through comments made by people linked to the research in various direct or indirect ways. One expert was a 62-year-old teacher of Inuktitut, with 25 years experience. She was a respected elder in the community. The other was a 38-year-old pedagogical counsellor, with 20 years teaching experience. These two cultural experts viewed all the videotapes made for the study; and they commented on the discourses used by the teachers. For Eriks-Brophy and Crago, these experts were able to clarify how the many practices in these classrooms actually reflected traditional Inuk values and socialization norms.

Again, there were several levels at which sets of data were collected. The first layer comprised 40 hours of videotaping, accompanied by several hundred pages of observation or field notes, and extensive interviews with teachers or with the two cultural experts. The observation notes and the transcribed interviews were coded using broad labels. These categories were derived from the literature, or from the Inuit teachers' own stated concepts about important aspects of their classroom work. As a result, some of these categories reflected the teachers' personal educational aims and their beliefs about what constitutes good teaching practice for them, rather than the aims that teachers in mainstream classrooms or experts in pedagogy might prefer. The list of categories was also informed by the long experience one of the researchers had teaching aboriginal children, and by her knowledge about what tends to work or not work in classrooms like these. A partial list of categories used in the coding appears below:

Teacher

Authority and discipline	*Correction and modelling*
ignoring bad behaviour	encouraging talk
singling out individuals	praise
Non-interference	physical closeness
following child's lead	repetition
supervision	individual/group help
control	checking in
teacher as helper	maintaining face
	evaluation

Students

Behaviour	*Peer interaction*
listening	overlaps
attentiveness	peer modes
talkativeness	peer coaching
teasing	cooperation
movement in class	sharing
active participation	competition
passive participation	physical closeness
independence	sex role differences
getting help	
obedience	

Lesson

Activities	*Values*
individual	cooperation
group	equality
repetition routines	non-interference

question-answer   maintaining face

storytelling   obedience

games   respect for others

free play   sharing

clean-up

transitions

The second layer of data began with commentaries on the videotapes offered by the teachers themselves, the cultural experts, or other Inuit teachers working in teacher education courses. The two cultural experts then helped select single, video-taped sequences showing each teacher giving an oral language lesson. Certain criteria informed their choice. First, the sequence had to conform to a linear lesson structure (Mehan, 1980) by comprising an opening phase, an instructional phase, and a closing phase. Second, the sequence had to be defined as the target activity for the lesson on the teacher's plan of work. And finally, the sequence had to be reasonably compact, to avoid unwieldly transcription and translation difficulties. This meant that the length of these target sequences ranged from about 7 to 16 minutes. Below are brief descriptions of two of the six sequences, one from each grade level:

Teacher 1: BLACK
Prior to the activity described, the children engaged in a whole group cut-and-paste activity making a flower. Children were then called to sit on the floor by the teacher. Not all the students had completed the previous activity. All the objects used in the lesson were previously assembled by the teacher. The lesson was an object-naming sequence centred on the Inuktitut word for "black."
Grade level: Kindergarten.
General activity type: Question-answer, repetition routine.
Full class of eight students was present.
Language used was Inuktitut, the first language of all the participants.

Teacher 4: Insect Names
The students were working on a math activity prior to the activity described. They were then called to sit on the floor by the teacher. The lesson was a picture-naming sequence about insects.
Grade level: Grade 1.
Materials used: picture cards of insects with the insect names written in Inuktitut on the back.
General activity type: Question-answer, repetition-routine, discussion.
Twelve students out of a total of 14 were present.
Language used was Inuktitut, the first language of all the participants.

Expert translators whose backgrounds were in the same Inuit region transcribed and translated each sequence from the Inuktitut into English. Then, the transcripts were entered into a data base system (MacWhinney & Snow, 1990) for storage and analysis. Coding categories were derived from four sources: categories compiled for research in multicultural classrooms by Ervin-Tripp and Wong Fillmore (1988), the actual discourses of aboriginal children, as described elsewhere in the research literature, a series of categories found in Mehan's description (1980) of classroom interactions and, finally, categories informed by the data itself. The different sets of coding categories reveal the researchers' interest in capturing a relatively wide range of verbal and non-verbal discourse types. They include things like exclamations, acknowledgments, and prompts. The categories also suggest the interest that the researchers had in exploring the real discursive worlds of the students. For example, under the broad heading of 'Communicative Intent' they included items that registered students seeking or giving an opinion, providing a personal experience, or revealing an internal state of mind or feeling.

Interpretation and Explanation. To reveal the different areas where transformations of discourse had occurred, the frequencies for the different sets of coding categories were calculated and compared with the frequencies found in Mehan's (1980) study of typical discourse norms in mainstream classrooms. Based on their data, it was clear to Eriks-Brophy and Crago that Inuit classroom discourse is not organized around the IRE pattern of lesson structuring (initiation, response, evaluation) that is so typical of mainstream classroom interactions (Cazden, 1988). Instead, the Inuit teachers tended to promote longer interactional sequences involving much more group participation. Overt teacher evaluation of student responses was usually missing unless some serious error had been made by the children; and, even here, more indirect forms of evaluation were normally used. For example, in most cases, student responses were signalled as 'correct' by the teacher simply moving the talk along, as the following extract reveals:

(Describing some birds they can see on a filmstrip)

Teacher: His beak. What colour is it?
Students: Orange.
Teacher: What about his head?
Students: Umm, black eyes, umm black. Black.
Teacher: What about his neck?
Students: White.
Teacher: What about his body?
Students: Umm, brown.
Teacher: At the end of his feathers, what colour is it?
Students: Umm, white. White.
         (pause)
Teacher: That one has some leaves.

Although the researchers report that overt evaluations of individual student performance were rare when compared with mainstream classrooms, there was some
variation in teacher interventions when the class as a whole was successful in producing a desired response; or when only a few members produced the desired response. But even this intervention usually involved indirect, rather than any
obvious, indication of evaluation. These indirect evaluations typically were repeti-
tions of student replies, or acknowledgements and requests for acknowledgment,
or the teacher modelling the desired response. This finding also contrasts with the
high level of teacher-intervention found in mainstream classrooms. When the Inuit
teachers intervened, they preferred to put emphasis on the information requested,
rather than on the correctness of the children's contributions. So, they avoided
making personal judgements about individual responses:

(Teacher shows a picture card)
Students: *Ammaukaluk* [a type of insect]
Teacher: *Ammaukaluk.* Where does it live?
Students: Inside the stomach.
Others: In the intestines.
Teacher: In the intestines.

(Teacher shows the next card)
Students: *Qaurulliq* [a black beetle with a white forehead]
Teacher: *Qaurulliq.* Why is it called *qaurulliq?*
Students: Because it has a forehead.
One Student: His forehead is white.
Teacher: His forehead has white on it. It's *qaurulliq.*

In addition, Eriks-Brophy and Crago (1994) found teachers using peer models
very effectively in the organization of discourse, the correction of errors, and
group activities. So, the discourse seemed to progress by repetition or subtle techniques for building onto peer models found inside the group responses, rather than
by the regulatory intervention of teacher discourse. One teacher commented on all
of this use of peer teaching: "Students can't learn by themselves. No one pushes
them to learn if they are by themselves, listening only to the teacher and not to each
other. Students don't learn alone. They need the others to learn from" (p. 114). But
there is more to all this than mere teacher preferences. It was clear that deep-seated
cultural values were playing themselves out in these discourse norms, as the researchers discovered for themselves during the interviews. The teachers freely ad-
mitted that their most important goal was to facilitate peer exchanges: "[my goal
is] that my students know how to get along and help each other"; "that my students
learn to cooperate"; and "that my students respect each other" (p. 114).

In general, the researchers found an emphasis in Inuit classroom exchanges on
listening to others, rather than on talkativeness, individual performance, or participation. This not only allowed teachers to make full use of peer models for eliciting
desired responses, which reduced their need to intervene as regulators and evalua-

tors, but it also promoted important Inuit values like respect for others, cooperation, and communal responsibility. At the same time, this organization of
classroom exchanges placed no obvious demands on the students to participate if
they felt uncomfortable doing so. They could remain silent, listening and observing the others in a setting where the equality of all group members was respected
without any competitive demands, potential loss of face, or fear of standing out
from the rest of the class. Yet, the students were still encouraged to take more than
usual responsibility for their own learning and for the progress of their group as a
whole, which Eriks-Brophy and Crago claim is more consistent with central Inuit
values about the importance of group cooperation.

Here, the use of teacher power was much reduced in every classroom observed. In its place, students were freer to vary certain aspects of the lessons and
shape classroom dialogue. Indeed, the evaluation tail of the IRE sequence was
removed entirely for these Inuit children or was so vestigial and unimportant as
to be hardly in evidence at all. Moreover, the teachers avoided both criticism and
praise of individuals within the peer groups. At the same time, these very different practices raised a concern for Eriks-Brophy and Crago about the later education of these same Inuit students when they contact very different discursive
norms and power arrangements in classrooms taught by non-Inuit teachers. In
this school board in Northern Quebec, that policy change usually happens at the
grade 3 level. And it involves more than a change from Inuktitut to English as the
language of instruction. Total changes occur in the cultural orientation of the
teachers, in the discourse norms used for learning and teaching, and in the cultural values and forms of cultural capital that inform and legitimate those norms.
But this is only one of the important power issues that these researchers raise for
others to think about.

Relatedly, at a time in their history when aboriginal peoples around the world are
demanding more control of their own community resources, including greater influence over the powerful social formations that position them as peoples, and greater
levels of emancipation in general, their ability to exploit future opportunities largely
rests with the education of their youth. As Eriks-Brophy and Crago (1994) conclude,
if aboriginal children as adults are going to help drive their cultures forward, they
need to be aware of the values and discourse norms that bind them to one another so
they can face their futures with confidence in themselves and awareness of their own
cultural background. Examining the ways that aboriginal teachers transform classroom interactions so as to incorporate community values and discourse norms into
those spaces seems a small but necessary step in that direction.

3.   A Study of Gendered Discourse Norms

Bourdieu's (1981) idea of symbolic capital is the starting point for Penny
Eckert's (1990) study of 'cooperative competition' in adolescent 'girl talk.' This
special form of cultural capital is important for young women to acquire and deploy in high schools where their influence commonly depends on the painstaking

accumulation of moral authority (see chap. 6). Through participating in single-sex talk, girls get valuable opportunities to develop the kinds of 'symbolic capital' so esteemed in high schools, where the stress on competitive interaction puts females at a disadvantage because it so often conflicts with their own acquired discourse norms. This 'girl talk' is a typically female speech event that involves long, detailed, and personal discussions about other people, norms, and beliefs. In it, girls learn about all these things, acquiring their own gendered discourse norms in the process and measuring their symbolic capital in respect to those norms.

A community of students scatters symbolic capital on its members by awarding different levels of popularity to different people. And being popular is a near-essential part of moral authority in high schools. It is especially valued by girls, again because they tend to have fewer avenues of influence open to them. Yet, their efforts to garner popularity provide girls with a dilemma that Eckert (1990) describes in her article: "Because popularity is accorded by the community as a whole, it requires not only likability but also sufficient, well-managed visibility to draw the community's attention to that likability" (p. 95). The very act of becoming visible means engaging in discreet acts of competition. It also means mixing with prestigious people. Unfortunately, either of these activities can easily compromise a girl's likability.

The conflict embedded in this dilemma is played out in the teenage talk Eckert analyzes. Choosing a form of participatory discourse analysis as her method, she examines a 2-hour stretch of group talk by six adolescent girls and herself. In this long session, the young women build an ephemeral but sheltered community for themselves, where their own norms are cooperatively defined through some careful processes of negotiation that always seem to end in consensus.

A "Participatory" Discourse Analysis.   This tape-recorded session was only a small part of a much larger participant observation study in a suburban high school, during which Eckert followed one graduating class right through their last two years of schooling. The six girls in this study were members of that graduating class. Eckert's knowledge of the broader ethnographic context, and her long-term familiarity with the participants and their classmates, allowed her to create a setting where this interaction could take place in a fairly naturalistic way. After asking one of the participants to gather some friends together, just to talk about 'stuff,' she joined in the talk herself. The six students, anonymously called Karen, Betty, Miriam, Carol, June, and Pamela, were at the end of their junior high school year. Each girl wore a microphone attached to a separate tape-recorder that each controlled herself. Eckert notes the preference in sociolinguistic studies for making any tape-recording as unobtrusive as possible, but she has found in her own work that, where individuals do their own recording in group sessions, they seem less aware of the machines than they would otherwise be.

The episode reported in the article was the first time these girls had met as a group since junior high school. Eckert says that, like any reunion, this meeting prompted the girls to measure their own social progress against each other, so the interaction became quite competitive at times, with each girl striving to prove to herself and to the others that she had 'done well' in the interim. As mentioned, this raised a dilemma for the participants. While still maintaining her likability, each had to show that she had succeeded in the competitive marketplace of the school. And just the act of flaunting her personal success meant competing with the others, although the on-going quest for likability made it impossible for the girls to compete too openly. Moreover, because all had followed different school trajectories, they needed to reach some agreement about what 'doing well' really meant for them as a group. So, they spent much of their time negotiating a set of norms that would cover the accomplishments and beliefs of each one of them.

The group's discussion spanned a variety of topics. After they had settled themselves around a table, Eckert began the interaction by asking how the girls managed to find things out in school. Discussion then moved quickly to ways of keeping unfavourable things from circulating too far, while still allowing more favorable information about themselves to leak out. This raised the subject of 'boys', especially how girls could let boys in the school know that they 'liked' them. In her article, Eckert focuses on this discussion of boys, because it reveals typical devices and strategies that helped the group establish norms of consensus negotiation. It also illustrates the two themes she discerns in the girls' meeting: concern about their popularity; and concern for their independence.

To show the girls' exchanges in a text of discourse analysis, Eckert shapes her transcript as a musical score written for seven different 'instruments'. This arrangement shows the contribution each speaker made, including her silences and her uses of prosody. So, this musical score is an attempt to represent as clearly as possible all the on-going relations between the utterances. In setting out her text in this way, Eckert also uses a standardized orthography, marking overlapping contributions as precisely as regularized spelling allows. She numbers the successive, uninterrupted lines of speech in sequence; and then she uses these numbers for reference purposes in her article's discussion. She indicates laughter with exclamation marks (!) but, sometimes, with the letter 'h' to suggest a different kind of inhaled laughter. Finally, her use of blank spaces indicates the length of pauses in the dialogue.

In the paper as a whole, four episodes of discourse are treated. The partial one cited below covers only the opening lines of the first episode. Here, the group had started to talk about how best to behave with boys, especially the pros and cons of using certain boys as go-betweens with other boys. Pamela has a disclosure to make on this topic, and the rest of the group are tantalized at the prospect of hearing about it:

1
June:	… it just didn't work out.
Miriam:	No they don't.
Betty:	
Karen:	Oh third parties NEVER work.
Carol:	
Pamela:	
Eckert:	

_____

2
June:	
Miriam:	I don't think so.
Betty:	
Karen:	DON'T EVER use a third party.
Carol:	They do SOMEtimes.
Pamela:	They do sometimes !!
Eckert:	

_____

3
June:	
Miriam:	
Betty:	hhh!!!
Karen:	It's never worked for me. !!!
Carol:	This is the voice of experience.
Pamela:	
Eckert:	Apparently it just worked over here.

_____

4
June:	
Miriam:	Yeah I know!!
Betty:	
Karen:	God now I'm dying to know !!!
Carol:	yeah
Pamela:	((Cough)) ! yeah !!
Eckert:	really?

_____

5
June:
Miriam: Let's see here's gossip. We all=
Betty: !
Karen:
Carol:
Pamela: ! ! !
Eckert: Are you dying to tell it or not?! !

———————

6
June:
Miriam: =want to hear it. Come on, tell us.
Betty: ! ! ! ! ! ! !   ! !   Come on Pam !
Karen: ! ! !   Come on, Pamela.
Carol: Everybody just lean =
Pamela:
Eckert:

———————

7
June:
Miriam: Yeah I know.
Betty: ! ! ! ! hhh
Karen: ! !
Carol: =forward. What was it? um Okay we might as well get it out.
Pamela: ((Cough))   ! !   yeah right.
Eckert:

Interpretation and Explanation.   When taken together, Eckert's rich collection of episodes allows her to make generalizations about the importance of shared norms for a community engaging in girl talk. She discusses how the negotiation of those norms reaffirms the group's sense of solidarity. Her episodes show a temporary community at work creating itself through its interaction as the girls link stories about their earlier lives and present selves. She describes their discussion as a long sequence of claims, counterclaims, and negotiated consensuses. First, one girl makes a statement of opinion or belief that someone else contradicts. Others then take sides in this dialectical process, until group consensus is negotiated by finding a new position that assimilates both original positions or perhaps by finding a position that reshapes the two into a new agreement. Indeed, not one topic is allowed to conclude without an ex-pression of consensus. By working their way towards an accumulation of these agree-ments on minor topics, the girls manage to reach a consensus on more general and important topics.

Sometimes, this process of reaching consensus positions the girls so that they seem to agree to things rather unwillingly. Seduced by the hegemony of the discourses that surround them, they cannot argue against the logic used to build that consensus. This happens partly because the logic itself depends on real-world illustrations. The girls use these as evidence to support minor points of agreement that they gradually weave into a greater consensus, even though in the end this can seem more flimsy for some girls than it is for others. Eckert argues that the special norms governing these forms of interaction are derived from the place that women and girls occupy in society. Their freedom to function in the world depends on them understanding and controlling the norms they learn in girl talk events, like the one she describes.

4.   Non-Standard Varieties: A Sociolinguistic Ethnography

Monica Heller's book (1999) could be used to illustrate research methods for any of the four main chapters of this book. In various ways, she deals with gendered norms of interaction, bilingualism, and different cultural discourse norms. However, I am using her work here just to illustrate the topic of non-standard varieties. Her sociolinguistic ethnography is the story of one Toronto school in the early 1990s. In it, Heller and her team of researchers describe and explain the language practices of everyday life in this school. Her aim was to uncover the social interests at play in that setting, interests that, for some students more than for others, are clearly prejudiced by the different levels of valuation allotted to different language varieties.

Heller sees the problem of evaluating language 'quality' as a long-standing one that has its roots in nineteenth-century Romantic nationalism, where the related ideology of giving social preferment to monolingualism is also rooted. For her, the differently ordered conceptions of language quality that have evolved, create he-gemonic relations among ethnocultural groups, among social classes, and among men and women. As indicated in chapter 4, France has built the most elaborate in-stitutional mechanism for regulating language quality, so the ideology of correct-ness seems even more pervasive for speakers of French varieties, wherever they are spoken, than it is for the users of other languages. Heller sees the half-million Franco-Ontarians as particularly beset by problems of language quality, inescap-ably positioned as they are by daily contacts with English, the dominant world lan-guage as well as the language of power in their province, and also enmeshed in disagreements about the social significance and functions of different varieties of French. Accordingly, Heller's study of the role and place of Franco-Ontarian vari-eties of French in this francophone school seems a valuable case study of 'non-standard' research methods at work.

An Ethnographic Account of a Single School's Discursive Sites.   Supported by a team of colleagues and research assistants, Heller worked at L'École
Champlain for more than 3 years. On the one hand, her team's long and close engagement with the school suggests that their study would fit properly under the *Adoption
Model* mentioned in an earlier section. At the same time, however, the *Centre de
recherches en éducation franco-ontarienne,* from which the team came, has a much
wider mandate: to study the education of this large francophone minority in Ontario
and disseminate findings and critical recommendations. Accordingly, their study fits
well within the *Empowering Outcomes Model* of culturally appropriate research.

Heller's aim was to understand the institutional perspectives of this school of
more than 400 students, including the perspectives of all its agents. To do this, she
studied participants at every level, including school board and school administrators, teachers, support staff, parents, and students. Her team's focus on the whole
school's perspective had consequences for how the researchers were seen by teachers and students. As Heller admits herself, in any school, an adult is more likely to be
viewed as a kind of teacher-figure than as a student, which constrains the kinds of relationship that researchers can readily have with students. In the previous study,
Penny Eckert (1990) was able to make herself a familiar and trusted sharer in the
girls' lives at school. But the focus of Heller's team went well beyond the immediate
discourses that position individuals or small groups of students. Rather, their project
tried to capture the school's role as an institution of sociocultural reproduction
where the children of a linguistic minority are exposed to the secondary socialization that helps shape that sociocultural reproduction. Some graduate students did
join the project later as research assistants, and they were able to work with students
in ways a little removed from the taint of school authority. Nevertheless, for the team
as a whole, that institutional association was always present.

Early in the project, the researchers tried to obtain from the school community
in general its perspective on the work the institution was doing. This meant interviewing administrators, including elected trustees and full-time administrators at
board and school level; it meant interviewing teachers and non-teaching staff, including guidance counsellors and social workers; it meant reading various policy
documents and notices that the school and its board published, including public
minutes of board meetings, the school calendar, and year book; it meant going
through collections of student work written in English and French, including displays in the hall and the corridors of the school. On average, the team spent about
two days a week at the school throughout the life of the project: in classrooms, in
the teachers' lounge, in the grounds, at school events. Also, early in the project,
they tried to get some insight into the different discursive practices that were valued or not valued in the school as a whole. This meant studying classrooms that
represented a range of situations by level and subject matter.

Beginning with Grade 10 classes, where streaming (tracking) began in earnest,
the team widened their search to include students at other levels too. But that cru-
cial Grade 10 cohort remained their major focus. *Français* classes provided the

most highly charged subject matter for them and for my discussion here, touching on the very issues of standardization and evaluation that concerned them, although the team balanced that focus by studying other classes, like Geography and Science. They observed classes of 90 minutes in length, tape-recording many of them. They also interviewed most of the students in each *Français* class. In these interviews, they asked students how they felt about the class, what their sociolinguistic history was, their language repertoire, their ambitions, and their feelings about being at Champlain.

In the second year, for periods ranging from 3 weeks to 3 months, the team worked closely with a group of 15 students who had been selected in the first year as representative of different linguistic practices and social positions. This group was made up of different social fractions: It included both boys and girls, both advanced and general-level students, some who preferred using French, Somali, or English as their first language, and a mixture of students with long or shorter life histories in Toronto. Members of the team followed these students around the place, spending time with them outside school, interviewing them singly or in focus groups, and interviewing some of their parents.

In the third and fourth years of the project, the team examined friendship networks made up of students from different social positions. For example, they met with a group of general-level students who defined themselves as smokers. The team invited some of these students to lunch on different occasions. Using tape-recordings of their lunchtime conversations and talk in the school's smoking area, the researchers learned about the ways in which these students were academically, socially, and linguistically marginalized in the school. The school also included groups of black students from Africa and Haiti. Some of their conversations were taped over lunch, too. Heller herself taped five half-hour conversations with six African girls, all engaged in spontaneous interactions in the cafeteria, the library, on the grass in front of the school, or over lunch at her house. Similar conversations were taped with a small group of boys from various backgrounds who identified themselves as multiculturals, and also with a group of academically successful but socially marginal girls who called themselves the "nerds" or "rejects." Finally, the team spent time with a group of academically successful and discursively dominant students who were identified by the "nerds" as the "popular group," or "the cute kids."

Throughout the research, the team attended all the public events held at Champlain. Heller says that the school used the public stage extensively to construct its image and to conduct its discursive struggles. So, just observing that public stage was vital to understanding the social construction of Champlain as a Franco-Ontarian minority school. Various events occurred with some regularity. Most frequent were meetings called by the student council to prepare for upcoming events, like council elections. There were also school assemblies and workshops where the staff talked to the students about their plans and concerns on issues like combating racism, domestic violence, and violence against women. Public performances by students were another source of data, including a cabaret night of songs, dances, and dramatic monologues, a literary café where works were recited in French, and a fashion show. Other shows were brought into the school to help make students aware of francophone culture. The interactions taking place at most of these events were recorded on video-tape by the school's audio-visual club, and the team had access to these tapes as an extra source of data. Outside the school, some members of its community took part in a student-run radio show on a local university station and an annual francophone festival.

Interpreting School Discourses About Language Quality.   As mentioned already, the problem of language 'quality' is a most important one for Franco-Ontarians. Yet, as Heller notes, public discourses on this issue in francophone Ontario occur mainly in the arena of education, and they place little stress on relations of power and social reproduction. Instead, the focus is on upholding a loose status quo of existing values by making appeals to universal criteria for judging language quality. Indeed, the team's data supported this point in various ways. For example, an extract from one of the school's course listings stressed the importance of mastering each language of instruction "perfectly," in order to get access to the best possible tool of thought and communication. Similarly, the team's content analysis of documents written for French-language schools in Ontario uncovered evaluative statements about the frequent differences between the language spoken by students arriving in school and the language the school should try to promote. But while these views, taken from the official discourses, seemed categorical about the deficit relationship the authorities believed existed between the different language varieties, elsewhere, official documents were much less sure about the 'superior quality' of school French. For instance, another system-level document suggested the distinction was merely one of 'difference' between 'a regional variety' of French and a 'language of instruction'. Heller describes this anomaly as 'a slippage' in policy, (p. 117) and it is a slippage that seemed to be echoed in life and practice at Champlain.

For example, the team's data allowed it to compile a picture of the so-called 'distant' or 'regional' variety that the school took care not to privilege. Apart from the usual sanctions on swearing and obscenities, which no school tolerates, other attributes of language 'quality' emerged from interviews with school personnel. For instance, when talking with an elected school trustee, Heller (1990) asked her about this topic directly: 'what do you understand by [language] quality?' The trustee's reply betrays the several, serious contradictions the school labours under:

> Quality of French uh I think that it is part of our desire for excellent education uh, that they express themselves, but that they express themselves in French; and here I will use something which which will be perhaps interpreted as racism, as we used to say in the old days: "not in Chinese"; it has to be a normal French; it has to be a French, period ... which does not mean a French with no accent uh, there, there is correct French which is normal French, but which can be used with x number of accents or even x number of variations between a vocabulary which is as rich and as important. (p. 118)

Heller interprets this text, along with other semi-official statements made by influential school leaders as evidence of the power that still lies behind the notion of an abstract, ideal, and 'normal' French. The prejudice of this ideal still lingers, even when its valuation conflicted in this case with the trustee's more democratic and up-to-date concern to respect diversity in matters beyond language.

Another type of non-standard variation that appears in the school's discourses was the students' frequent use of English expressions in their French. In fact, teacher concern about these traces of contact with English was stronger than their concern about other non-standard features. An influence at work here is the fact that, in Canada, anglicisms are more likely to appear in the language of marginal French Canadian groups, providing a source of contempt for many French-speaking immigrants who are not French but still feel they speak better French than French Canadians do. In contrast, attaining French language purity helps reproduce the social standing and power of various élite sections of the Canadian population.

So, the use of English expressions by students at Champlain linked them with sociocultural positions whose capital is not much valued in schools. As a result, the scrambling hunt for anglicisms occurred frequently in pedagogy and evaluation at Champlain as teachers and others sought to limit the extent to which the students' French contained these terrible marks of contact with English. Textbooks in French were one source of evidence here. Some contained explicit sections on anglicisms, marking them out as forms to be avoided. Yet, while the school was carrying on a tradition of tracking down anglicisms and expunging them from the formal, school French of students, there was much variation in commitment and ambiguity in practice.

For instance, in tapes of their work in classrooms, even advanced Français teachers were ambivalent about the use of anglicisms if the English word chosen expressed a meaning not easily represented by a single French expression. But here too, they still made it plain to students that they were tolerating the anglicism only under great duress. Meanwhile, other teachers were more or less careful, depending on their personal or professional attachments to the norm. For example, in the extract below a teacher was working with a Grade 10 advanced French class:

Martine:	pourquoi lit-on? *[why do we read?]*
Student:	pour relaxer *[to relax]*
Martine:	pour se détendre, 'relaxer' c'est anglais *[to* 'se détendre' *(relax),* 'relaxer' *is English]*

Later, the same teacher corrected her students' use of Belgian and Swiss variants of French, and she even corrected a Canadian variant found in the mainstream French used by students in her classroom. Heller's team discovered similar examples in the other classes observed, but many of these revealed the teachers' ambivalence about what to value and what not to value. They also revealed real uncertainty among the students about what the school was demanding from them.

In other texts presented as evidence, the team found examples of the student body subtly interpreting the school's concentration on high-status language norms. The students did this by linking low-status norms with figures of fun from the real world. For example, the student council often presented its messages through a series of dramatic skits designed to persuade students to participate in extra-curricular activities. Often, these skits satirized authentic, working-class Canadian French. In one, for instance, two boys played stereotypical French-Canadian lumberjacks who were using exaggerated but excellent Quebec French, a variety that contrasts markedly with the language valued in the school. In another, two students played a working-class couple, he with a pot belly, she in rollers and fluffy pink slippers, both sitting on the couch watching television. Again, the dialogue was in exaggerated Quebec French, mocking that usage by associating it with figures of ridicule.

Finally, a row of students interrogated a vernacular-speaking old woman on the evils of irresponsible garbage disposal. At the end, the students ask whether old grannies (speaking old-fashioned dialects) should be thrown out too; they decide to toss her into the recycling bin. Indeed, all these skits suggested that vernacular forms of French were worthy of contempt. And even these native speakers of 'French' as a first language frequently found their own French was not quite good enough for the school. The students revealed that contradiction in interviews with Heller's team. One boy, for example, complained that he always thought of himself as a native speaker of French, and as a serious student, too, a view of himself that his parents supported in an interview with the researchers but a view that was subtly contradicted by the biased language valuations of the school. These evaluative practices, in their turn, managed to contradict the many enlightened discourses of respect for diversity, anti-racism, and a sense of ethnolinguistic community that appeared in the school's other public spaces.

My concentration here on the non-standard issue understates the breadth of this study and the many insights it achieves through its ingenious interpretation of different types of evidence, careful triangulation of methods, coding, structuring, and presentation. All these things reveal a team of researchers committed to understanding and explaining their piece of a complex web of relations, networks, and discourses. In doing so, they provide their own practical and well demonstrated answers to questions about the source of dominant discourses, their circulation, and their effects. Despite all this, there were limits to the team's penetration of the students' daily lives outside school, and these set certain constraints on the range of interpretation and explanation that was possible. Yet, as Heller notes, this huge collection of data did allow a close reading of the broad range of sites where the school's public discourse was constructed and where students were positioned in different ways with respect to the constraining definitions offered by the school.

CONCLUSION

This chapter began with a brief discussion of changes currently affecting language diversty and education research practices and the new and old methods those changes seem to favour. Then, by providing four examples of methods at work, I tried to highlight the greater depth of insight these new approaches offer researchers as they go about interpreting and explaining the real social world found in the reasons and accounts of participants in that world. In line with this ongoing turn toward an interpretative alternative in social research, I suggested that a priority for new approaches to language diversity research is to seek out the views and interests of those whose language, lives, and social arrangements provide the focus of any study undertaken. Accordingly, I included studies of methods in action that give their own searching answers to key questions: where is discourse, how does it operate, and what does it do? In these four studies, the various researchers interpret emergent phenomena that arise from the reasons and accounts of people positioned by different language games, all played out within educational institutions. To explain the structural influences at work, the researchers also set their evidence against an interpretative background that integrates the reasons and accounts of others who are influenced by other theories and disciplinary language games. The findings, in every case, offer interesting and important insights into the real world of language diversity and education.

In contrast to all this, many of the approaches to language study that evolved in the Western academic world over the last century, seem rather divorced from the reasons and accounts of peoples living outside that narrow world, and even divorced from many living within it. In more recent times, by putting greater emphasis on the actual context of language studies, some applied linguists and some sociolinguists have managed to soften the exclusively 'linguistic' nature of mainstream linguistics in their own work. Yet, the kind of 'context' that usually interests workers in applied linguistics, and even many workers in sociolinguistics, often pulls up well short of contextual issues that go much beyond natural language itself. And regarding natural language as the exclusive social semiotic that shapes discursive practices and positions people as individuals and groups, leaves us with a rather impoverished conception of context. This is because the contextual signs that constrain and liberate human practices depend on rules of use that reach well beyond natural language. And all these different sign systems are bound up with questions of cultural dominance; and the language games that they structure are affected by historic power differentials maintained largely in the non-linguistic discourses of wider social formations. It is these that provide the real social context and the real subject matter for language diversity studies in education.

DISCUSSION STARTERS

1. "The training and development of language teaching experts has been very insensitive to economic, social, and political implications of what happens." Do you agree that the training and development of language teachers is and should be the central focus of applied linguistics? Supposing it is the central focus, how would this affect the way that language teaching experts look at their world? How could their professional development be made more sensitive?

2. Put the phrase, 'a field of possible options,' into your own words. Suggest some practical research questions that might arise from such a field. How might these

questions be studied in a research project? Does this approach from Foucault have appeal as a way of deciding research topics and directions?

3. Sketch out an imaginary study using the activities Hymes (1964) recommends for doing ethnography of communication. At what points in your study would you consult the reasons and accounts of the community under study? What different human science disciplines would offer important insights for your study?

4. Look at the original version of Freeman (1998) and the explanations she offers for her findings. How does she take the influence of wider social formations into account in deriving her explanations? Are there other structural factors that she might have considered? How would consideration of these other factors change her conclusions?

5. Look at the original version of Eriks-Brophy and Crago (1994). In what way do these researchers consult the reasons and accounts of relevant actors in other theories and disciplines? How were their research findings informed by these different acts of consultation? Are there other theories and other disciplines that they overlooked?

6. After looking at the original versions of Eckert (1990) and Eriks-Brophy and Crago (1994), list the research methods the two studies employ. How do the studies differ in the methods chosen? Are the methods appropriate for the studies undertaken? How would you improve on them if you could?

7. "Bourdieu's idea of 'symbolic capital' is the starting point for Penny Eckert's study." Look at the original version of Eckert (1990). In what ways does this idea from Bourdieu inform her study? Does her study make Bourdieu's idea clearer? How important is that idea for understanding Eckert's aims and her conclusion? Is it relevant to the personal goals the girls are trying to achieve through their interactions? In what way?

8. "Her aim was to uncover the social interests at play in that setting, interests that for some students more than for others are clearly prejudiced by the different levels of valuation allotted to different language varieties." Look at the original version of Heller (1999). How successful was her research team in achieving that aim? What techniques helped them? How did they take account of wider social formations in arriving at their explanations?

9. Do you agree that Heller's study "fits well within the *Empowering Outcomes Model* of culturally appropriate research"? In what specific ways does it produce empowering outcomes? How could it be more productive of empowering outcomes?

References

Abbott, C. (1997). IT and literacy. In V. Edwards & D. Corson (Eds.), *Literacy* (pp. 181–188). Boston: Kluwer Academic.

Agnihotri, R. K. (1997). Sustaining local literacies. In V. Edwards & D. Corson (Eds.), *Literacy* (pp. 173–179). Boston: Kluwer Academic.

Albert, M., & Obler, L. (1979). *The bilingual brain.* New York: Academic Press.

Alloway, L., & Gilbert, P. (1997). Boys and literacy: Lessons from Australia. *Gender and Education, 9,* 49–58.

Allwright, D. (1997). Classroom-oriented research in second language learning. In G. R. Tucker & D. Corson (Eds.), *Second language education* (pp. 63–73). Boston: Kluwer Academic.

AAUW [American Association of University Women]. (1995). *How schools shortchange girls: A study of major findings on girls and education.* New York: Marlowe & Company.

Ammon, U. (1972). *Dialekt, soziale ungleichheit und schule.* Weinheim/Basel, Switzerland: Beltz.

Ammon, U., Dittmar, N., & Mattheier, K. (Eds.). (1987). *Sociolinguistics.* Berlin, Germany: Walter de Gruyter.

Andersson, L.-G., & Trudgill, P. (1990). *Bad language.* Oxford, England: Basil Blackwell.

Appel, R. (1988). The language education of immigrant workers' children in the Netherlands. In T. Skutnabb-Kangas & J. Cummins (Eds.), *Minority education: From shame to struggle* (pp. 57–77). Philadelphia: Multilingual Matters.

Apple, M. (1982). *Education and power.* London: Routledge.

Artiles, A., & Trent, S. (1994). Overrepresentation of minority students in special education: A continuing debate. *Journal of Special Education, 27,* 410–437.

Au, K., & Mason, J. (1983). Cultural congruence in classroom participation structures: Achieving a balance of rights. *Discourse Processes, 6,* 145–167.

Auerbach, E. R. (1997). Family literacy. In V. Edwards & D. Corson (Eds.), *Literacy* (pp. 153–161). Boston: Kluwer Academic.

Baker, C. (1988). *Key issues in bilingualism and bilingual education.* Clevedon, England: Multilingual Matters.

Baker, C. (1997). Survey methods in researching language and education. In N. Hornberger & D. Corson (Eds.), *Research methods in language and education* (pp. 35–45). Boston: Kluwer Academic.

Baker, R., & Chenery, H. J. (1997). The assessment of speech and language disorders. In C. Clapham & D. Corson (Eds.), *Language testing and assessment* (pp. 211–225). Boston: Kluwer Academic.

Bakhtin, M. (1975/1981). *The dialogic imagination: Four essays.* Austin, TX: University of Texas Press.

Baldwin, J. (1997). If Black English isn't a language, then tell me what is? *The Black Scholar: Journal of Black Studies and Research, 27,* 5–6.

Ballenger, C. (1997). Science talk in a bilingual classroom. *Language and Education, 11,* 1–14.

Baran, G. (1987). Teaching girls science. In M. McNeil (Ed.), *Gender and expertise.* London: Free Association Books.

Barnes, D., Britton, J., & Rosen, H. (1969) *Language, the learner and the school.* London: Penguin.

Barry, B. (1989). *A treatise on social justice: Vol. 1. Theories of justice.* Berkeley, CA: University of California Press.

Bascia, N. (1996). Inside and outside: minority immigrant teachers in Canadian schools. *Qualitative Studies in Education, 9,* 151–165.

Baudoux, C., & Noircent, A. (1993). Ropports sociaux de sexe dans les classes du collégial québécois. *Revue canadienne de l'éducation, 18,* 150–167.

Baugh, J. (1997a). Research on race and social class in language acquisition and use. In N. Hornberger and D. Corson (Eds.), *Research methods in language and education* (pp. 111–121). Boston: Kluwer Academic.

Baugh, J. (1997b). Linguistic discrimination in education. In R. Wodak & D. Corson (Eds.), *Language policy and political issues in education* (pp. 33–41). Boston: Kluwer Academic.

Baugh, J. (2000). *Beyond Ebonics: Linguistic pride and racial prejudice.* New York: Oxford University Press.

Baxter, J. (1999). Teaching girls to speak out: the female voice in public contexts. *Language and Education, 13,* 81–98.

Bernstein, B. (1990). *Class, codes and control. Vol. 4: The structuring of pedagogic discourse.* London: Routledge & Kegan Paul.

Bhaskar, R. (1986). *Scientific realism and human emancipation.* London: Verso.

Bigelow, B., Christensen, L., Karp, S., Miner, B., & Peterson, B. (1994). *Rethinking our classrooms.* Milwaukee, WI: Rethinking Schools.

Biggs, N., & Edwards, V. (1991). "I treat them all the same": Teacher-pupil talk in multi-ethnic classrooms. *Language and Education, 5,* 161–176.

Bjerrum Nielsen, H., & Davies, B. (1997). The construction of gendered identity through classroom talk. In B. Davies & D. Corson (Eds.), *Oral discourse and education* (pp. 125–136). Boston: Kluwer Academic.

Black, D. (1997, May 3). Educator honored for her work with deaf. *The Toronto Star,* p. A5.

Blair, H. (1986). Teacher's attitudes toward the oral English of indigenous children in Saskatchewan and Queensland. In *Mokakit: Selected papers from the First Mokakit Conference, July 25–27, 1984* (pp. 22–35). Vancouver, BC: Mokakit.

Blake, B. E. (1998). "Critical" reader response in an urban classroom: creating cultural texts to engage diverse readers. *Theory Into Practice, 37,* 238–243.

Blount, J. M. (1999). Manliness and the gendered construction of school administration in the USA. *International Journal of Leadership in Education, 2,* 55–68.

Bogoch, B. (1994). Power, distance and solidarity: Models of professional-client interaction in an Israeli legal aid setting. *Discourse & Society, 5,* 65–88.

Bortoni-Ricardo, S. (1985). *The urbanization of rural dialect speakers: A sociolinguistic study in Brazil.* Cambridge, England: Cambridge University Press.

Bourdieu, P. (1966). L'école conservatrice. *Revue Française de sociologie, 7,* 225–226, 330–342, 346–347.

Bourdieu, P. (1981). *Ce que parler veut dire: L'économie des échanges linguistique.* Paris: Fayard.

Bourdieu, P. (1984). *Distinction: A social critique of the judgement of taste.* Cambridge, MA: Harvard University Press.

Brandl, M. (1983). A certain heritage: women and their children in north Australia. In F. Gale (Ed.), *We are bosses ourselves: The status and role of aboriginal women today.* Canberra, Australia: Australian Institute of Aboriginal Studies.

Branson, J., & Miller, D. (1995). Sign language and the discursive construction of power over the Deaf through education. In D. Corson (Ed.), *Discourse and power in educational organizations* (pp. 167–89). Cresskill, NJ: Hampton.

Branson, J., & Miller, D. (1997a). National sign languages and language policies. In R. Wodak & D. Corson (Eds.), *Language policies and political issues* (pp. 89–98). Boston: Kluwer Academic.

Branson, J., & Miller, D. (1997b). Research methods for studying the language of the signing Deaf. In N. Hornberger & D. Corson (Eds.), *Research methods in language and education* (pp. 175–185). Boston: Kluwer Academic.

Briggs, C. (1986). *Learning how to ask: A sociolinguistic appraisal of the role of the interview in social science research.* Cambridge: Cambridge University Press.

Britton, J. (1970). *Language and learning.* London: Penguin.

Brouwer, D. (1982). The influence of the addressee's sex on politeness in language use. *Linguistics, 20,* 697–711.

Brouwer, D., Gerritsen, M., & De Haan, D. (1979). Speech differences between women and men: On the wrong track? *Language in Society, 8,* 33–50.

Brown, P. (1993). Gender, politeness and confrontation in Tenejapa. In D. Tannen (Ed.), *Gender and conversational interaction* (pp. 144–162). New York: Oxford University Press.

Bruck, M. (1984). The suitability of immersion education for children with special needs. In C. Rivera (Ed.), *Placement procedures in bilingual education: Education and policy issues.* Philadelphia: Multilingual Matters.

Bruner, J. (1973). *Beyond the information given: Studies in the psychology of knowing.* New York: Norton.

Bruner, J. (1990). *Acts of meaning.* Cambridge, MA: Harvard University Press.

Bruner, J. (1996). *The culture of education.* Cambridge, MA: Harvard University Press.

Buck, G. (1997). The testing of listening in a second language. In C. Clapham & D. Corson (Eds.), *Language testing and assessment* (pp. 65–73). Boston: Kluwer Academic.

Burnaby, B. (1997). Language policy and education in Canada. In R. Wodak & D. Corson (Eds.), *Language policy and political issues in education* (pp. 151–159). Boston: Kluwer Academic.

Burns, J., & Bird, L. (1987). Girls' cooperation and boys' isolation in achieving understanding in chemistry. *GASAT Conference Proceedings,* Victoria University, Wellington, New Zealand.

Burns, J., Clift, C., & Duncan, J. (1991). Understanding of understanding: implications for learning and teaching. *British Journal of Educational Psychology, 61,* 276–289.

Cameron, D. (1985). *Feminism and linguistic theory.* London: Macmillan.

Cameron, D. (1997). Theoretical debates in feminist linguistics: questions of sex and gender. In R. Wodak (Ed.), *Gender and discourse* (pp. 21–36). Thousand Oaks, CA: Sage.

Cameron, D., & Coates, J. (1985). Some problems in the sociolinguistic explanation of sex differences. *Language and Communication, 5,* 143–151.

Campos, S., & Keatinge, H. (1988). The Carpinteria language minority student experience: from theory, to practice, to success. In T. Skutnabb-Kangas & J. Cummins (Eds.), *Minority education: From shame to struggle* (pp. 299–306). Philadelphia: Multilingual Matters.

Canadian Association of the Deaf. (1990). Vision 2000 Conference a huge success. *The Deaf Canadian Advocate, 5*(12), 1–2.

Cazden, C. (1988). *Classroom discourse: The language of teaching and learning.* Portsmouth, England: Heinemann.

Cazden, C. (1990). Differential treatment in New Zealand: Reflections on research in minority education. *Teaching and Teacher Education, 6,* 291–303.

Chamot, A. (1988). Bilingualism in education and bilingual education: The state of the art in the United States. *Journal of Multilingual and Multicultural Development, 9,* 11–35.

Cheshire, J., & Edwards, V. (1993). Sociolinguistics in the classroom: Exploring linguistic diversity. In J. Milroy & L. Milroy (Eds.), *Real English* (pp. 34–52). London: Longman.

Cheshire, J., & Jenkins, N. (1991). Gender differences in the GCSE Oral English Examination: Part 2. *Language and Education, 5,* 19–40.

Chouliaraki, L. (1996). Regulative practices in a 'progressivist' classroom: 'Good habits' as a 'disciplinary technology'. *Language and Education, 10,* 103–118.

Christian, D., & Wolfram, W. (1989). *Dialects and education: Issues and answers.* Englewood Cliffs, NJ: Prentice-Hall.

Christie, M. (1985). *Aboriginal perspectives on experience and learning: The role of language in Aboriginal education.* (pp. 5–19). Geelong, Australia: Deakin University Press.

Christie, M. (1988). The invasion of aboriginal education. In Institute of Applied Aboriginal Studies, *Learning my way (Waikaru 16).* Perth: Western Australia College of Advanced Education.

Churchill, S. (1986). *The education of linguistic and cultural minorities in OECD countries.* Philadelphia: Multilingual Matters.

Churchill, S., Frenette, N., & Quazi, S. (1986). *Éducation et besoins des Franco-Ontariens: Le diagnostic d'un système d'éducation.* Toronto, ON: Le Conseil de l'Éducation Franco-Ontarienne.

Clapham, C., & Corson, D. (Eds.). (1997). *Language testing and assessment.* Boston: Kluwer Academic.

Clark, R., & Ivanic, R. (1997). Critical discourse analysis and educational change. In L. van Lier & D. Corson (Eds.), *Knowledge about language* (pp. 217–227). Boston: Kluwer Academic.

Clegg, J. (1996). *Mainstreaming ESL.* Philadelphia: Multilingual Matters.

Clyne, M. (1997). Language policies and education in Australia. In R. Wodak & D. Corson (Eds.), *Language policy and political issues in education* (pp. 129–137). Boston: Kluwer Academic.

Coates, J. (1998). Women behaving badly: female speakers backstage. *Journal of Sociolinguistics, 3,* 65–80.

Coates, J., & Cameron, D. (1988). *Women in their speech communities: New perspectives on language and sex.* London: Longman.

Collier, V. (1992). A synthesis of studies examining long-term language-minority student data on academic achievement. *Bilingual Research Journal, 16,* 187–212.

Commonwealth Schools Commission. (1984). *A review of the commonwealth English as a Second Language (ESL) program.* Canberra: Author.

Corson, D. (1993). *Language, minority education and gender.* Clevedon, England: Multilingual Matters.

Corson, D. (Ed.). (1995a). *Discourse and power in educational organizations.* Cresskill, NJ: Hampton Press.

Corson, D. (1995b). *Using english words.* Boston: Kluwer Academic.

Corson, D. (1997). Critical realism: an emancipatory philosophy for applied linguistics? *Applied Linguistics, 18,* 166–188.

Corson, D. (1998). *Changing education for diversity.* London: Open University Press.

Corson, D. (1999). *Language policy in schools.* Mahwah, NJ: Lawrence Erlbaum Associates.

Corson, D., & Lemay, S. (1996). *Social justice and language policy in education: The Canadian research.* Toronto, ON: OISE Press/University of Toronto Press.

Crago, M. (1992). Communicative interaction and second language acquisition: An Inuit example. *TESOL Quarterly, 26,* 487–505.

Crandall, J. -A. (1997). Language teaching approaches for school-age learners in second language contexts. In G. R. Tucker & D. Corson (Eds.), *Second language education* (pp. 75–83). Boston: Kluwer Academic.

Crosby, F., & Nyquist, L. (1977). The female register: an empirical study of Lakoff's hypotheses. *Language in Society, 6,* 313–322.

Crystal, D. (1987). *The Cambridge encyclopedia of language.* Cambridge, England: Cambridge University Press.

Cumming, A. (1997). The testing of writing in a second language. In C. Clapham & D. Corson (Eds.), *Language testing and assessment* (pp. 51–63). Boston: Kluwer Academic.

Cummins, J. (1981). *Bilingualism and minority language children.* Toronto, ON: Ontario Institute for Studies in Education.

Cummins, J. (1984). *Bilingualism and special education: Issues in assessment and pedagogy.* Clevedon, England: Multilingual Matters.

Cummins, J. (1986). Empowering minority students: a framework for intervention. *Harvard Educational Review, 56,* 18–36.

Cummins, J. (1989). A theoretical framework for bilingual special education. *Exceptional Children, 56,* 111–119.

Cummins, J. (1996). *Negotiating identities: Education for empowerment in a diverse society.* Ontario, CA: California Association for Bilingual Education.

Cummins, J., & Corson, D. (Eds.).(1997). *Bilingual education.* Boston: Kluwer Academic.

Cummins, J., & Danesi, M. (1990). *Heritage languages.* Toronto, ON: Garamond Press.

Cummins, J., & Sayers, D. (1995). *Brave new schools: Challenging cultural illiteracy.* New York: St Martin's Press.

Dahrendorf, R. (1978). *Life chances.* Chicago: University of Chicago Press.

Danby, S., & Baker, C. (1998). How to be masculine in block area. *Childhood, 5,* 151–175.

Dannequin, C. (1987) Les enfants bâillonnés: The teaching of French as mother tongue in elementary school. *Language and Education, 1,* 15–31.

Davies, B., & Corson, D. (Eds.). (1997). *Oral discourse and education.* Boston: Kluwer Academic.

DeFrancisco, V. (1991). The sounds of silence: how men silence women in marital relations. *Discourse & Society, 2,* 413–423.

Delpit, L. (1995). *Other people's children: Cultural conflict in the classroom.* New York: The New Press.

Department of Education and Science. (1975). *A language for life* (The Bullock Report). London: HMSO.

Department of Education and Science. (1988). *Report of the Committee of Inquiry into the Teaching of the English Language* (The Kingman Report). London: HMSO.

DeStefano, J. S. (1991). Ethnolinguistic minority groups and literacy: Tom, Dick and Harry at home and at school. In M. E. McGroarty & C. J. Faltis (Eds.), *Languages in school and society: Policy and pedagogy* (pp. 443–464). Berlin, Germany: de Gruyter.

Dittman, A. (1977). Developmental factors in conversational behaviour. *Journal of Communication, 22,* 404–423.

Duranti, A. (1997). *Linguistic anthropology.* New York: Cambridge University Press.

Durkheim, E. (1894/1966). *The rules of sociological method.* New York: The Free Press.

Eckert, P. (1989). *Jocks and Burnouts.* New York: Teachers College Press.

Eckert, P. (1990). Cooperative competition in adolescent "girl talk". *Discourse Processes, 13,* 91–122.

Eckert, P., & McConnell-Ginet, S. (1992a). Communities of practice: where language, gender and power all live. In K. Hall, M. Bucholtz & B. Moonwomon (Eds.), *Locating power* (pp. 89–99). Berkeley, CA: University of Berkeley Women and Language Group.

Eckert, P., & McConnell-Ginet, S. (1992b). Think practically and look locally: language and gender as community-based practice. *Annual Review of Anthropology, 21,* 461–490.

Edelman, M. (1984). The political language of the helping professions. In M. Shapiro (Ed.), *Language and politics.* Oxford, England: Basil Blackwell.

Edwards, A. D. (1976). *Language in culture and class: The sociology of language and education.* London: Heinemann.

Edwards, A. D. (1997). Oral language, culture and class. In B. Davies and D. Corson (Eds.), *Oral discourse and education* (pp. 65–73). Boston: Kluwer Academic.

Edwards, A. D., & Westgate, D. (1994). *Investigating classroom talk.* Brighton, England: Falmer.

Edwards, J. (1989). *Language and disadvantage: Studies in disorders of communication* (2nd ed.). London: Cole & Whurr.

Edwards, V. (1986). *Language in a Black community.* Clevedon, England: Multilingual Matters.

Edwards, V. (1989). Dialect and education in Europe: a postscript. *Journal of Multilingual and Multicultural Development, 10,* 317–323.

Edwards, V., & Redfern, A. (1992). *The world in a classroom: Language in education in Britain and Canada.* Philadelphia, PA: Multilingual Matters.

Egbo, B. (1997). Female literacy and life chances in rural Nigeria. In V. Edwards & D. Corson (Eds.), *Literacy* (pp. 215–224). London: Kluwer Academic.

Egbo, B. (2000). *Female literacy and life chances in Sub-Saharan Africa.* Clevedon, England: Multilingual Matters.

Erickson, F. (1975). Gatekeeping and the melting pot. *Harvard Educational Review, 45,* 44–70.

Erickson, F. (1984). Rhetoric, anecdote and rhapsody: Coherence strategies in a conversation among Black American adolescents. In Tannen, D. (Ed.), *Coherence in spoken and written discourse* (pp. 81–154). Norwood, NJ: Ablex.

Erickson, F. (1996). Transformation and school success: the politics and culture of educational achievement. In E. Jacob and C. Jordan (Eds.), *Minority education: Anthropological perspectives.* Norwood, NJ: Ablex.

Eriks-Brophy, A., & Crago, M. (1994). Transforming classroom discourse: an Inuit example. *Language and Education, 8,* 105–122.

Ervin-Tripp, S., & Wong Fillmore, L. (1988). *Interactional coding manual.* Unpublished manuscript.

Escobar, G. (1999, January 17). Immigrant numbers in US triple. *Guardian Weekly* ("The Washington Post" section), p. 17.

Esposito, A. (1979). Sex differences in children's conversation. *Language and Speech, 22,* 213–220.

Evans, C., & Zimmer, K. (1993). Sign talk development project, Winnipeg, Manitoba. *ACEHI/ACEDA, 19,* 62–70.

Fairclough, N. (1985). Critical and descriptive goals in discourse analysis. *Journal of Pragmatics, 9,* 739–763.

Fairclough, N. (Ed.). (1992). *Critical language awareness.* London: Longman.

Fairclough, N. (1995). Critical language awareness and self-identity in education. In D. Corson (Ed.), *Discourse and power in educational organizations* (pp. 257–272). Cresskill, NJ: Hampton Press.

Faltis, C. (1997). Case study methods in researching language and education. In N. Hornberger & D. Corson (Eds.), *Research methods in language and education* (pp. 145–151). Boston: Kluwer Academic.

Farah, I. (1997). Ethnography of communication. In N. Hornberger & D. Corson (Eds.), *Research methods in language and education* (pp. 125–133). Boston: Kluwer Academic.

Fasold, R. (1984). *The sociolinguistics of society.* Oxford, England: Basil Blackwell.

Fasold, R. (1990). *The sociolinguistics of language.* Oxford, England: Basil Blackwell.

Fennema, E., & Peterson, P. (1985). Autonomous learning behaviour: a possible explanation of gender-related differences in mathematics. In L. Wilkinson & C. Marrett (Eds.), *Gender influences in classroom interaction.* Orlando, FL: Academic Press.

Fettes, M. (2000). *The linguistic ecology of education.* Unpublished doctoral thesis, University of Toronto, Toronto, ON.

Feuerverger, G. (1997). On the edges of the map: a study of heritage language teachers in Toronto. *Teaching and Teacher Education, 13,* 39–54

Fichtelius, A., Johansson, I., & Nordin, K. (1980). Three investigations of sex-associated speech variation in day school. *Women's Studies International Quarterly, 3,* 219–225.

Fishman, J. (1969). *Readings in the sociology of language.* The Hague, Netherlands: Mouton.

Fishman, J. (Ed.). (1978). *Advances in the study of societal multilingualism.* The Hague, Netherlands: Mouton.

Fishman, J. (1980). Minority language maintenance and the ethnic mother tongue school. *Modern Language Journal, 64,* 167–172.

Fishman, J. (1996). Maintaining languages: What works and what doesn't? In G. Cantoni (Ed.), *Stabilizing indigenous languages* (pp. 186–198). Flagstaff, AZ: Northern Arizona University.

Fishman, P. (1983). Interaction: The work women do. In B. Thorne, C. Kramarae, & N. Henley (Eds.), *Language, gender and society.* Rowley, MA: Newbury House.

Fitzpatrick, F. (1987). *The open door.* Philadelphia: Multilingual Matters.

Fordham, S. (1999). Dissin' the standard: Ebonics as guerrilla warfare at Capital High. *Anthropology and Education Quarterly, 30,* 272–293.

Foster, M. (1997). Ebonics: The children speak up. *Quarterly of the National Writing Project, 19,* 7–12.

Foucault, M. (1972). *The archaeology of knowledge.* London: Tavistock.

Foucault, M. (1977). *Discipline and punish: The birth of the prison.* New York: Pantheon.

Foucault, M. (1980). *Power/knowledge: Selected interviews and other writings 1971–1977.* New York: Pantheon.

Foucault, M. (1982). The subject and power. In H. Dreyfus & P. Rabinow (Eds.), *Michel Foucault: Beyond structuralism and hermeneutics.* New York: Harvester.

Foucault, M. (1984a). In P. Rabinow (Ed.), *The Foucault reader.* London: Penguin.

Foucault, M. (1984b). The order of discourse. In M. Shapiro (Ed.), *Language and politics* (pp. 108–138). New York: New York University Press.

Freeman, R. D. (1996). Dual-language planning at Oyster bilingual school: "It's much more than language". *TESOL Quarterly, 30,* 557–582.

Freeman, R. D. (1998). *Bilingual education and social change.* Clevedon, England: Multilingual Matters.

Furby, L. (1986). Psychology and justice. In R. L. Cohen (Ed.), *Justice: Views from the social sciences.* New York: Plenum.

Gal, S. (1988). The political economy of code choice. In M. Heller (Ed.), *Codeswitching: Anthropological and sociolinguistic perspectives* (pp. 245–264). Berlin, Germany: Mouton de Gruyter.

Gándara, P. (1994). The impact of the Education Reform Movement on limited English proficient students. In B. McLeod (Ed.), *Language and learning.* Albany, NY: State University of New York Press.

Garcez, P. (1997). Micro-ethnography. In N. Hornberger & D. Corson (Eds.), *Research methods in language and education* (pp. 187–196). Boston: Kluwer Academic.

García, O., & Otheguy, R. (1987). The bilingual education of Cuban-American children in Dade County's ethnic schools. *Language and Education, 1,* 83–95.

Gee, J. P. (1997). Meanings in discourse: coordinating and being coordinated. In Muspratt, S., Luke, A. & Freebody, P. (Eds.), *Constructing critical literacies* (pp. 273–302). St. Leonards, Australia: Allen & Unwin.

Geertz, C. (1973). *The interpretation of cultures.* New York: Basic Books.

Gersten, R., & Woodward, J. (1994). The language minority student and special education: Issues, trends and paradoxes. *Exceptional Children, 60,* 310–322.

Gibson, H., Small, A., & Mason, D. (1997). Deaf bilingual bicultural education. In J. Cummins & D. Corson (Eds.), *Bilingual education* (pp. 231–241). Boston: Kluwer Academic.

Giles, H., Hewstone, M., Ryan, E. B., & Johnson, P. (1987) Research on language attitudes. In U. Ammon, N. Dittmar, & K. Mattheier (Eds.), *Sociolinguistics* (pp. 1068–1081). Berlin, Germany: de Gruyter.

Gillett, J. (1987). Ethnic bilingual education for Canada's minority groups. *The Canadian Modern Language Review, 43,* 337–356.

Goldstein, B. (1988). In search of survival: the education and integration of Hmong refugee girls. *The Journal of Ethnic Studies, 16,* 1–27.

Goodwin, M. H. (1980). Directive/response speech sequences in girls' and boys' task activities. In S. McConnell-Ginet, R. Borker, & N. Furman (Eds.), *Women and language in literature and society* (pp. 157–173). New York: Praeger.

Goodwin, M. H. (1988). Cooperation and competition across girls' play activities. In J. Coates (Ed.), *Language and gender: A reader* (pp. 121–146). Oxford, England: Basil Blackwell.

Goodwin, M. H. (1990). *He-said-she-said: Talk as social organization among Black children.* Bloomington: Indiana University Press.

Gramsci, A. (1948/1966). *Opere di Antonio Gramsci (Quaderni del carcere XVIII).* Vols I–XI. Turin, Italy: Einaudi.

Greenfield, T. (1976). Bilingualism, multiculturalism, and the crisis of purpose. *Canadian Society for the Study of Education Yearbook, 3,* 107–136.

Grieshaber, S., & Danby, S. (1999, June). *The pervasiveness of gender in a childcare classroom.* Paper presented at the Eighth Reconceptualising Early Childhood Education Conference, Columbus, OH.

Grimshaw, A. (1987). Sociolinguistics versus sociology of language: tempest in a teapot or profound academic conundrum? In U. Ammon, N. Dittmar, & K. Mattheier (Eds.), *Sociolinguistics* (pp. 9–15). Berlin, Germany: de Gruyter.

Gumperz, J. (1976). Language, communication and public negotiation. In P. Sanday (Ed.), *Anthropology and the public interest.* New York: Academic Press.

Gumperz, J. (1977). Sociocultural knowledge in conversational inference. In M. Saville-Troike (Ed.), *Twenty-eighth annual roundtable monograph series in language and linguistics.* Washington, DC: Georgetown University Press.

Gumperz, J. (1982). *Discourse strategies.* Cambridge, England: Cambridge University Press.

Guskey, T. (1986). Staff development and the process of teacher change. *Educational Researcher, 15,* 5–12.

Hagman, T., & Lahdenperä, J. (1988). Nine years of Finnish-medium education in Sweden: What happens afterwards? The education of minority children in Botkyrka. In T. Skutnabb-Kangas & J. Cummins (Eds.), *Minority education: From shame to struggle* (pp. 328–337). Philadelphia, PA: Multilingual Matters.

Hall, K. & Buckholtz, M. (Eds.) (1995). *Gender articulated: Language and the socially constructed self.* New York: Routledge.

Hamayan, E. (1997). Teaching exceptional second language learners. In G. R. Tucker & D. Corson (Eds.), *Second language education* (pp. 85–94). Boston: Kluwer Academic.

Hamp-Lyons, L. (1997). Ethics in language testing. In C. Clapham & D. Corson (Eds.), *Language testing and assessment* (pp. 323–333). Boston: Kluwer Academic.

Harker, R. (1990). Bourdieu: education and reproduction. In R. Harker, C. Mahar & C. Wilkes (Eds.), *An introduction to the work of Pierre Bourdieu.* London: Macmillan.

Harré, R. (1987). *The social construction of emotions.* Oxford, England: Basil Blackwell.

Harré, R., & G. Gillett. (1994). *The discursive mind.* Thousand Oaks, CA: Sage Publications.

Harris, S., & Devlin, B. (1997). Bilingual programs involving Aboriginal languages in Australia. In J. Cummins & D. Corson (Eds.), *Bilingual education* (pp. 1–14). Boston: Kluwer Academic.

Hastings, W. K. (1997). International law and education in a minority language. In R. Wodak & D. Corson (Eds.), *Language policy and political issues in education* (pp. 67–75). Boston: Kluwer Academic.

Haw, K. (1998). *Educating Muslim girls: Shifting discourses.* Philadelphia: Open University Press.

Heath, S. (1983). *Ways with words: Ethnography of communication in communities and classrooms.* Cambridge, England: Cambridge University Press.

Heath, S. (1986). Critical factors in literacy development. In S. de Castell, A. Luke, & K. Egan (Eds.), *Literacy, society and schooling: A reader.* Cambridge, England: Cambridge University Press.

Heath, S., & Branscombe, A. (1986). The book as narrative prop in language acquisition. In B. Schieffelin, & P. Gilmore (Eds.), *The acquisition of literacy: Ethnographic perspectives.* Norwood, NJ: Ablex.

Heller, M. (1994). *Crosswords: Language, education and ethnicity in French Ontario.* Berlin, Germany: Mouton.

Heller, M. (1995). Language choice, social institutions, and symbolic domination. *Language and Society, 24,* 373–405.

Heller, M. (1997). Language choice and symbolic domination. In B. Davies & D. Corson (Eds.), *Oral discourse and education* (pp. 87–94). Boston: Kluwer Academic.

Heller, M. (1999). *Linguistic minorities and modernity: A sociolinguistic ethnography.* London: Longman.

Herriman, M., & Burnaby, B. (1996). *Language policies in English-dominant countries.* Clevedon, England: Multilingual Matters.

Herring, S., Johnson, D. A., & DiBenedetto, T. (1995). "This discussion is going too far!": Male resistance to female participation on the Internet. In K. Hall & M. Bucholz (Eds.), *Gender articulated: Language and the socially constructed self* (pp. 67–96). New York: Routledge.

Hewitt, R. (1989) Creole in the classroom: Political grammars and educational vocabularies. In R. Grillo (Ed.), *Social anthropology and the politics of language.* London: Routledge.

Hingangaroa Smith, G. (1990). *Models for culturally appropriate research.* Seminar paper presented at Massey University, Palmerston North, New Zealand.

Hobsbawm, E. (1989). *The Age of Empire: 1875–1914.* New York: Vintage Books.

Holmes, J. (1995). *Women, men and politeness.* London: Longman.

Holmes, J. (1998). Narrative structure: some contrasts between Maori and Pakeha story-telling. *Multilingua, 17,* 25–58.

Hornberger, N. H. (1990a). Creating successful learning contexts for bilingual literacy. *Teachers College Record, 92,* 212–229.

Hornberger, N. H. (1990b). Teacher Quechua use in bilingual and non-bilingual classrooms of Puno, Peru. In R. Jacobson & C. Faltis (Eds.), *Language distribution issues in bilingual schooling* (pp. 162–173). Clevedon, England: Multilingual Matters.

Hornberger, N. H. (1995). Ethnography in linguistic perspective: understanding school processes. *Language and Education, 9,* 233–248.

Hornberger, N. H., & Corson, D. (Eds.). (1997). *Research methods in language and education.* Boston: Kluwer Academic.

Hornberger, N. H., & Skilton-Sylvester, E. (in press). Revisiting the continua of biliteracy. *Language and Education.*

Horvath, B. (1980). *The education of migrant children: A language planning perspective* (ERDC Report No. 24). Canberra, Australia: AGPS.

Hudson, R., & Holmes, J. (1995). *Children's use of spoken standard English.* London: School Curriculum and Assessment Authority.

Hughes, J. (1990). *The philosophy of social research.* London: Longmans.

Hymes, D. (1964). Introduction: toward ethnographies of communication. *American Anthropologist, 66*(6, Pt 2), 1–35.

Hymes, D. (1971). On linguistic theory, communicative competence and the education of disadvantaged children. In M. Wax, S. Diamond & F. Gearing (Eds.), *Anthropological perspectives in education.* New York: Basic Books.

Hymes, D. (1974). *Foundations in sociolinguistics: An ethnographic approach.* Philadelphia: University of Pennsylvania Press.

Iglesias, A. (1985). Cultural conflict in the classroom. In D. Ripich & F. Spinelli (Eds.), *School discourse problems.* London: Taylor & Francis.

Israelite, N., Ewoldt, C., & Hoffmeister, R. (1992). *Bilingual/bicultural education for Deaf and hard of hearing students: A review of the literature on the effects of native sign language on majority-language language acquisition.* A report to the Ontario Ministry of Education. Toronto, ON: Queen's Printer for Ontario.

Jackson, J. J. (1997). On Oakland's ebonics: some say gibberish, some say slang, some say did-den-dat, me say dem dumb, it be mother tongue. *The Black Scholar: Journal of Black Studies and Research, 27,* 18–25.

Janks, H. (1997). Teaching about language and power. In R. Wodak & D. Corson (Eds.), *Language policy and political issues in education* (pp. 241–251). Boston: Kluwer Academic.

Jaworski, A., & Sachdev, I. (1998). Beliefs about silence in the classroom. *Language and Education, 12,* 273–292.

Jenkins, N., & Cheshire, J. (1990). Gender issues in the GCSE Oral English Examination: Part 1. *Language and Education, 4,* 261–292.

Johnson, R., Liddell, S., & Erting, C. (1989). *Unlocking the curriculum: Principles for achieving access in Deaf education.* Gallaudet Research Institute working paper. Washington, DC: Gallaudet University.

Jones, A. (1987). Which girls are 'learning to lose'? In S. Middleton (Ed.), *Women and education in Aotearoa.* Wellington, New Zealand: Allen and Unwin.

Jordan, C. (1985). Translating culture: from ethnographic information to educational program. *Anthropology and Education Quarterly, 16,* 105–123.

Joshee, R. & Bullard, J. (1992). Tensions between homogeneity and diversity: governmental roles in multicultural education. *Canadian Ethnic Studies, 24,* 113–126.

Kanaris, A. (1999). Gendered journeys: children's writing and the construction of gender. *Language and Education, 13,* 254–268.

Keenan, E. (1974). Norm makers, norm breakers: uses of speech by men and women in a Malagasy community. In R. Bauman & J. Scherzer (Eds.), *Explorations in the ethnography of speaking* (pp. 125–143). Cambridge, England: Cambridge University Press.

Kelly, A. (1988). Gender differences in teacher-pupil interactions: a meta-analytic review. *Research in Education, 39,* 1–23.

Kendall, S., & Tannen, D. (1997). Gender and language in the workplace. In R. Wodak (Ed.), *Gender and discourse* (pp. 81–105). Thousand Oaks, CA: Sage Publications.

Kessler, S., Ashenden, D., Connell, R., & Dowsett, G. (1985). Gender relations in secondary schooling. *Sociology of Education, 58,* 34–48.

Khubchandani, L. (1997). Language policy and education in the Indian sub-continent. In R. Wodak & D. Corson (Eds.), *Language policy and political issues in education* (pp. 179–187). Boston: Kluwer Academic.

Kincheloe, J. L. (1991). *Teachers as researchers: Qualitative paths to teacher empowerment.* New York: Falmer.

Klann-Delius, G. (1987). Sex and language. In U. Ammon, N. Dittmar & K. Mattheier (Eds.), *Sociolinguistics* (pp. 767–780). Berlin, Germany: Walter de Gruyter.

Krahnke, K. (1987). *Approaches to syllabus design for foreign language teaching.* Englewood Cliffs, NJ: Prentice Hall.

Kuhn, T. S. (1970). *The structure of scientific revolutions.* Chicago: University of Chicago Press.

Kyle, J., & Woll, B. (1985). *Sign language: The study of Deaf people and their language.* Cambridge, England: Cambridge University Press.

Kymlicka, W. (1989). *Liberalism, community and culture.* Oxford, England: Clarendon Press.

Labov, W. (1966). Finding out about children's language. *Working Papers in Communication, 1,* 1–30.

Labov, W. (1971). *Pidginization and Creolization of languages.* New York: Cambridge University Press.

Labov, W. (1972a). *Language in the inner city.* Philadelphia: University of Pennsylvania Press.

Labov, W. (1972b). The logic of non-standard English. In P. Giglioli (Ed.), *Language and social context.* Harmondsworth, England: Penguin.

Labov, W. (1982). Objectivity and commitment in linguistic science: the case of the Black English trial in Ann Arbor. *Language in Society, 11,* 165–201.

Labov, W. (1994). Can reading failure be reversed? A linguistic approach to the question. In V. Gadsden & D. Wagner (Eds.), *Literacy among African American youth* (pp. 39–68). Cresskill, NJ: Hampton Press.

Ladd, P. (1991). Making plans for Nigel: the erosion of identity by mainstreaming. In G. Taylor & J. Bishop (Eds.), *Being Deaf: the experience of Deafness.* London: Pinter.

Lakoff, R. (1975). *Language and women's place.* New York: Harper and Row.

Lambert, W. (1975). Culture and language as factors in learning and education. In A. Wolfgang (Ed.). *Education of immigrant students: Issues and answers.* Toronto, ON: Ontario Institute for Studies in Education.

Landry, R., & Allard, R. (1987). Étude du développement bilingue chez les Acadiens des provinces maritimes. In R. Théberge & J. Lafontant (Eds.), *Demain, la francophonie en milieu minoritaire?* (pp. 63–112). Saint Boniface, MB: Centre de Recherche Collège Saint-Boniface.

Lanehart, S. J. (1998). African American vernacular English and education. *Journal of English Linguistics, 26,* 122–136.

Lee, V. E., Marks, H., & Byrd, T. (1994). Sexism in single-sex and coeducational independent secondary school classrooms. *Sociology of Education, 67,* 92–120.

Leman, J. (1997). School as a socialising and corrective force in inter-ethnic urban relations. *Journal of Multilingual and Multicultural Development, 18,* 125–134.

Lemke, J. (1990). *Talking science: Language, learning and values.* Norwood, NJ: Ablex.

LeVine, R. A. (1984). Properties of culture: ethnographic view. In R. A. Shweder & R. A. LeVine (Eds), *Culture theory: Essays on mind, self, and emotion.* (pp. 67–87). Cambridge, England: Cambridge University Press.

LeVine, R. A., & White, M. (1986). *Human conditions: The cultural basis of educational development.* New York: Routledge and Kegan Paul.

Lindholm, K. (1997). Two-way bilingual education programs in the United States. In J. Cummins & D. Corson (Eds.), *Bilingual education* (pp. 271–279). Boston: Kluwer Academic.

Lindsay, A. (1992). Oral narrative discourse style of First Nations children and the language of schooling. *Reflections on Canadian Literacy, 10,* 205–209.

Lippi-Green, R. (1997). *English with an accent: Language, ideology, and discrimination in the United States.* London: Routledge.

Llewellyn, R. (1968). *How green was my valley.* Toronto, ON: Signet.

Lockhart, J. (1991)."We real cool": dialect in the middle school classroom. *English Journal, 80* (December), 53–58.

Long, M. H., & Crookes, G. (1992). Three approaches to task-based syllabus design. *TESOL Quarterly, 26,* 27–56.

Luke, A. (1997). Critical approaches to literacy. In V. Edwards & D. Corson (Eds.), *Literacy* (pp. 143–152). London: Kluwer Academic.

Luria, A. R. (1973). *The working brain.* Harmondsworth, England: Penguin.

Mackey, W. F. (1991). Language education in bilingual Acadia. In O. García (Ed.), *Bilingual education* (pp. 239–252). Amsterdam: Benjamins.

MacKinnon, K., & Densham, J. (1989). Ethnolinguistic diversity in Britain: Policies and practice in school and society. *Language, Culture and Curriculum, 2,* 75–89.

Maclear, K. (1994). The myth of the "model minority": Rethinking the education of Asian Canadians. *Our Schools/Our Selves, 5*(3), 54–76.

MacPhail, B. (1999, May 12). Reaping what we sow in the way we rear our boys [On-line Editorial]. Available: www.houstonchronicle.com.

MacWhinney, B., & Snow, C. (1990). The child language data exchange system: An update. *Journal of Child Language, 17,* 457–472.

Mael, F. A. (1998). Single-sex and coeducational schooling: relationships to socioemotional and academic development. *Review of Educational Research, 68,* 101–129.

Malcolm, I. (1979). The West Australian Aboriginal child and classroom interaction: a sociolinguisitc approach. *Journal of Pragmatics, 3,* 305–320.

Malcolm, I. (1982). Speech events of the aboriginal classroom. *International Journal of the Sociology of Language, 36,* 115–134.

Malcolm, I. (1994). Aboriginal English inside and outside the classroom. *Australian Review of Applied Linguistics, 17,* 147–180.

Maltz, D., & Borker, R. (1983). A cultural approach to male-female miscommunication. In J. Gumperz (Ed.), *Language and social identity.* Cambridge, England: Cambridge University Press.

Martin-Jones, M. (1997). Bilingual classroom discourse. In N. Hornberger & D. Corson (Eds.), *Research methods in language and education* (pp. 249–258). Boston: Kluwer Academic.

Masemann, V. (1984). Multicultural programs in Toronto schools. In J. Mallea & J. Young (Eds.), *Cultural diversity and Canadian education* (pp. 349–369). Ottawa, ON: Carleton University Press.

Mason, D. (1994). *Bilingual/bicultural deaf education is appropriate.* (Association of Canadian Educators of the Hearing Impaired Occasional Monograph series No. 2). Toronto, ON: Association of Canadian Educators of the Hearing Impaired.

May, S. (1997). Critical ethnography. In N. Hornberger & D. Corson (Eds.), *Research methods in language and education* (pp. 197–206). Boston: Kluwer Academic.

McCarty, T. (1997). Teacher research methods in language and education. In N. Hornberger & D. Corson (Eds.), *Research methods in language and education* (pp. 227–237). Boston: Kluwer Academic.

McConnell-Ginet, S., Borker, R., & Furman, N. (Eds.). (1980). *Women and language in literature and society.* New York: Praeger.

McDonald, M. (1989). The exploitation of linguistic mis-match: towards an ethnography of customs and manners. In R. Grillo (Ed.), *Social anthropology and the politics of language.* London: Routledge.

McElhinny, B. (1995). Challenging hegemonic masculinities: Female and male police officers handling domestic violence. In K. Hall & M. Buckholtz (Eds.), *Gender articulated: Language and the socially constructed self* (pp. 217–243). New York: Routledge.

McFeatters, D. (1995, March 27). Editorial. *Globe & Mail,* A11.

McGonigal, J. (1997). Using oral discourse in literary studies. In B. Davies & D. Corson (Eds.), *Oral discourse and education* (pp. 249–257). Boston: Kluwer Academic.

McWhorter, J. H. (1997). Wasting energy on an illusion. *The Black Scholar: Journal of Black Studies and Research, 27,* 9–13.

Meara, P. (1982). Vocabulary acquisition: a neglected aspect of language learning. In V. Kinsella (Ed.), *Surveys 1: Eight state-of-the-art articles on key areas in language teaching* (pp. 100–126). Cambridge, England: Cambridge University Press.

Mehan, H. (1980). The competent student. *Anthropology and Education Quarterly, 11,* 32–64.

Mehan, H. (1984). Language and schooling. *Sociology of Education, 57,* 174–183.

Michaels, S. (1981). 'Sharing time': children's narrative styles and differential access to literacy. *Language in Society, 10,* 423–442.

Michaels, S., & Cazden, C. (1986). Teacher/child collaboration as oral preparation for literacy. In B. Schieffelin & P. Gilmore (Eds.), *The acquisition of literacy: Ethnographic perspectives.* Norwood, NJ: Ablex.

Moffett, J. (1968). *Teaching the universe of discourse.* London: Houghton Mifflin.

Moffett, J. (1989). Censorship and spiritual education. *English Education, 21,* 70–87.

Moll, L. C. (1992). Bilingual classroom studies and community analysis. *Educational Researcher, 21,* 20–24.

Moorfield, J. (1987). Implications for schools of research findings in bilingual education. In W. Hirsh (Ed.), *Living languages.* Auckland, New Zealand: Heinemann.

Morgan, B. D. (1998). *The ESL classroom: Teaching, critical practice, and community development.* Toronto, ON: University of Toronto Press.

Morse, L., & Handley, H. (1985). Listening to adolescents: gender differences in science class interaction. In L. Wilkinson & C. Marrett (Eds.), *Gender influences in classroom interaction.* Orlando, FL: Academic Press.

Mougeon, R., & Nadasdi, T. (1998). Sociolinguistic discontinuity in linguistic minority communities. *Language, 74,* 40–55.

Much, N. C. (1992). The analysis of discourse as methodology for a semiotic psychology. *American Behavioural Scientist, 36,* 52–72.

Myths and facts of immigration. (1999, April 10). *The Toronto Star,* p. D7.

Nichols, P. C. (1989). Storytelling in Carolina: continuities and contrasts. *Anthropology and Education Quarterly, 20,* 232–245.

Nielsen, K. (1978). Class and justice. In J. Arthur & W. H. Shaw (Eds.), *Justice and economic distribution.* Englewood Cliffs, NJ: Prentice Hall.

Norton, B. (1997). Critical discourse research. In N. Hornberger and D. Corson (Eds.), *Research methods in language and education* (pp. 207–215). Boston: Kluwer Academic.

Nwoye, O. G. (1998). Linguistic gender difference in Igbo. *International Journal of the Sociology of Language, 129,* 87–102.

O'Barr, W., & Atkins, B. (1980). "Women's language" or "powerless language?" In S. McConnell-Ginet, R. Borker & N. Furman (Eds.), *Women and language in literature and society.* New York: Praeger.

Ochs, E., & Taylor, C. (1995). The "Father Knows Best" dynamic in dinnertime narratives. In K. Hall & M. Bucholz (Eds.), *Gender articulated: Language and the socially constructed self* (pp. 97–120). New York: Routledge.

234   REFERENCES

Oevermann, U. (1972). *Sprache und soziale Herkunft: Ein Beitrag zur Analyse schichtspezifischer Sozialisationsprozesse und ihrer Bedeutung fuer den Studienerfolg.* Frankfurt am Main, Germany: Suhrkamp.
Ogbu, J. (1983). Minority status and schooling in plural societies. *Comparative Education Review, 27,* 168–190.
Ogbu, J. (1987). Variability in minority school performance: a problem in search of an explanation. *Anthropology and Education Quarterly, 18,* 312–334.
Oryan, S. (1997). 'Modest language - humble souls': Speech patterns among Israeli Orthodox women and girls. *Hebrew Linguistics, 41–42,* 7–20.
Pakir, A. (1997). Innovative second language education in South-east Asia. In G. Tucker & D. Corson (Eds.), *Second Language Education* (pp. 221–230). Boston: Kluwer Academic.
Pauwels, A. (1991). Gender differences in Australian English. In S. Romaine (Ed.), *Language in Australia* (pp. 318–326). Cambridge, England: Cambridge University Press.
Pennycook, A. (1990). Towards a critical applied linguistics for the 1990s. *Issues in Applied Linguistics, 1,* 8–28.
Philips, S. (1972). Participant structures and communicative competence: Warm Springs children in community and classroom. In C. Cazden, V. John, & D. Hymes (Eds.), *Functions of language in the classroom.* New York: Teachers College Press.
Philips, S. (1980). Sex differences and language. *Annual Review of Anthropology, 9,* 523–544.
Philips, S. (1983). *The invisible culture: Communication in classroom and community on the Warm Springs Indian Reservation.* New York: Longman.
Philips, S., Steele, S., & Tanz, C. (Eds.). (1987). *Language, gender, and sex in comparative perspective.* Cambridge, England: Cambridge University Press.
Phillipson, R. (1992). *Linguistic imperialism.* Oxford, England: Oxford University Press.
Pollack, W. (1973). *Strategien zur Emanzipation: Bildungspolitik, Didaktik und Soziolinguistik.* Wien: Jugend und Volk.
Popper, K. R. (1972). *Objective knowledge: An evolutionary approach.* Oxford, England: Clarendon Press.
Poulson, L., Radmor, H., & Turner-Bisset, R. (1996). From policy to practice: Language education, English teaching and curriculum reform in secondary schools in England. *Language and Education, 10,* 33–46.
Quine, W. V. O. (1953). *From a logical point of view.* New York: Harper Torch Books.
Quine, W. V. O. (1966). *The Ways of Paradox and Other Essays.* New York: Random House.
Ramirez, J. (1992). Executive summary. *Bilingual Research Journal, 16,* 1–62.
Rampton, M. B. (1995). *Crossing: Language and ethnicity among adolescents.* New York: Longman.
Randall, G. (1987). Gender differences in pupil-teacher interaction in workshops and laboratories. In G. Weiner & M. Arnot (Eds.), *Gender Under Scrutiny.* London: Hutchinson.
Rassool, N. (1997). Language policies for a multicultural Britain. In R. Wodak & D. Corson (Eds.), *Language policy and political issues in education* (pp. 113–127). Boston: Kluwer Academic.
Rawls, J. (1972). *A theory of justice.* Oxford, England: Oxford University Press.
Rawls, J. (1980). Kantian constructivism in moral theory: The Dewey Lectures. *Journal of Philosophy, 77,* 515–572.
Rawls, J. (1993). *Political liberalism: John Dewey essays in philosophy.* New York: Columbia University Press.
Reay, D. (1991). Intersections of gender, race and class in the primary school. *British Journal of Sociology of Education, 12,* 163–182.
Reid, E. (1988). Linguistic minorities and language education: the English experience. *Journal of Multilingual and Multicultural Development, 9,* 181–191, 220–223.
Rezai-Rashti, G. (1994). The dilemma of working with minority female students in Canadian high schools. *Canadian Woman's Studies/Les cahiers de la femme, 14*(2), 76–82.
Ricento, T. (1997). Language policy and education in the United States. In R. Wodak & D. Corson (Eds.), *Language policy and political issues in education* (pp. 139–149). Boston: Kluwer Academic.
Rickford, J., & Rickford, A. E. (1995). Dialect readers revisited. *Linguistics and Education, 7,* 107–128.
Rodda, M., Grove, C., & Finch, B. (1986). Mainstreaming and the education of Deaf students. *The Alberta Journal of Educational Research, 32,* 140–153.
Romaine, S. (1978). Postvocalic /r/ in Scottish English: sound change in progress? In P. Trudgill (Ed.), *Sociolinguistic patterns in British English.* London: Edward Arnold.

Rosen, C., & Rosen, H. (1973). *The language of primary school children.* London: Penguin.

Ross, R. (1996). *Returning to the teachings: Exploring Aboriginal justice.* Toronto, ON: Penguin.

Royal Commission on Learning in Ontario (1995). *For the love of learning.* Toronto, ON: Queen's Printer for Ontario.

Ruíz, R. (1984). Orientations in language planning. *Journal of the National Association for Bilingual Education, 8,* 15–34.

Rundle, B. (1990). *Wittgenstein and contemporary philosophy of language.* Oxford, England: Basil Blackwell.

Ryan, J. (1992). Formal schooling and deculturation: nursing practice and the erosion of Native communication styles. *The Alberta Journal of Educational Research, 38,* 91–103.

Ryan, J. (1994). Organizing the facts: Aboriginal education and cultural differences in school discourse and knowledge. *Language and Education, 8,* 251–271.

Ryan, J. (1999). *Race and ethnicity in multi-ethnic schools.* Philadelphia: Multilingual Matters.

Sadker, M., & Sadker, D. (1985, March). Sexism in the schoolroom of the '80s. *Psychology Today,* 54–57.

Sanchez, G. (1934). Bilingualism and mental measures: a word of caution. *Journal of Applied Psychology, 18,* 765–772.

Sandel, M. (1982). *Justice and the limits of liberalism.* London: Cambridge University Press.

Sato, C. J. (1989). A nonstandard approach to standard English. *TESOL Quarterly, 23,* 259–282.

Saville-Troike, M. (1979). Culture, language and education. In H. Trueba & C. Barnett-Mizrahi (Eds.), *Bilingual multicultural education and the professional: From theory to practice.* Rowley, MA: Newbury House.

Saville-Troike, M. (1987). The ethnography of speaking. In U. Ammon, N. Dittmar, & K. Mattheier (Eds.), *Sociolinguistics* (pp. 660–671). Berlin, Germany: de Gruyter.

Saville-Troike, M. (1989). *The ethnography of communication: An introduction.* Oxford, sxEngland: Basil Blackwell.

Schieffelin, B. (1987). Do different worlds mean different words? An example from Papua New Guinea. In S. Philips, S. Steele, & C. Tanz (Eds.), *Language, gender, and sex in comparative perspective.* Cambridge, England: Cambridge University Press.

Schlank, C. H., & Metzger, B. (1997). *Together and equal: Fostering cooperative play and promoting gender equity in early childhood programs.* Needham Heights, MA: Allyn & Bacon.

Scollon, R., & Scollon, S. (1979). *Linguistic convergence: An ethnography of speaking at Fort Chipewyan.* New York: Academic Press.

Scollon, R., & Scollon, S. (1981). *Narrative literacy and face in inter-ethnic communication.* Norwood, NJ: Ablex.

Scollon, R., & Scollon, S. (1984). Cooking it up and boiling it down: abstracts in Athabaskan children's story retellings. In D. Tannen (Ed.), *Coherence in spoken and written discourse.* Norwood, NJ: Ablex.

Shakeshaft, C., & Perry, A. (1995). The language of power vs the language of empowerment: Gender differences in administrative communication. In D. Corson (Ed.), *Discourse and power in educational organizations* (pp. 17–30). Cresskill, NJ: Hampton Press.

Shaw, G.B. (1903/1951) *Man and superman, the revolutionist's handbook,* "Maxims for revolutionists." In *Seven Plays by George Bernard Shaw* (pp. 517–743). New York: Dodd, Mead.

Sheldon, A. (1997). Talking power: Girls, gender enculturation and discourse. In R. Wodak (Ed.), *Gender and discourse* (pp. 225–244). Thousand Oaks, CA: Sage.

Silverstein, M., & Urban, G. (Eds.) (1996). *Natural histories of discourses.* Chicago: University of Chicago Press.

Singleton, D. (1997). Age and second language learning. In G. R. Tucker & D. Corson (Eds.), *Second language education* (pp. 43–49). Boston: Kluwer Academic.

Skehan, P. (1996). A framework for implementation of task-based instruction. *Applied Linguistics, 17,* 38–62.

Skutnabb-Kangas, T. (1997). Human rights and language policy in education. In R. Wodak & D. Corson (Eds.), *Language policy and political issues in education* (pp. 55–65). Boston: Kluwer Academic.

Smith, D. (1986). The anthropology of literacy acquisition. In B. Schieffelin & P. Gilmore (Eds.), *The acquisition of literacy: Ethnographic perspectives.* Norwood, NJ: Ablex.

Smith, J. S. (1992). Women in charge: politeness and directives in the speech of Japanese women. *Language in Society, 21,* 59–82.

Smith, P. (1985). *Languages, the sexes and society.* Oxford, England: Basil Blackwell.

Smitherman, G. (1977). *Talkin' and testifyin': The language of Black America.* Boston: Houghton Mifflin.

Smitherman, G. (1992). Black English, diverging or converging?: The view from the National Assessment of Educational Progress. *Language and Education, 6,* 47–61.

Smitherman, G. (1997). Black language and the education of Black children - one mo once. *The Black Scholar: Journal of Black Studies and Research, 27,* 28–35.

Speicher, B., & McMahon, S. (1992). Some African American perspectives on Black English vernacular. *Language in Society, 21,* 383–407.

Stanworth, M. (1983). *Gender and schooling: A study of sexual divisions in the classroom.* London: Hutchinson.

Street, B. (1997). Social literacies. In V. Edwards & D. Corson (Eds.), *Literacy* (pp. 133–141). London: Kluwer Academic.

Sullivan, M., Douglas, A., Mason, J., McAlpine, L., Pittinger, C., & Smith, D. (1991). Reading and writing with the Algonquin, Cree, Micmac and Mohawk: a learning experience for McGill instructors. *McGill Journal of Education, 26,* 209–217.

Sylvester, E. (1996). Inside, outside and in-between: Identities, literacies and educational policies in the lives of Cambodian women and girls in Philadelphia. Unpublished doctoral dissertation, University of Philadelphia.

Takahara, K. (1991). Female speech patterns in Japanese. *International Journal of the Sociology of Language, 92,* 61–85.

Tannen, D. (1982). Ethnic style in male-female communication. In J. J. Gumperz (Ed.), *Language and social identity* (pp. 217–231). Cambridge, England: Cambridge University Press.

Tannen, D. (1993). What's in a frame: surface evidence for underlying expectations. In D. Tannen (Ed.), *Framing in discourse* (pp. 14–56). New York: Oxford University Press.

Tannen, D., Kendall, S., & Adger, C. (1997). Conversational patterns across gender, class and ethnicity: implications for classroom discourse. In B. Davies & D. Corson (Eds.), *Oral discourse and education* (pp. 75–85). Boston: Kluwer Academic.

Taylor, C. (1979). Interpretation and the sciences of Man. In P. Rabinow & W. M. Sullivan (Eds.), *Interpretive social science: A reader.* Berkeley, CA: University of California Press.

Taylor, C. (1992). *Multiculturalism and "the politics of recognition".* Princeton, NJ: Princeton University Press.

Taylor, O., & Matsuda, M. (1988). Storytelling and classroom discrimination. In G. Smitherman-Donaldson & T. van Dijk, *Discourse and discrimination.* Detroit, MI: Wayne State University Press.

Telles, J. (1996). *Being a language teacher: Stories of critical reflection on language and pedagogy.* Unpublished doctoral thesis, Ontario Institute for Studies in Education, Toronto, ON.

Thompson, J. B. (1990). *Ideology and modern culture: Critical social theory in the era of mass communication.* Stanford, CA: Stanford University Press.

Thorne, B. (1986). Girls and boys together … but mostly apart: Gender arrangements in elementary schools. In W. Hartup & Z. Rubin (Eds.), *Relationships and development.* Hillsdale, NJ: Erlbaum.

Tiede, K. (1996). Appropriating the discourse of science: A case study of a grade eight science class. Unpublished doctoral thesis, University of Toronto, Toronto, ON.

Tompkins, J. (1998). *Teaching in a cold and windy place: Change in an Inuit school.* Toronto, ON: University of Toronto Press.

Treichler, P., & Kramarae, C. (1983). Women's talk in the ivory tower. *Communication Quarterly, 31,* 118–132.

Troemel-Ploetz, S. (1994). "Let me put it this way, John": Conversational strategies of women in leadership positions. *Journal of Pragmatics, 22,* 199–209.

Troike, R. (1981). A synthesis of research on bilingual education. *Educational Leadership, 14,* 498–504.

Tsolidis, G. (1990). Ethnic minority girls and self-esteem. In J. Kenway & S. Willis (Eds.), *Hearts and minds: Self-esteem and the schooling of girls* (pp. 53–69). London: Falmer.

Valdés, G. (1997). Bilinguals and bilingualism: language policy in an anti-immigrant age. *International Journal of the Sociology of Language, 127,* 25–52.

Vallen, T., & Stijnen, S. (1987). Language and educational success of indigenous and non-indigenous minority students in the Netherlands. *Language and Education, 1,* 109–124.

van Leeuwen, T. (1997). Media in education. In R. Wodak & D. Corson (Eds.), *Language policy and political issues in education* (pp. 211–218). Boston: Kluwer Academic.

van Lier, L., & Corson, D. (Eds.). (1997). *Knowledge about language.* Boston: Kluwer Academic.

Verhoeven, L. (1994). Transfer in bilingual development: The linguistic interdependence hypothesis revisited. *Language Learning, 44,* 381–415.

Vogt, L., Jordan, C., & Tharp, R. (1987). Explaining school failure, producing school success: two cases. *Anthropology and Education Quarterly, 19,* 276–286.

Wagner, S. (avec la collaboration de P. Granier). (1991). *Analphabétisme de minorité et alphabétisation d'affirmation nationale à propos de L'Ontario Français. Volume 1: Synthèse théorique et historique.* Ottawa, ON: Mutual Press.

Waite, D. (1997). Language, power and teacher-administrator discourse. In R. Wodak & D. Corson (Eds.), *Language policy and political issues in language and education* (pp. 43–52). Boston: Kluwer Academic.

Walkerdine, V. (1987). Sex, power and pedagogy. In M. Arnot & G. Weiner (Eds.), *Gender and the politics of schooling.* London: Unwin Hyman.

Warner, S. L. N. (1999). *Kuleana:* the right, responsibility, and authority of indigenous peoples to speak and make decisions themselves in language and cultural revitalization. *Anthropology and Education Quarterly, 30,* 68–93.

Watson-Gegeo, K. (1997). Classroom ethnography. In N. Hornberger & D. Corson (Eds.), *Research methods in language and education* (pp. 135–144). Boston: Kluwer Academic.

Watts, R. (1997). Language policy and education in New Zealand and the South Pacific. In R. Wodak & D. Corson (Eds.), *Language policy and political issues in education* (pp. 191–200). Boston: Kluwer Academic.

Weber, M. (1969). *The theory of social and economic organisation.* New York: The Free Press.

Weir, C. J. (1997). The testing of reading in a second language. In C. Clapham & D. Corson (Eds.), *Language testing and assessment* (pp. 39–49). Boston: Kluwer Academic.

Whiteman, M. (Ed.). (1981). *Writing: The nature, development and teaching of written communication. Volume 1. Variation in writing: Functional and linguistic-cultural differences.* Hillsdale, NJ: Lawrence Erlbaum Associates.

Williams, R. (1981). *Culture.* Glasgow, Scotland: Fontana.

Williamson, J., & Hardman, F. (1997). Non-standard dialect and children's writing. *Language and Education, 11,* 287–299.

Willis, P. (1977). *Learning to labour.* Aldershot, England: Gower.

Willms, J. D., & Jacobsen, S. (1990). Growth in mathematics skills during the intermediate years: sex differences and school effects. *International Journal of Educational Research, 14,* 157–174.

Winch, C. (1989). Standard English, normativity and the Cox Committee Report. *Language and Education, 3,* 275–293.

Winch, C. & Gingell, J. (1994). Dialect interference and difficulties with writing. *Language and Education 8,* 157–182.

Wittgenstein, L. (1953). *Philosophical investigations.* (G. E. M. Anscombe, Trans.). Oxford, England: Basil Blackwell.

Wittgenstein, L. (1972). *On Certainty.* New York: Harper Torchbooks.

Wodak, R. (1975). *Das Sprachverhalten von Angeklagten bei Gericht.* Tuebingen: Scriptor.

Wodak, R. (1981). Women relate, men report: sex differences in language behaviour in a therapeutic group. *Journal of Pragmatics, 5,* 261–285.

Wodak, R. (1995). Power, discourse, and styles of female leadership in school committee meetings. In D. Corson (Ed.), *Discourse and power in educational organizations* (pp. 31–54). Cresskill, NJ: Hampton Press.

Wodak, R. (Ed.). (1997). *Gender and discourse.* Thousand Oaks, CA: Sage.

Wodak, R., & de Cillia, R. (Eds.). (1995). *Sprachenpolitik in Mittel und Osteuropa.* Vienna, Austria: Passagen.

Wolfram, W. (1991). *Dialects and American English.* Englewood Cliffs, NJ: Prentice-Hall.

Wolfram, W. (1993). Ethical considerations in language awareness programs. *Issues in Applied Linguistics, 4,* 225–255.

Wong Fillmore, L., Ammon, P., McLaughlin, B., & Ammon, M. S. (1985). *Final report for learning English through bilingual instruction.* Berkeley/Santa Cruz, CA: University of California.

Wong Fillmore, L., & Valdez, C. (1986). Teaching bilingual learners. In M. Wittrock (Ed.), *Handbook of research on teaching.* New York: Macmillan.

Woodford, M. (1997). Introduction. *The Black Scholar: Journal of Black Studies and Research, 27,* 2–3.

Wrong, D. (1979). *Power: Its forms, bases and uses.* Oxford, England: Basil Blackwell.

Young, I. (1981). Towards a critical theory of justice. *Social Theory and Practice, 7,* 279–302.

Young, R. E. (1992). *Critical theory and classroom talk.* Clevedon, England: Multilingual Matters.

Zinsser, C. (1986). For the Bible tells me so: Teaching children in a fundamentalist church. In B. Schieffelin & P. Gilmore (Eds.), *The acquisition of literacy: Ethnographic perspectives.* Norwood, NJ: Ablex.

Author Index

A

Abbott, C., 146
Adger, C., 82, 87
Agnihotri, R. K., 94
Albert, M., 112
Allard, R., 127
Alloway, L., 167, 172
Allwright, D., 139
AAUW [American Association of University Women], 168, 172, 175
Ammon, M. S., 115
Ammon, P., 115
Ammon, U., 70, 189
Andersson, L.-G., 91
Appel, R., 115
Apple, M., 20
Artiles, A., 120
Ashenden, D., 184
Atkins, B., 161
Au, K., 60
Auerbach, E. R., 92, 94

B

Baker, C., 112, 124, 166
Baker, R., 145
Bakhtin, M., 62
Baldwin, J., 80
Ballenger, C., 61
Baran, G., 176
Barnes, D., 74
Barry, B., 27

Bascia, N., 144
Baudoux, C., 169
Baugh, J., 67, 80, 92
Baxter, J., 172, 184
Bernstein, B., 73
Bhaskar, R., 7, 30, 188, 192
Bigelow, B., 94
Biggs, N., 57, 169, 178
Bird, L., 182
Bjerrum Nielsen, H., 168, 170
Black, D., 132
Blair, H., 75, 84, 96
Blake, B. E., 93
Blount, J. M., 161
Bogoch, B., 162
Borker, R., 155, 159, 160, 167
Bortoni-Ricardo, S., 70
Bourdieu, P., 21, 70, 71, 194
Brandl, M., 43
Branscombe, A., 50
Branson, J., 128, 129, 130, 131, 134
Briggs, C., 196
Britton, J., 74
Brouwer, D., 162
Brown, P., 159
Bruck, M., 134, 135
Bruner, J., 8
Bucholtz, M., 162
Buck, G., 145
Bullard, J., 122
Burnaby, B., 71, 103
Burns, J., 182
Byrd, T., 184

C

Cameron, D., 155, 159, 167
Campos, S., 116
Canadian Association of the Deaf, 132
Cazden, C., 40, 44, 52, 56, 57, 58, 59, 178, 207
Chamot, A., 115
Chenery, H. J., 145
Cheshire, J., 82, 164, 165
Chouliaraki, L., 62
Christensen, L., 94
Christian, D., 79
Christie, M., 41, 57
Churchill, S., 102, 117, 127
Clapham, C., 78
Clark, R., 90
Clegg, J., 135
Clift, C., 182
Clyne, M., 104
Coates, J., 155, 159
Collier, V., 116
Commonwealth Schools Commission, 135
Connell, R., 184
Crago, M., 57, 60, 64, 203, 208, 221
Crandall, J.-A., 139, 141, 145
Crookes, G., 138
Crosby, F., 162
Crystal, D., 112
Cumming, A., 145
Cummins, J., 19, 87, 94, 99, 105, 106, 112,
        113, 114, 119, 120, 121, 127, 131,
        142, 147

D

Dahrendorf, R., 153
Danby, S., 166
Danesi, M., 131
Dannequin, C., 69
Davies, B., 62, 168, 170
de Cillia, R., 70
DeFrancisco, V., 157
de Haan, D., 162
Delpit, L., 49, 88, 89, 90
Densham, J., 131
Department of Education and Science, 75, 77
DeStefano, J. S., 54
Devlin, B., 70
DiBenedetto, T., 10
Dittman, A., 165
Dittmar, N., 189
Douglas, A., 42
Dowsett, G., 184
Duncan, J., 182
Duranti, A., 196
Durkheim, E., 3

E

Eckert, P., 156, 159, 162, 165, 166, 170, 210,
        221
Edelman, M., 19
Edwards, A. D., 54, 74, 77, 85, 190
Edwards, J., 82
Edwards, V., 57, 82, 83, 87, 88, 142, 169, 178
Egbo, B., 94, 153
Erickson, F., 18, 48, 52, 87, 88, 92
Eriks-Brophy, A., 64, 203, 208, 221
Erting, C., 134
Ervin-Tripp, S., 207
Escobar, G., 104
Esposito, A., 165
Evans, C., 133
Ewoldt, C., 132, 133, 134

F

Fairclough, N., 19, 76, 90
Faltis, C., 124
Farah, I., 195, 198
Fasold, R., 22, 67, 77, 83, 158
Fennema, E., 169
Fettes, M., 9
Feuerverger, G., 122
Fichtelius, A., 169
Finch, B., 131
Fishman, J., 85, 118, 127, 190
Fishman, P., 157
Fitzpatrick, F., 117
Fordham, S., 89, 92
Foster, M., 80
Foucault, M., 1, 17, 192, 195
Freeman, R. D., 125, 198, 199, 201, 221
Frenette, N., 117, 127
Furby, L., 29
Furman, N., 155

G

Gal, S., 100, 101
Gándara, P., 116
Garcez, P., 198
García, O., 115, 116
Gee, J. P., 9, 52
Geertz, C., 9
Gerritson, M., 162
Gersten, R., 120
Gibson, H., 129, 130, 133, 134
Gilbert, P., 167, 172
Giles, H., 82
Gillett, G., 7, 9, 10, 12, 17
Gillett, J., 119
Gingell, J., 86

Goldstein, B., 179
Goodwin, M. H., 165, 167
Gramsci, A., 18, 76
Greenfield, T., 106
Grieshaber, S., 166
Grimshaw, A., 190
Grove, C., 131
Gumperz, J., 36, 48, 198
Guskey, T., 84

H

Hagman, T., 116
Hall, K., 162
Hamayan, E., 121, 134, 137
Hamp-Lyons, L., 145
Handley, H., 169
Hardman, F., 70
Harker, R., 24
Harré, R., 7, 9, 10, 12, 17
Harris, S., 70
Hastings, W. K., 102
Haw, K., 180
Heath, S., 50, 53, 54
Heller, M., 23, 62, 81, 82, 152, 170, 214, 217, 221
Herriman, M., 71
Herring, S., 10
Hewitt, R., 88
Hewstone, M., 82
Hingangaroa Smith, G., 193
Hobsbawm, E., 25
Hoffmeister, R., 132, 133, 134
Holmes, J., 49, 70, 158
Hornberger, N. H., 94, 116, 119, 195, 196, 198
Horvath, B., 105
Hudson, R., 70
Hughes, J., 2, 6
Hymes, D., 36, 47, 195

I

Iglesias, A., 119
Israelite, N., 132, 133, 134
Ivanic, R., 90

J

Jackson, J. J., 80
Jacobsen, S., 184
Janks, H., 90
Jaworski, A., 62
Jenkins, N., 164, 165
Johansson, I., 169

Johnson, D. A., 10
Johnson, P., 82
Johnson, R., 134
Jones, A., 56, 178
Jordan, C., 55, 63
Joshee, R., 122

K

Kanaris, A., 167
Karp, S., 94
Keatinge, H., 116
Keenan, E., 162
Kelly, A., 168, 169
Kendall, S., 82, 87, 158, 161
Kessler, S., 184
Khubchandani, L., 70
Kincheloe, J. L., 84
Klann-Delius, G., 158, 165
Krahnke, K., 141
Kramarae, C., 159
Kuhn, T. S., 5
Kyle, J., 129, 130
Kymlicka, W., 30

L

Labov, W., 18, 73, 74, 78, 85, 86, 87
Ladd, P., 131
Lahdenperä, J., 116
Lakoff, R., 155
Lambert, W., 104
Landry, R., 127
Lanehart, S. J., 74, 87
Lee, V. E., 184
Leman, J., 118
Lemay, S., 32, 79, 103, 125, 127, 172
Lemke, J., 61
LeVine, R. A., 10, 153
Liddell, S., 134
Lindholm, K., 124, 125
Lindsay, A., 51
Lippi-Green, R., 76, 79
Llewellyn, R., 99
Lockhart, J., 90
Long, M. H., 138
Luke, A., 94
Luria, A. R., 12

M

Mackey, W. F., 125
MacKinnon, K., 131

Maclear, K., 180
MacPhail, B., 173
MacWhinney, B., 207
Mael, F. A., 168, 184
Malcolm, I., 43, 47, 60
Maltz, D., 159, 160, 167
Marks, H., 184
Martin-Jones, M., 198
Masemann, V., 106
Mason, D., 129, 130, 131, 133, 134
Mason, J., 42, 60
Matsuda, M., 49
Mattheier, K., 189
May, S., 198
McAlpine, L., 42
McCarty, T., 84, 198
McConnell-Ginet, S., 155, 156, 162
McDonald, M., 37
McElhinny, B., 160
McFeatters, D., 66
McGonigal, J., 94, 147
McLaughlin, B., 115
McMahon, S., 88
McWhorter, J. H., 80
Meara, P., 139
Mehan, H., 87, 204, 206
Metzger, B., 182
Michaels, S., 36, 50, 52
Miller, D., 128, 129, 131, 134
Miner, B., 94
Moffett, J., 93, 109
Moll, L. C., 116
Moorfield, J., 115
Morgan, B. D., 142
Morse, L., 169
Mougeon, R., 81
Much, N. C., 10

N

Nadasdi, T., 81
Nichols, P. C., 52
Nielsen, K., 29
Noircent, A., 169
Nordin, K., 169
Norton, B., 145
Nwoye, O. G., 158
Nyquist, L., 162

O

O'Barr, W., 161
Obler, L., 112
Ochs, E., 18

Oevermann, U., 70
Ogbu, J., 38, 106
Oryan, S., 156
Otheguy, R., 115, 116

P

Pakir, A., 77
Pauwels, A., 155
Pennycook, A., 189
Perry, A., 161
Peterson, B., 94
Peterson, P., 169
Philips, S., 44, 45, 50, 155
Phillipson, R., 190, 191
Pittinger, C., 42
Pollack, W., 70
Popper, K. R., 4
Poulson, L., 68, 75

Q

Quazi, S., 117, 127
Quine, W. V. O., 5, 190

R

Radmor, H., 68, 75
Ramirez, J., 116
Rampton, M. B., 198
Randall, G., 182
Rassool, N., 104
Rawls, J., 27, 29
Reay, D., 160
Redfern, A., 142
Reid, E., 135
Rezai-Rashti, G., 177
Ricento, T., 104
Rickford, A. E., 79, 83, 85, 90
Rickford, J., 79, 83, 85, 90
Rodda, M., 131
Romaine, S., 155
Rosen, C., 74
Rosen, H., 74
Ross, R., 20
Royal Commission on Learning in Ontario, 110
Ruíz, R., 199
Rundle, B., 11
Ryan, E. B., 82
Ryan, J., 16, 46, 61

S

Sachdev, I., 62

Sadker, D., 169
Sadker, M., 169
Sanchez, G., 106
Sandel, M., 29
Sato, C. J., 85
Saville-Troike, M., 39, 196
Sayers, D., 94, 142, 147
Schieffelin, B., 155
Schlank, C. H., 182
Scollon, R., 40, 49
Scollon, S., 40, 49
Shakeshaft, C., 161
Shaw, G. B., 28
Sheldon, A., 166, 174
Silverstein, M., 196
Singleton, D., 141
Skehan, P., 138
Skilton-Sylvester, E., 94
Skutnabb-Kangas, R., 102
Small, A., 129, 130, 133, 134
Smith, D., 42, 92
Smith, J. S., 158
Smith, P., 159, 162
Smitherman, G., 75, 78, 80, 86
Snow, C., 207
Speicher, B., 88
Stanworth, M., 169, 170
Steele, S., 155
Stijnen, S., 114
Street, B., 94
Sullivan, M., 42
Sylvester, E., 180

T

Takahara, K., 158
Tannen, D., 82, 87, 158, 161, 162, 199
Tanz, C., 155
Taylor, C., 5, 18, 30
Taylor, O., 49
Telles, J., 70, 75, 96
Tharp, R., 55
Thompson, J. B., 197
Thorne, B., 166
Tiede, K., 61
Tompkins, J., 119
Treichler, P., 159
Trent, S., 120
Troemel-Ploetz, S., 161
Troike, R., 106
Trudgill, P., 91
Tsolidis, G., 176, 177
Turner-Bisset, R., 68, 75

U

Urban, G., 196

V

Valdés, G., 30
Valdez, C., 116
Vallen, T., 114
van Leeuwen, T., 10
van Lier, L., 34, 143
Verhoeven, L., 115
Vogt, L., 55

W

Wagner, S., 91, 94
Waite, D., 173
Walkerdine, V., 162
Warner, S. L. N., 42
Watson-Gegeo, K., 198
Watts, R., 104
Weber, M., 5
Weir, C. J., 145
Westgate, D., 54
White, M., 153
Whiteman, M., 86
Williams, R., 9
Williamson, J., 70
Willis, P., 89
Willms, J. D., 184
Winch, C., 76, 86
Wittgenstein, L., 4
Wodak, R., 70, 155, 160, 161, 173
Wolfram, W., 78–79
Woll, B., 129, 130
Wong Fillmore, L., 115, 116, 207
Woodford, M., 80
Woodward, J., 120
Wrong, D., 18

Y

Young, I., 29
Young, R. E., 62, 87

Z

Zimmer, K., 133
Zinsser, C., 54

Subject Index

A

AAVE, *see* African American Vernacular English
Aboriginal Australians, *see* Indigenous peoples
Aboriginal languages, 70, 104, 108
Aboriginal peoples, *see* Indigenous peoples
Academic words, 62, 139–143
Académie Française, 69
Acadian French, 81, 102, 125
Accent, 22, 66–67, 70, 79, 87, 217
Accountability, 15, 145
Achievement, 41–42, 53, 67, 85, 93, 110, 113, 116, 125, 169, 175, 185
Adjectives, 20
Administration, 2, 65, 70, 126, 161
Administrators, 31, 35, 78, 111, 123–124, 144, 184, 199–203, 215
Adolescents, 52, 74, 88–89, 92–94, 124, 134, 139–143, 159–160, 165–166, 170–171, 179, 182, 210
Advertising, 10, 82, 173
Africa, *see also* Malagasy Republic, the, Nigeria, South Africa, 67, 72–74, 79–80, 82, 153–154, 170, 216
African Americans, 37–38, 45, 50–54, 67, 74, 79–80, 86–89, 92, 97, 120, 162
African American Vernacular English (AAVE), 67, 79–81, 85–88, 92, 97
Aggression, verbal, 159–160
Alberta, 130
Algonquin, *see* Indigenous peoples
Alienation, 26
American Sign Language (ASL), 129–134

Analytic competence, 87
Anglicisms, 126, 218
Anglophones, 79, 91, 103, 112, 117, 123–129
Anglo-Saxon, 109, 139
Ann Arbor, MI, 74, 77–80
Anthropology, 7, 190–191, 194, 197,
Appropriateness, 76–78, 97
Arapaho, *see* Indigenous peoples
Archaic values, 158
Aristophanes, 69
Arizona, 55–56
ASL, *see* American Sign Language
Assessment, 15, 77–78, 86, 97, 119–121, 132–133, 135, 145, 172, 198
    communicative proficiency, 78, 97
    language testing, 77–78, 121, 145
Assimilation, 26, 91, 126, 127
    linguistic, 101
Assimilationary pressures, reducing, 127
Athabaskan, *see* Indigenous peoples
Audience, 49, 52, 88, 152
Australasia, *see also* Australia, New Zealand, Papua New Guinea, 42, 56, 66, 104, 177–178, 182
Australia, 41, 43, 47, 57, 71, 75, 83–84, 103–108, 113, 122, 147, 160, 166, 172, 177

B

Basal readers, 54
Behaviour, 2–3, 6, 14, 17–20, 39–40, 45, 48, 53–54, 64, 69, 84–85, 97, 153,

157–158, 164–168, 171, 179, 183, 186, 190, 205
Behaviourism, 3
Beliefs, 6–7, 18, 29, 62, 84–85, 97, 105, 149, 166, 192, 199, 204, 210–211
Bias, 28–29, 67, 70, 74, 78, 148, 154, 169, 177, 202, 219
    systemic bias, 19–20
Biculturalism, 38–39, 108, 129, 132–134
Bilingual education, 30, 32, 80, 99–151, 179, 200–202
    active, 116
    additive, 104, 201
    advantages of, 112–113
    immersion, 112–119, 125–126, 131, 133, 148
    maintenance programs, 104–107
    subtractive, 105
    two-way, 60, 103, 124–125, 201–202
Bilingual Education Act (US), 100, 103, 201
Bilingualism, 30–34, 80–81, 99–151, 170, 179, 198–202, 214
Black Americans, see African Americans
Black English, see African American Vernacular English
Books, see Literacy
Boys, 152–187, 211, 216, 219
Brain, 8, 12, 14, 111
Brazil, 75, 96, 159
Britain, see also England, Scotland, Wales, 30, 57, 66, 83–88, 103–104, 117, 122–125, 129–131, 160, 170, 177–180
British Sign Language (BSL), 129
BSL, see British Sign Language
Bullock Report, the, 75, 77, 79, 96
Buraku, 106

C

California, 79–82, 100, 126, 133, 147
California School for the Deaf, 133
Cambodians, 116, 180
Canada, 20, 30, 32, 38–42, 46, 51, 56–57, 61–62, 66, 71, 75, 77, 79–83, 88, 91, 100, 102, 103–108, 115–134, 170, 174, 177–180, 218–219
Canadian French, 81, 126, 219
Capital
    cultural, 21–25, 34–35, 57, 72, 105, 119, 176, 181, 194, 209–210
    linguistic, 21–23, 35–38, 44, 48, 50, 65, 68, 72, 91, 106–108, 122, 157, 171, 180
    high status, 22, 72, 91

symbolic, 21, 35, 157, 166, 210, 221
Capitalism, 25–26, 154–159, 161, 177
Caribbean, the, 80–88
Cariño, 40, 58
Celtic languages, 104, 123–125, 129
Center for Immigration Studies, the, 104
Centre de recherches en éducation franco-ontarienne, 215
Chemistry, 182
Chinese, 115, 217
CLA, see Language awareness
Code switching, 88–90, 134
Cognition, 8–12
Comics, 50
Communicative method, 138
Communicative proficiency assessment, 78, 97
Communities, 6–7, 19, 23, 26, 30–74, 81–88, 94–133, 136, 142, 147–150, 154–160, 165, 171, 174–181, 184, 192–204, 209–221
    of practice, see also Language games, 156–165, 192–196
    consulting participants in, 193–194
Community consultation, 118, 193–194
Community languages, 68, 88, 103–104, 108, 122, 129, 149
Competence
    communicative, 47, 80, 137
    discourse, 137
    linguistic, 137
    social, 137
    sociocultural, 137
    sociolinguistic, 137
    strategic, 137
Compulsory schooling, 117, 141
Computer technology, 10, 142, 146
Comte, Auguste, 2
Conception of discovery, 1, 30
Conceptual frameworks, see also Language games, 21, 176–177, 18
Conflict, 17, 33–37, 74, 160, 163, 166, 174, 179, 200–201, 210
Conrad, Joseph, 94
Consciousness, 12–13, 18, 28–29, 34, 156
Consensus, 27, 67, 70, 159, 210–214
    negotiation, 211
Consultation, 31, 33, 107, 128, 190–194, 198, 221
Context, 2, 6, 17–18, 22–37, 46–50, 56, 64, 68, 72, 74, 77–79, 86–94, 116, 119, 127, 137, 140, 157, 161–184, 195–200, 203, 210, 220
    cultural, 24, 105
Conversation, 44, 139–141, 157–165, 171, 197, 204

Cooperation, 43, 46, 164, 185, 205, 209
Cooperative competition, 210
Cooperative practice, 163–164
Correctness, 71, 76–78, 91, 97, 208
Correlation, principle of, 2–3
Cree, *see* Indigenous peoples
Creole, 88
Critical awareness, 13, 34, 67–68, 85, 96
Critical language awareness (CLA) *see* Language awareness
Critical literacy, 68, 94, 126, 184
Critical realism, 30–33, 58, 188, 195
Cultural background, 17, 64, 115, 175, 176, 187, 194, 209
Cultural capital, *see* Capital
Cultural identity, 37–39, 49, 116, 128
Cultural interests, 38, 154–157, 163, 172
Cultural mismatches, 37–39, 51, 177
Cultural value, 36–50, 56–58, 64–65, 106, 175, 178, 203, 208–209
Culture, 4–13, 20–29, 36–65, 72–76, 83, 88–93, 97, 103–137, 148, 156, 160, 169–179, 203–204, 217
  academic, 62, 93, 127–128
  dominant, 21, 38–43, 54, 72, 91, 106–107, 123, 179
  of education, 72
  home, 63, 178
  of literacy, 23, 127–128
  of power, 88–89
  youth, 88
Curriculum, 1, 12–14, 34, 39, 42, 51–65, 76, 79, 91–109, 121–149, 171–172, 179–185, 197–202
  anti-bias, 149
  literacy, 95
Cyberspeak, 146

D

Daily rounds, 88
Deaf, the, *see also* Signing Deaf, the, 33, 99, 108–109, 121, 128–134, 150
Decision making, 31–33, 95
Devolution, 25, 31
Dialects, *see* Language varieties
Dialogue, 29, 51, 60, 63, 96, 109, 209–211, 219
Disciplines, academic, 1, 10, 42, 109, 188–197, 221
Discourse, 1, 6–24, 34–67, 72–91, 109–111, 119, 137–186, 190–220
  competitive, 157–167
  cooperative, 157–167

  colonial, 177
  games, *see* Language games
  oral, 62
Discourse analysis, 197, 210–211
  participatory, 210–214
Discourse norms, 23–24, 36–65, 79, 90, 119, 152–187, 201–210
  audience participation, 49
  chanting, 55
  co-occurrence expectations, 36
  cultural, 36–65, 115, 203, 214
  eye contact, 56
  female, 154–157
  gendered, 152–187, 210–214
  greeting style, 37
  hesitation, 45
  interruption, 51, 54, 158, 163, 165
  reticence, 48, 56
  rhythm, 157
  silences, 158, 211
  talk story, 55
  teasing behaviour, 37
  turn-taking, 36, 55, 81, 166
Discrimination, 16, 69–71, 84, 91–93, 105, 143, 177, 185, 190, 198, 202–203
  gender, 175
Discursive bias, 143
Discursive turn, the, 7–8, 13
Distortion, 20, 34, 71
Diversity
  cultural, 112, 189, 199
  human, 4, 41
  language, 13–16, 25–30, 35, 77, 90, 104–106, 188–189, 193–199, 220
Drama, 94, 120
Dutch, 114

E

Early childhood education (ECE), 110–111
Early childhood educators, 181–182
Ebonics, 66–98
ECE, *see* Early childhood education
Education
  bilingual, 30–32, 80, 99–151, 201
  elementary, 12, 134
  post-secondary, 110, 132
Educational policy, 25, 30, 33, 68, 72, 79, 102, 113, 128, 130
Egalitarianism, 30, 41, 161, 166
El Salvador, 202
Emancipation, 188–190, 209
Emergent phenomena, 10, 188, 192, 220
Emotion, 12, 37, 61, 145, 156, 173
Enfants baîllonnés, les (gagged children), 69

England, *see also* Britain, 70–75, 165, 172, 182
English, 6, 20, 28–37, 47, 57, 66–149, 165, 170, 193, 201–202, 207–209, 214–218
 as a Second Language, *see* ESL
English Only policies, 28–30, 32, 104
Epistemology, 2, 189–192
Equality, 161, 205, 209
Equity, 182
ESL (English as a Second Language), 62, 99–151, 199
 education
 high school students, 136–137
 older immigrant children, 134–148
 specialists, 135, 141–144
Ethnic groups, 17, 67–68, 168
Ethnic identity, 112, 124
Ethnography, 78, 82, 155, 178, 180, 194–200, 204, 210, 215, 221
 classroom, 198
 of communication, 194–200, 221
Europe, *see also* Britain, France, Germany, Ireland, Italy, Netherlands, the, Scandinavia, Switzerland, Turkey, 2, 70, 103, 110, 124
Evaluation, 2, 15, 43, 65, 140, 145, 202–209, 216, 218
Expertise, 144–145, 162
Experts, 42, 97, 136, 162, 190, 204, 206, 221

F

Families, *see also* Parents, Home and family, 18–21, 26, 42–43, 46, 53–55, 59, 63, 66, 73, 94–95, 101, 103, 118, 126–130, 149, 154, 157, 163, 176–178, 181
Feminism, 159, 173, 175
Finland, 106
Finnish, 106, 116–117
First languages, 32–33, 61–62, 78, 86, 99, 100, 107–137, 145, 148, 149, 150, 151, 177, 201, 206, 216, 219
First Nations, *see* Indigenous peoples
Florida, 123
Frame analysis, 199
Framingham, MA, 133
France, 69, 82, 127, 134, 214
Franco-Ontarians, 23, 81–82, 89, 91, 102, 125–126, 150, 214, 216–217
Francophones, 23, 38, 72, 79, 82, 103, 117, 123–129, 169–170, 214–217
Free will, 3

French, 6, 21, 23, 32, 37, 57, 69, 71, 79–83, 88, 92, 102, 112, 117, 125–134, 143, 170, 214–219
 Acadian, *see* Acadian French
 Canadian, *see* Canadian French

G

Gaelic, *see* Celtic languages
Gender, *see* Sex and gender
German, 70
Germany, 85
Girl talk, 166, 170, 210, 213–214
Girls, 51–57, 85, 99, 152–187, 210–216, 221
 immigrant, 153, 169, 174–185
 different norms of, 174–180
Goals, 26, 29–30, 84–85, 160–161, 169, 196, 199, 201, 221
Golden Rule, the, 28–29
Graeco-Latin vocabulary, 139–142
Grammar, 67, 70, 74, 78, 86, 115, 129, 147
Great Britain, *see* Britain
Greece, 156
Greek, Ancient, 69, 139, 140–144
Guns, 173, 186

H

Harvard Project on Human Potential, the, 153
Hawaii, 55, 56, 63, 119
Hegemony, 17–19, 24, 26, 33–34, 48, 56, 65, 81, 86, 89, 101, 163, 170, 184, 214
Heritage languages, 79, 117–119, 122–123
 programs, 79, 117–119, 122–123
 teachers, 122–123
Hermeneutics, 189, 197
Hispanic Americans, 28, 38, 40–41, 58, 104, 115, 123, 201
History, 4,, 9, 28–29, 33, 38, 41, 69–75, 79, 113, 123–124, 150, 157, 160–164, 188–189, 194, 196–197
Hmong, the, 178–179, 187
Holland, *see* Netherlands, the
Home and family, *see also* Families, Parents, 18–21, 26, 32, 38, 42–46, 53–55, 59–68, 73, 80, 83, 87, 92–95, 101–103, 117–119, 126–130, 148–149, 154, 157, 163, 175–181
Human sciences, the, 1, 6–9, 188–192, 221

I

Identity, 9, 14, 17–19, 23, 29, 34, 37, 39, 41, 60, 66–67, 71, 80–81, 87–96, 105,

117, 122, 126, 129, 131, 156,
160–162, 165, 168–170, 178, 180,
190, 201
Ideology, 2, 4, 13, 25, 33, 62, 69–72, 75–76,
81, 91, 94, 96, 105–106, 107, 113,
155, 158, 160, 163, 167, 169, 183,
191–192, 196–199, 214
  of correctness, 69–75, 214
Idiolects, 6
Illiteracy, 91–92, 126
  of oppression, 91–92, 126
  of resistance, 91–92, 126
Immersion, *see* Bilingual education
Immigrant languages, 104, 119–123, 150
Immigrants, 30, 39, 61, 66, 69, 79, 82, 88,
101–124, 134–135, 139, 150–154,
169, 174–185, 218
India, 113
Indiana School for the Deaf, 133
Indigenous peoples, 37–48, 56, 65–66, 79, 83,
108, 123, 129, 154, 193, 194, 209
  Aboriginal Australians, 41–43, 47, 108
    Milingimbi Yolngu, 57
  First Nations
    Algonquin, 42
    Athabaskan, 40–41, 48–49, 56
    Cree, 42
    Mohawk, 42
  Inuit, 57, 60– 64, 102, 203–209
  Maori, 41–46, 104
  Native Americans, 20, 44–50
    Arapaho, 49
    Navajo, 55–56
Individualism, 26–27, 30, 43, 171
Inequality, 20, 29, 73, 96, 105, 119, 153, 162,
178
Informal interaction, 46, 160
In-groups, 87, 170
Initiation-Response-Evaluation (IRE), 203–209
Injustice, 16, 65, 71, 82, 83
Interactions, single-sex, 171
Interdependence hypothesis, 114–115, 130
Internet, the, 146–147, 167
Interviews, 90, 149, 157, 190, 196–201, 204,
208, 215–219
Intolerance, 19, 33, 51, 71, 118, 124
Inuit, *see* Indigenous peoples
Inuktitut, 204–209
IQ tests, 78, 105
IRE, *see* Initiation-Response-Evaluation
Ireland, 38, 123–124
Islam, 156, 180
Israeli Orthodox, 156
Italian, 143
Italy, 113

J

Japan, 85, 106
Japanese, 106, 158

K

Kamehameha program, 63
Key situations, 48–56, 65, 88
Kingman Report, the, 75
Kula Kaiapuni, 42
Kura Kaupapa Maori, 42

L

Langue des Signes Québécoise, la (LSQ),
129–131
Labeling, 20, 54, 143
Language
  arts, 79
  development, 110, 124, 148, 150
  first, 32
  and gender, 152–161
  maintenance, 108, 113, 122–126
  modes, 133
  natural, 3, 4, 10, 12, 16, 129–130, 141, 143,
    193–194, 220
  observational, 3
  and power, 16–35, 195
  powerless, 161
  problems, 106
  proficiency, 6, 11, 32, 78, 87, 97, 101, 114,
    117–118, 121, 125–126,
    130–138, 142, 145, 165, 184,
    201
  quality, 214–217
  second, 62
  and social justice, 16–35
  in society, 191
  standardization, 81, 216
  testing, *see* Assessment
  in use, 78
  'women's', 156, 161–162
Language awareness, 33, 82, 109, 140, 143
  critical (CLA), 34, 68, 90–91, 96–97, 140,
    143, 146
Language games, 4–5, 9–11, 15, 21, 42, 50,
    62–63, 83, 95–96, 154–156,
    163–167, 170–176, 180, 184–195,
    199, 203, 220
Language teaching, 139, 141, 190, 191, 221
Language varieties, 6, 17, 24–29, 32, 36,
    66–96, 101, 126–129, 149–150,
    196, 214, 217, 221
  non-standard, 19, 22–23, 66–98, 100–101,
    126–129, 150, 214, 218–219

in North America, 79–82
Language-as-problem, 199–201
Language-as-resource, 199–201
Languages, *see also individual languages*
  majority, 28, 101–106, 112–115, 118,
    125–127
  minority, 22, 28–34, 92, 99–120, 125–128,
    132, 148–150, 193, 199, 201
  as vehicle of instruction, 127
Laos, 179
Latin, 139–144
Latino (American), 29, 201–202
Learning, 1, 7, 12, 20, 36, 40–44, 53–63, 69,
    78, 84, 94–95, 100–149, 168, 172,
    179, 182, 185, 198, 203, 209
Learning Center for Deaf Children, 133
L'École Champlain, 214–219
Legislation, 103, 126
Lexico-semantic range, 74
Liberalism, 30
Libraries, 93, 118, 149, 216
Ligatures, *see* Options and ligatures
Linguistic capital, *see* Capital
Linguistic discrimination, 68
Linguistics, 7, 188–195, 220
  anthropological, 196
  applied, 188–192, 220–221
Listening, 20, 57, 81, 111, 145–146, 160, 164,
    205–209
Literacy, 39, 49–54, 65, 76, 85, 91–95, 115,
    121–122, 128–133, 137, 146–149,
    153, 184
  academic, 49, 65, 81, 91–94, 120, 126, 184
  books and, 7, 9, 17, 21–26, 46, 50, 53, 90,
    95, 109, 139, 149, 189, 194–196,
    198, 214–215
  text, 43, 54, 61, 86, 94, 103, 139, 218
  computer, 93
  critical, 68, 94, 126, 184
  cultural, 93
  media, 93, 145–147
  political, 93
  technological, 93
  visual, 93
London, England, 176
Los Angeles, CA, 33
LSQ, *see Langue des Signes Québécoise, la*

M

Ma (shame), 57, 178
Mainstreaming, 130–131, 150
Malagasy Republic, the, 162
Manitoba, 130
Mathematics, 172, 184, 206

Meaning systems, 8–13, 21, 61, 73, 140–141
  cultural, 5, 9–12, 74, 174
Media, the, 10, 84–85, 93, 103, 105, 109, 111,
    133, 145–147, 174, 202–203
Media studies, 145–147
Medium of instruction, 14, 99, 115–117, 133
Mental events, 9
Mexico, 115, 123, 158
Michigan, 74
Milingimbi yolngu, *see* Indigenous peoples
Minorities, 20, 22, 25, 27–34, 38–39, 79, 81,
    88, 92, 99–129, 132, 143–144,
    148–150, 155, 176–177, 180, 193,
    199, 201, 215–216
  established, 123–128
  involuntary, 38–39, 65, 116, 123
  linguistic, 31, 82, 91–92, 99–102, 107–109,
    112–131, 136, 150, 200–201, 215
  voluntary, 39, 65
Model minority, the, 180
Models
  Adoption, 193, 215
  content-based, 141
  for doing culturally appropriate research,
    193–194
  Empowering Outcomes, 193, 199, 215, 221
  Mentor, 193, 204
  Power-Sharing, 193
  task-based, 141–142
Mohawk, *see* Indigenous peoples
Monolingualism, 67–68, 75, 81, 108, 114, 116,
    201–202, 214
Montreal, QC, 112
Moral authority, 210
Moral value, 3
MOTET project, the, 117
Mother tongue, 80–81, 105, 108, 116–117,
    121, 127, 128
Multilingualism, 31–32, 95, 103, 113, 149

N

Narrative, 8, 40, 47–55, 60, 106–107, 181, 182,
    190
Native Americans, *see* Indigenous peoples
Navajo, *see* Indigenous peoples
Negotiation, 40, 48, 210, 213
Netherlands, the, 114–115
New Brunswick, 125
New Mexico, 82, 126
New Testament, the, 28
New York, NY, 33, 79, 147
New Zealand, 42, 56, 66, 104, 177–182
Nigeria, 153

Norms, 8–10, 16–26, 31, 32, 36–65, 70–85,
        121, 125, 152–184, 196–198,
        203–204, 209–214, 219
    behavioral, 6
    discourse, *see* Discourse norms
North America, *see also* Canada, Caribbean,
        the, Mexico, United States, the, 20,
        38, 41, 46, 56, 61–62, 77, 79, 83,
        102–103, 115, 120, 124, 129, 131,
        134, 158, 170, 174, 177, 179
Norway, 85
Nouns, 20

O

Oakland Board of Education, 80
Objectivity, 1, 5, 15
Observation, 78, 80, 84, 97, 121, 197–200,
        204, 210
OECD, *see* Organization for Economic Coop-
        eration and Development
Ontario, 23, 82, 91, 102, 110, 117, 122–127,
        130, 132, 170, 172, 215–217
Ontology, 18, 30–31, 192
Oppression, 33, 38, 48, 92, 128, 163, 170, 186,
        196
Options and ligatures, 153–158, 164, 172–174,
        181–186
    building, 172
Oral language activities, 60–63, 182
Oregon, 44
Organization for Economic Cooperation and
        Development (OECD), 102–107
Outcomes, 14, 49, 91, 107–110, 145, 193, 196,
        221
Over-representation, 120
Oyster Bilingual School, 125, 198–203

P

Pacific Islanders, 56, 178
Panjabi, 57, 117, 178
Papua New Guinea, 155
Paradigms, 5, 196
Parents, *see also* Families, Home and family,
        24, 43, 48, 53–57, 74, 85–86, 97,
        118, 126, 132–135, 145–149,
        163–165, 176–177, 181, 199, 201,
        215–216, 219
    education of, 132
Participation, 10, 13, 49, 54, 60–61, 167,
        171–172, 182, 201–209
Pedagogy, 43, 65, 84, 98, 128, 185, 198, 204,
        218
Peer tutoring, 55

Personalization, 58–59
Philadelphia, PA, 22, 67, 116, 180
Philosophy, 3, 4, 14, 30, 42, 188–192
    of science, 4
Phonology, 67, 74
Physiology, 8
Play activity, 165–166
Pluralism, 32–33, 148, 174, 202
Police, 160–164, 202
Policy
    educational, 25, 30, 33, 68, 72, 79, 102, 113,
        128, 130
    language, 26, 29, 34, 35, 68, 76–77, 84,
        102–104, 124, 144, 149, 183,
        199–200
    principles, 32–33
Policymakers, 28, 31–33, 38, 76–77, 106
Policymaking, 31–34, 107, 195
Politics, 1, 9, 13, 27, 30, 38, 70, 76, 93, 96,
        101–104, 124, 159, 168, 186,
        189–199, 221
Polynesia, 41–43, 46, 50, 55–57, 59, 63, 119
Portuguese, 70, 143
Positivism, 2–7, 14, 189, 196–197
Postmodernism, 25–26, 33, 189, 193
Poverty, 34, 80
Power, 8, 10, 16–35, 50–51, 60, 67–72, 77,
        81–82, 86–91, 96–97, 101, 122,
        129, 140, 144, 152–169, 173–176,
        186, 190, 194, 197–199, 203, 209,
        214, 217–218, 220
    classroom, 89
    of classroom context, 56–58
    male, 154–157, 175
    symbolic, 22, 129
Powerlessness, 51, 93, 173
Prejudice, 69, 77, 84, 143–147, 218
Prestige, 25, 70, 76–77, 85, 90–91, 101, 118,
        127, 156–157, 163, 172, 202, 210
Prince Charles, 66, 70–71
Privatization, 58
Privilege, cultural, 122
Professional development, *see also* Teacher ed-
        ucation, 74, 77, 84–85, 95–96, 120,
        122, 142, 149, 221
Pronunciation, 78–79, 87
Propaganda, *see also* Media education, Critical
        literacy, 13
Psycholinguistics, 189
Psychology, 3, 7–8, 12, 190–191, 197
    cognitive, 8, 12
    discursive, 7–8, 189, 195
    ecological, 9
    social, 8, 189
Publilius Cyrus, 69

Puerto Rico, 73, 116
Pygmalion effect, the, 98

Q

Québec, 30–32, 38, 81, 103, 125–127, 147,
    169, 203, 209, 219
Queensland, 84
Questionnaires, 197

R

Race, 13, 23, 34, 70, 76, 81, 88, 105, 175, 185
Racism, 38, 80, 106–107, 122, 177–178, 184,
    216–217
    systemic, 76, 84, 177–178
Rationalization, 20, 34
Reading, 46, 50–55, 78–80, 85–87, 128, 134,
    139–141, 145–146, 168, 173, 201
Reception units, 136
Reform, 34, 76, 150, 157, 182–183, 195
Religion, 4, 13, 28, 32, 105, 157
    fundamentalist, 54, 156
Repression, 20, 34
Research
    action, 84
    cross-cultural, 165
    methods, 13, 82–84, 125, 166, 188–221
    small-scale, 178
    social, 2–4, 8, 15, 188, 192, 196–197, 220
Role play, 90
Romance languages, 142–143
Rough Rock, AZ, 55
Rules of use, 7, 9, 11, 15, 36–37, 40, 48, 83,
    95, 119, 137–141, 153, 161–169,
    173, 176, 182–183, 186–187,
    191–192, 197, 220
Russian, 12

S

Samoa, 41
Saskatchewan, 83
Scandinavia, *see also* Finland, Norway,
    Sweden, 134, 168–169
Schools
    elementary, 42, 44, 136, 165, 168, 193
    high, 34, 54, 56, 61–62, 92–93, 109–110,
        134–150, 165–172, 178–179,
        210–211
    relational, 161, 170
Science, 75, 77, 216
Scotland, *see also* Britain, 38, 123, 147
Second languages, 57, 69, 78, 80, 99–152, 190,
    204
Self-esteem, 59–60, 115, 170
Semantics, 194

Semiotics, 6
Separatism, 42
Sex and gender, 23, 28–29, 32, 51–57, 70, 76,
    85, 99, 105, 109, 152–187, 195,
    205, 210–221
Sexism, 143, 177–178, 184
    systemic, 76, 84, 177–178
Sharing time, 49–53
Show and tell, *see* Sharing time
Sign language, 121, 128–134
    and mainstreaming, 129–131
Sign systems, 5
Signed English, 129–130
Signing, 33, 99, 108–109, 128–134, 150
Signing Deaf, the, 128–134
Signs, 4–15, 20–23, 36, 40, 43–45, 49, 62–63,
    91, 109, 111, 119, 129, 137–140,
    149, 153, 158–174, 181–187,
    191–192, 197, 199, 201, 220
    non-verbal, 10, 15, 158, 166, 174
Sign systems, 5–7
Silence, 22, 43, 56, 62, 75, 111
Skepticism, 4–5
Social groups, 4, 21–22, 27, 33, 95, 150,
    155–156, 186
Social institutions, 19, 27–28, 199
Socialization, 29, 36, 40, 46, 50–51, 55, 153,
    158, 163–164, 204, 215
Social justice, 16–35, 64, 67, 81, 95, 97,
    99–101, 105, 113, 148, 168, 184,
    197, 202
Social life, 1, 14, 25, 172
Social science, 2, 4, 9, 188, 191
Social world, the, 1–7, 10, 14–15, 26, 31, 33,
    164, 171, 186, 192, 220
Sociocultural reproduction, 20–24, 215
Sociolinguistics, 18, 36, 74, 76–77, 87, 101,
    137, 155, 188–192, 196, 198, 210,
    214, 216, 220
Sociology of language, 189–190
Solidarity, 23, 74, 106, 115, 129, 155–156,
    159, 190, 213
South Africa, 38
South America, *see also* Brazil, 70, 201
Spanish, 6, 32, 70, 116, 123–126, 143, 150,
    201–202
Speaking, 18–19, 26, 36, 43–9, 52–55, 61, 65,
    69–72, 75, 81–89, 93, 96, 101–102,
    109, 115, 125–126, 128–130, 133,
    140–146, 155, 158–170, 185, 200,
    202, 210–211, 217, 219
Special education, 80, 102, 120–121, 179
Spelling, 86, 146–147, 211
Sport, 164
St Lucia, 86

Staff, 15, 77, 84, 97, 118, 133, 135–136, 142–148, 184–185, 194, 199, 201–202, 215–216
Staffing, 135
Stereotypes, 13, 20, 64, 69, 73–77, 82–83, 96, 103, 105, 116, 156, 170, 173–177, 180–184, 202–203
  linguistic, 68
Stigma, 19, 22, 75, 91
Stockholm, Sweden, 116
Storytelling, 49–50, 133, 134, 206
Stratification, 156, 190
Student councils, 152, 216, 219
Students
  deaf signing, *see also* Signing Deaf, the
    partial integration of, 131
    school and classroom practices for, 131–134
  ESL, 62, 114, 130, 135–150
  exceptional, 121, 130, 134–135, 144
    minority language, 121
  gifted and talented, 121, 135
Surveys, 86, 104, 125, 195, 196
Sweden, 106, 115–117, 134, 159
Switzerland, 85, 134
Symbolic capital, *see* Capital
Symbolic domination, 101, 107
Syntax, 22, 49, 67, 139

T

Taboo language, 159
Talking about text, 109, 128, 133, 140–142, 146
Teacher attitudes, 82–85
Teacher education, *see also* Professional development, 65, 74, 83, 96–97, 135, 142, 206
Teacher practice, 15, 187
Teachers, 15–16, 20, 40, 43, 45, 47, 51–66, 74, 77, 81–87, 90, 94–98, 120–121, 133, 135, 141–142, 150, 162, 168–169, 176, 178, 181–183, 187, 198, 202–209, 218
Teaching
  incidental, 136
  paired, 136 144
  parallel, 136, 144
  rotation, 136, 144
  withdrawal, 136
Teaching the Universe of Discourse, 109
Television, 46, 50, 69, 90, 139–140, 152, 219
Test norms, 78
Testing, language, *see* Assessment
Tests, intelligence, *see also* IQ tests, 120
Theories of knowledge, 2, 191–192

Theorists, 30, 36, 72, 74, 79, 109, 192
Theory, 2–7, 12, 15, 29–30, 60, 63, 73, 112–114, 129, 175, 188–197, 220–221
Threshold hypothesis, the, 113
Tolerance, 2, 71
Toronto, ON, 33, 66, 106, 214, 216
Translation, 6, 115, 145, 206
Translators, 149, 206
Triangulation, 197, 200, 219
Turkey, 114–115
Turkish, 114–115
Turn-allocation, 203
Two-way programs, 103, 125, 201

U

United Kingdom, *see* Britain
United Nations, the, 37, 91
United States, the, 5, 8, 27–29, 32, 38–40, 45, 67, 71, 74–76, 79–86, 90, 100–110, 115–127, 133, 135, 147, 150, 156, 159, 166, 169, 172–180, 195–203
  Office of Civil Rights, 105
  Office of Education, 105
Unz Initiative, the, 100

V

Values, cultural, 36–37, 40–42, 48, 50, 56, 58, 64–65, 106, 175, 203, 208–209
Verbs, 20, 86, 185
Vernaculars, 23, 73, 81, 88–89, 94, 101, 126, 127, 219
Vertical grouping, 55
Violence, 10, 37, 173, 174, 176, 186, 216
  male, 173
  symbolic, 22, 101, 106, 163
Vocabulary, 6, 22–23, 49, 67, 70, 74, 78, 109, 115, 139–142, 217
  academic, 34, 62, 139–143
  diversity, 22
  high status, 22

W

Wait-time, 59
Wales, *see also* Britain, 38, 75, 123, 165, 172
Warm Springs, OR, 44–50
Welsh, 99, 124, 129
Western cultures, 153, 155, 159–160, 203, 220
White Americans, 22, 41, 67, 153, 207
Writing, 52–53, 70, 86, 109, 128, 134, 145–147, 167
Written language, 76, 92, 129, 134, 146